U T T H A E H

DINING CAR

JUNIOR LEAGUE OF OGDEN

COOK
BOOK

The purpose of the Junior League is exclusively educational and charitable. Our aims are:
· to promote voluntarism;
· to develop participation in community affairs, and
· to demonstrate the effectiveness of trained volunteers.

Proceeds from the sale of **THE UTAH DINING CAR** will be returned to the community to support the many projects and programs undertaken by the Junior League of Ogden, Utah.

First Printing · September 1984 · 5,000 copies

Second Printing · May 1985 · 5,000 copies

Third Printing . January 1988 · 5,000 copies

Additional copies of **THE UTAH DINING CAR** can be obtained by using the order blanks in the back of the book or by writing to:

THE UTAH DINING CAR
Junior League of Ogden
2580 Jefferson
Ogden, Utah 84401

Library of Congress Catalog Number: 84-80830
International Standard Book Number: 0-9613453-0-6

COVER: Depicted on the cover is a reinactment of the driving of the Golden Spike at Promontary Point, Utah

Graphic Designer: Dale Bryner, Ogden, Utah

Printed in the United States of America by
Artistic Printing Company
Salt Lake City, Utah

I.S.B.N.: 0-9613453

TABLE OF CONTENTS

HIGH ALTITUDE COOKING

Atmospheric pressure at high altitudes (over 3,000 feet) is lower than that at sea level, and water boils at a lower temperature. These differences affect those foods that rely on boiling water or leavening.

When making yeast breads, use only half the amount of yeast and punch the bread down more times. Use the lesser amount of flour the recipe calls for and bake the bread in an oven that is 25 degrees hotter than the recipe suggests so it doesn't rise as much when first exposed to the heat.

Cakes have the same problem as bread when it comes to heights. Be careful not to overbeat eggs and raise the oven temperature about 25 degrees. In addition, cut the baking powder or baking soda by one-third (ie., 2 teaspoons instead of 3 teaspoons) or increase the amount of flour by 1 tablespoon and decrease the leavening by one-half teaspoon.

When making candy, lower the temperature two degrees for every 1,000 feet or about 8 degrees for 4,000 foot elevations. If in doubt, use the ice-water test for candymaking.

THE UTAH

DINING CAR
has been organized around a railroad theme because of the significance of the meeting of the Union Pacific and the Central Pacific railroads near Ogden in 1869.

The first transcontinental travelers to venture through Ogden did not enjoy the luxury of dining cars. Until well into the 1880's, the railroads fed their passengers at dining stations along the way. Thirty minutes were allowed for ordering and bolting food, (usually thin, shoe-leather steak and corn cake for all meals) before continuing on the journey. One of the few recommended dining spots was kept by a man in Evanston, Wyoming. He served fresh mountain trout. This was greatly appreciated then, and remains a great favorite to this day.

PAN FRIED TROUT

4 trout, cleaned, with head and tail left on
2 tablespoons flour
4 tablespoons butter or bacon fat
juice of ½ lemon
4 tablespoons of sliced almonds

DIRECTIONS:

This trout can be made just as easily on the trail as at home. Just pack in the butter, flour, (or corn meal), lemon and almonds. Roll the fish in the flour or corn meal, or put it into a plastic bag and shake it gently. Melt the butter or fat in a skillet, and fry the trout over medium heat until it resists a finger push, and is no longer translucent from the inside. Remove the trout, heat the almonds in the butter, and pour almonds, butter, and lemon juice over the trout. If using corn meal, omit the almonds.

The town of Ogden is placed squarely upon the junction of two great transcontinental routes: North-south from Canada to Mexico, and east-west from New York and Chicago to the Pacific northwest and California. The easiest east-west transcontinental route passes through the Wasatch range of the Rocky Mountains just to the east of Ogden, and skirts the Great Salt Lake just to the north of Ogden.

Long before the first transcontinental railroad took this route in 1869, Ogden was a "Junction City," and the easy north-south route through the Salt Lake Valley was used by Indians, explorers, and trappers following the north-south orientation of the Rockies.

Ogden takes its name from Peter Skeene Ogden, a trapper for the Hudson's Bay Company, who trapped beaver in the mountain valley just above Ogden in 1825. The valley was called Ogden's Hole, and there were frequent trappers' "rendevous" in those days, complete with Indian wives and the daughters of Indian Chiefs. The hunting is still good in the mountains above Ogden.

VENISON STEW

In 1840 Osborne Russell spent Christmas Day near the site of Ogden among fifteen lodges of Snake Indians. His journal describes the Christmas dinner, including a large tin plate, eighteen inches in diameter, heaping full of stewed deer meat. The Indians spoke French, learned from French-Canadian trappers. This "deer meat" recipe also has a French accent.

3 pounds venison, cut into 2 inch squares	1 bay leaf
1½ cups dry red wine	2 cloves garlic, mashed
¼ cup gin (for the juniper taste)	2 cups onions, sliced
2 tablespoons cooking oil	2 cups carrots, sliced
2 teaspoons salt	½ pound lean bacon, diced
5 peppercorns	1½ cups fresh mushrooms, sliced
1 teaspoon thyme	2 cups tomatoes, diced
	2 cups beef stock

DIRECTIONS: OVEN TEMPERATURE: 350°

Combine all ingredients, up to but not including the bacon, in a glass bowl. Cover and marinate three hours, stirring frequently. Simmer the bacon for 10 minutes in a pot of water. Drain and dry.

Remove the venison from the marinade and drain in a sieve over a bowl. Put ⅓ of the bacon in a large (5 quart) casserole dish. Layer some of the marinade, vegetables, mushrooms, and tomatoes over them. Shake the meat in a sack containing 1 cup of flour. Layer meat, vegetables, and bacon, ending with bacon. Strain the wine from the marinade into the cassrole, and add enough beef stock to almost cover the meat and vegetables.

Cover tightly and bake in a 350 degree oven for 4 hours. Skim off fat before serving. This is good hot or cold. It can be made ahead and reheated.

A trapper and trader named Miles Goodyear built himself a stockade on the site of the present day Ogden in 1844-45. Goodyear's wife was the daughter of a Ute Chief. There were many Chief's daughters in those days. Almost every trapper was married to one.

Goodyear saw the potential of Ogden as a trading center. His idea was to trade – not with the Indians, but with the settlers traveling over the Oregon Trail. In 1846, Goodyear took furs to Southern California, and returned with a herd of horses to trade with the wagon trains passing over the Trail near Evanston, Wyoming. This is the same Evanston famous for trout dinners in later generations.

While Goodyear was in California, the tragic Donner-Reed party attempted to force a way through the heavily wooded, narrow and rocky Weber Canyon into the Salt Lake Valley near Ogden. The transcontinental railroad subsequently used this route, but the Donner-Reed party had neither the man power nor the engineering skills to cope. They were so delayed by this episode that they were caught by Fall snows in the Sierra Nevada passes, and nearly half of the party perished.

On November 25, 1847, Miles Goodyear executed a deed to the land of present-day Ogden to Mormon settlers. This was a piece of calculated showmanship on Goodyear's part, since his right to the land was based on a "Mexican Land Grant," which had no legal foundation. The purchase price was $1,950, money which had been earned by Mormon soldiers in California.

Ogden became a pioneer settlement in 1848, settled by hearty souls who frequently walked beside their carts across the plains. In this respect, as in others, Ogden is representative of the heart of America. The pleasant, economically prosperous suburbs of today are built upon a foundation of terrible hardship, heartbreak, and sacrifice. There was considerable cultural diversity in Ogden from the start, since the Mormons brought many of their converts from Europe. One traveler of the 1850's, making his way from Salt Lake City to Ogden, complained that it was impossible to obtain directions, since every dwelling housed Dutchmen, Welchmen, and Scandanavians!

MORMON MUFFINS

These are essentially a national pioneer muffin, popular because they are hearty and flavorful, but need no time to rise.

1⅓ cups flour	2 tablespoons brown sugar
1 teaspoon baking soda	1 egg
½ teaspoon salt	½ cup molasses
4 tablespoons shortening	⅔ cup buttermilk

DIRECTIONS:　　　　　　　　　　　　　　　　**OVEN TEMPERATURE: 400°**

Grease 12 muffin tins. Sift together the flour, soda, and salt. Blend the shortening, sugar, egg, and molasses. Add the dry ingredients to the shortening mixture alternately with the buttermilk. Bake in 400 degree oven for 15 to 18 minutes.

The driving of the Golden Spike was the last step in the completion of the first transcontinental railroad. It occurred on May 10, 1869, a short distance from Ogden at Promontory Point. The telegraph wires flashed the message from Ogden across the waiting nation, over the trail walked at such cost by the pioneers. The message was: "DOT, DOT, DOT, DONE!" Celebrations were held all over the continent. The event represented not only the conquering of a continent by a determined people, it also represented the tying together of the manifest diversities of those people. Many thousands of Chinese workers labored on the Central Pacific section of the road, coming from California over the Sierras Nevada, tunnelling inch by inch with picks and shovels. The Chinese had their own representatives, who divided the pay and provided the food. The Chinese had a varied diet, and were sick much less often than the Union Pacific workers, who ate only salted meat, potatoes and cornbread, and who didn't routinely boil water for tea. Corned beef remains an American institution.

HOME CURED CORNED BEEF

A 5 pound beef brisket
¼ teaspoon salt peter
¼ cup warm water
2 tablespoons sugar
2 cloves garlic, minced
2 teaspoons paprika
1 tablespoon pickling spice
¾ cup canning salt
2 quarts water

Fruit glaze:
½ cup brown sugar
2 teaspoons grated orange rind
1 teaspoon grated lemon rind
½ teaspoon dry mustard
½ cup apple juice
⅓ cup orange juice
2 tablespoons lemon juice

DIRECTIONS: **OVEN TEMPERATURE: 350°**

Place the brisket in a crock, cutting it in half if necessary. Do not use a tin or aluminum pot. Dissolve the salt peter in ¼ cup warm water. Mix all the other ingredients together, stir in the salt peter, and pour over the beef. Weight the meat with a plate to keep it under the brine, cover, and refrigerate for three weeks. Keep it under the brine, or it will spoil. Simmer the corned beef brisket 2½ to 3 hours. Drain when done. Mix together the fruit glaze ingredients, press into the top of the corned beef, and bake at 350 degrees for 30 minutes.

SOUTHERN PACIFIC SPRING LAMB WITH VEGETABLES   6 SERVINGS

This recipe is from a collector's notebook. The famous "Southern Pacific" lamb stew which was the specialty of their dining car service years ago.

2 pounds stewing lamb
4 tablespoons butter
½ cup celery, chopped
2 medium onions, chopped
3 tablespoons flour

2½ cups beef broth
3 carrots, quartered
3 turnips, quartered
2 cups boiling onions, peeled
1 · 12-ounce package frozen peas

DIRECTIONS:

Dry lamb carefully, and sauté in butter until lightly browned. Add chopped onions and celery, and sauté until vegetables are soft. Add flour, and cook until flour is golden brown.

Pour in the beef broth, and simmer, tightly covered, for 1½ hours, stirring occasionally. Brown the carrots, turnips, and onions in an additional 3 tablespoons butter. Add the vegetables to the meat, and simmer an additional hour, covered.

Freshness of taste is the charm of this recipe, and it must be made fresh. At this point, however, it can sit for an hour or so off the heat.

To serve, reheat gently, but do not boil. Add frozen peas fifteen minutes before serving. Serve with browned potatoes or boiled new potatoes.

In Ogden, Jefferson Avenue is lined with the extravagant homes of ninteenth century entrepreneurs, brothers in spirit to the men who founded, and profited enormously from, the transcontinental railroad. The Eccles Circle, further towards the mountains, is a perfectly preserved example of American Prairie School Architecture of the twentieth century, built by families with roots deep in the commercial growth of the West and the Nation.

One such family collected and preserved authentic Dining Car recipes. In an age of microwave, plastic tray meals, it is interesting to contemplate the explicit requirement: "Must be cooked fresh." Imagine such a thing in a public dining car.

Ogden is a "junction" city, and a representative city, in its cooking as well as its history. Like the train tracks which tie Ogden to the nation and to the American experience, American regional cooking ties all of us to our historical roots, to our present reality, and to the future. There is such a thing as true American cooking. Exploring the basics of that cooking provides us with a key to the love and care, as well as the diversity, handed down from the past. Exploring the basics gives us a better understanding of our own origins as Americans. Even though fashions in cooking and lifestyles change, the basics remain, the track which ties us together.

LAYING THE TRACKS

Waterskiing is possible on many Utah Lakes and reservoirs. It is especially scenic on Lake Powell, amid the splendors of Glen Canyon.

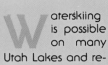

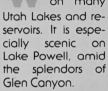

Laying the Track

The purpose of this section is two-fold: to provide a logical layout of the basics for the inexperienced cook, and to provide the experienced cook with a handy reference and (optional) food for thought about American cooking. The key to good American cooking lies in the essential great abundance of the land itself. Good American cooking takes the best and freshest of what is available and emphasizes the essence of the food itself. The following recipes are all lessons in how to emphasize the essence, and they all follow in logical sequence from basic techniques.

BROTHS

Broths are at the heart of good cooking. They are essential to soups, sauces, and gravies. We are so used to the canned and dried broths, that the taste of a homemade broth comes as a real shock. Homemade broth is an excellent way to save on salt content. Add salt sparingly, to taste.

CHICKEN BROTH
(and POACHED CHICKEN)　　　　　　YIELD: 2 Quarts

This is the easiest broth to make, and very good.

4 pounds of chicken, necks and wings,
　all white or dark, or mixed
4 quarts of cold water

3¼ inch slices fresh ginger
2 clove garlic
1 leek or medium onion, chopped

DIRECTIONS:

Rinse the chicken under running water and remove any visible fat. Put the chicken and vegetables in the pot, bring to a boil over high heat, and reduce heat to a simmer. With a large spoon, skim the foam from the surface. Simmer, uncovered, without stirring, for three hours.

Line a sieve with a double thickness of dampened cheesecloth. Strain the stock through the sieve into a bowl. Let cool to room temperature, then refrigerate overnight.

Remove the fat from the surface of the stock, and refrigerate for three days, or freeze in pint containers.

HINT:

Strip the meat from the bones to use for salad and casseroles.

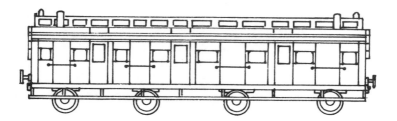

BEEF BROTH

YIELD: 2 Quarts of Broth

4 pounds of beef bones, cracked or sawed
2 large onions, roughly chopped
2 carrots, sliced
1 leek, sliced into 1 inch pieces
4 sprigs of parsley

1 bay leaf
10 whole black peppercorns
¼ teaspoon thyme
2 cloves garlic

DIRECTIONS:

OVEN TEMPERATURE: 400°

Put the bones, onion, and carrot in a large roasting or lasagna pan. Roast for 1½ hours, turning the bones, until they are very brown. Remove the bones and vegetables to a large kettle, using a slotted spoon. Add two cups of cold water to the pan, and return it to the turned off oven for 5 minutes.

Cover the bones and vegetables in the stock pot or kettle with cold water, about four quarts. Scrape the roasting pan well, dissolving the brown bits in the water. Pour this dark brown flavoring into the stock pot. Bring the pot to a boil, and reduce the heat to a simmer. Skim the froth from the top with a large spoon for ½ hour. Add the leek and the remaining ingredients, and simmer the stock, uncovered, for 4 to 5 hours.

Line a strainer with a double thickness of dampened cheesecloth. Ladle the broth through the strainer into a bowl, then carfully remove the bones and set aside. Do not try to pour from the pot directly into the strainer. The bones fall out and make a terrible mess. After the bones are removed from the pot, strain the rest of the broth.

Cool the broth, and refrigerate it overnight. Remove the fat from the top, and it is ready to use within five days, or freeze. To save freezer space, the broth can be reduced over a high heat to one quart, once the fat has been removed. Dilute with equal parts of water to use.

BUTTER AND FLOUR BASED WHITE SAUCE

YIELD: 2 Cups

This is the same as the classic French Béchamel sauce. In some parts of this country, it's called cream sauce, causing endless confusion. All of our modern recipes using cream of mushroom soup are derived from this sauce. White sauce can be substituted for the soup and liquid in any modern casserole recipe.

4 tablespoons flour
4 tablespoons butter
2 cups milk

salt and white pepper
nutmeg

DIRECTIONS:

Melt the butter in a heavy medium saucepan. Blend in the flour, using a spoon or a whisk. Heat the milk in another pan, or in the microwave. This step can be omitted without serious chance of disaster. Cook the butter and flour together for 1 to 2 minutes, to cook out the taste of flour. Don't let it brown unless you want a brown sauce. Add the milk, bring to a boil, and stir constantly for 3 to 5 minutes. Season with salt, pepper, and nutmeg.

CREAMED VEGETABLES
CREAMED TUNA
CHIPPED BEEF ON TOAST
HAMBURGER GRAVY

SEE BUTTER AND FLOUR BASED WHITE SAUCE

DIRECTIONS:

Add 1½ cups of whatever you want "creamed" to 2 cups of white sauce. Thin the mixture out, if necessary, with ½ cup milk or cream. Put the vegetables into a serving dish, and keep warm in a low oven. Add choppped onion to the tuna, chipped beef, or hamburger. Serve with toast, rice, or mashed potatoes. This much will serve 4 children or 2 hungry adults.

PAN GRAVY
BEEF, PORK, CHICKEN, or TURKEY

SEE BUTTER AND FLOUR BASED WHITE SAUCE

DIRECTIONS:

There are two kinds of pan gravy. "Natural" gravy results in a pure reduction of the essence of flavor. American pan gravy results in more gravy for everyone. It is interesting to note the evolution of natural gravy into plenty for everyone.

TO MAKE NATURAL GRAVY (AU JUS): Roast beef in an uncovered pan in which one quartered onion has also been roasted. For medium rare, roast 20 mintues per pound in a 350 degree oven. Remove the beef and allow it to rest on a warmed serving platter. Tilt the pan, and remove all visible clear fat. Pour 1½ cups of water or beef broth into the pan, and return the pan to the oven for 5 minutes. Take the pan from the oven, stir well to loosen all of the brown bits, and strain this "natural" gravy into a serving bowl.

TO MAKE PAN GRAVY: Remove the beef, chicken, pork, or turkey from the roasting pan. Tilt the pan, and remove all visible clear fat from the pan, using a spoon. Add liquid to equal the amount of gravy you want. Two cups serves four. Use water or broth; or part broth, part milk or cream. Return the pan to the oven.

In a medium saucepan, follow the directions for making white sauce. Use 2 tablespoons of butter and 2 tablespoons of flour for every cup of liquid. Remove the pan from the oven, scrape well to loosen the brown bits, and strain into the saucepan containing the flour and butter. Bring the mixture to a boil, stirring well. Taste the gravy and season it with salt and pepper. This is a sure winner: no lumps ever.

CHEESE SAUCE

SEE BUTTER AND FLOUR BASED WHITE SAUCE

DIRECTIONS:

Add ½ cup of grated sharp Cheddar, Swiss, or American cheese to white sauce. Flavor with a few drops of Tabasco Sauce (optional).

BISCUITS AND GRAVY

SEE BUTTER AND FLOUR BASED WHITE SAUCE

DIRECTIONS:

Make biscuits with treasured family recipe, or use Bisquick. Roll and cut out for the proper effect. Split the hot biscuits when done, and butter generously. Cover the biscuits with white sauce made with an additional ½ cup cream. If served with fried chicken, pan gravy variation (see previous page), can be used. Biscuits and gravy are a traditional Rocky Mountain skiers' breakfast, served with scrambled eggs and sausage. Allow ¼ cup white sauce for each biscuit.

EGG BASED SAUCES:

GENERAL INSTRUCTIONS:

These sauces are more difficult than white sauce and its variations, because they depend on the combination of oil or butter and egg yolks for thickening. The trick is to warm the egg yolks so that they will receive the maximum amount of butter or oil. They can't be warmed too much, or they will turn into scrambled eggs. The oil or butter can't be added too fast, or the yolks will refuse to absorb them, and the sauce will separate. The real trick to making these sauces is understanding them.

These sauces can be made in a blender or food processor. They are easy to make by hand, however, and the cleaning up is much faster. If the sauce does curdle or separate, beat an egg yolk with a tablespoon of water over low heat until it is creamy. Then, turn off the heat, add the separated mixture by teaspoons until the sauce is thick.

HOLLANDAISE

YIELD: 1 Cup

For Eggs Benedict, Fish, and Vegetables

½ cup butter
3 tablespoons water

3 egg yolks
juice of ½ lemon

DIRECTIONS:

Melt the butter in a small glass pitcher, or pour it into a glass or plastic measuring cup after melting. Let the butter cool to luke-warm. In a small heavy saucepan or bowl, beat the water and egg well for 30 seconds. Put the pan or bowl over very low heat. Place the bowl over a pan of simmering water. Whisk the yolks and water until the heat thickens the yolks, and you can see the trail of the wisk on the bottom of the bowl. Do not let the bottom of the bowl or pan become more than hand hot.

Take the bowl or pan from the heat, and whisk in the butter, drop by drop. When the sauce begins to thicken, the butter can be added faster. Do not add the sediment at the bottom of the butter. Stir in the lemon juice, and salt and pepper to taste. Serve warm, not hot.

BEARNAISE SAUCE

YIELD: 1 Cup

SEE EGG BASED SAUCES AND HOLLANDAISE

Traditional American steak butter is a variation of Bearnaise. It is made exactly the same way as hollandaise. Serve with steak, lamb, or salmon.

1½ sticks (¾ cup) butter
3 tablespoons vinegar
3 tablespoons dry white wine
10 peppercorns crushed
2 shallots or green onions, chopped

2 teaspoons dried tarragon, or
1 tablespoon fresh tarragon, chopped
3 egg yolks
2 tablespoons fresh tarragon, chopped, or dried tarragon soaked in wine

DIRECTIONS:

In a small saucepan, boil the vinegar and wine with the peppercorns, shallot or green onion, and the tarragon until the liquid is reduced to 2 tablespoons. Strain the mixture into your bowl or saucepan, pressing hard on the solids. Beat the egg yolks with this flavoring instead of the water in the hollandaise recipe, and proceed exactly as in the hollandaise recipe. Add chopped or dried tarragon for flavoring instead of lemon juice. Add plenty of freshly ground pepper, if pepper taste is not strong enough.

MAYONNAISE

YIELD: 2 Cups

SEE EGG BASED SAUCE AND HOLLANDAISE

3 egg yolks
¼ teaspoon dry mustard
½ teaspoon salt

2 teaspoons lemon juice
2 cups olive oil or vegetable oil
salt and white pepper

DIRECTIONS:

Beat the egg yolks for 2 or 3 minutes, until thick. Add the mustard, salt, and lemon juice. Beat for another minute over very low heat, as in the hollandaise recipe. Slowly add the oil by ½ teaspoons, until ½ cup has gone in. Begin to add oil by tablespoons, and thin out the mayonnaise with drops of lemon juice if it becomes too thick. If the sauce separates, a tablespoon of Dijon mustard may be used instead of the egg yolk to reconstitute the sauce. Season with salt, white pepper, and lemon juice.

TOMATO BASED SAUCES

Fresh tomatoes can be one of the glories of American cooking. These recipes depend on the enhancement of the fresh tomato taste. Wait until you can use vine ripened tomatoes to make them. The fresh tomato sauce freezes beautifully.

To skin and seed tomatoes: With a fork in each hand, spear two tomatoes and plunge them into a pot of boiling water for 20 seconds. Line them up in front of you as they are finished, and spear two more. When all are scalded, slip the skins off of them, and remove the core. Cut them each in half crosswise and dig out the seeds with your finger.

FRESH TOMATO SAUCE

YIELD: 2 Cups

2 tablespoons oil
½ cup onion, chopped
2 pounds (4 cups) fresh tomatoes,
  peeled, seeded, and chopped

1 clove garlic, minced
  (optional)
½ teaspoon dried thyme or oregano

DIRECTIONS:

Cook the onion slowly in the oil until cooked, but not brown. Add the tomatoes, the garlic, and the herb. Cook over medium heat until reduced to 2 cups. This will take about 30 minutes. Freezes very well.

FRESH HOT SALSA

YIELD: 1½ Cups

Small hot chilies grow very well in the high valleys near Ogden. This sauce is common when the chilies are ripe. It is borrowed from our New Mexican neighbors.

1 clove garlic
½ teaspoon salt
3 tablespoons oil
1 tablespoon vinegar

1 cup tomato, cored seeded,
  and chopped
3 small green chilies (serranos)
½ cup onion, chopped

DIRECTIONS:

Peel the garlic clove, slice it, and cover it with salt in a medium bowl. Mash with a fork into a paste. Add the oil and the vinegar, then the onion, the tomato and chilies, finely chopped. Be very careful when chopping the chilies. Wear rubber gloves if you have them. Wash your hands very well, and rub with lemon juice. Excellent as a dip for chips, with eggs. An all around fresh hot sauce.

FAVORITE FAMILY
GREEN CHILI SALSA

YIELD: 16 Pints

¾ bushel tomatoes, skins removed
  and chopped
1½ pounds assorted chile peppers,
seeds removed, ground or diced small
10 very large onions, diced

8 to 10 green bell peppers, diced
2 cloves garlic, minced
10 tablespoons uniodized salt
less than 1 cup vinegar

DIRECTIONS:

Combine all ingredients in very large pot and bring to a boil. Simmer at least 6 hours (till thick). Stir often; be careful to not let stick on bottom. Hot pack 20 minutes for pints and 30 minutes for quarts.

HINT:

Pour some salsa over an 8-ounce cube of softened cream cheese and serve with crackers or tortilla chips or serve just plain with tortilla chips. Great over eggs and with Mexican dishes.

APPETIZERS & BEVERAGES

Utah's lakes are freshened morning and evening by canyon breezes. Pineview reservoir above Ogden is perfect for sailing.

CHILLED VEGETABLES

SERVES 12-15

6 cups carrots, sliced diagonally
2 green peppers, sliced
1 large Bermuda onion, sliced
2 heads cauliflower, cut into pieces

Marinade:
1 cup tomato soup concentrate

½ cup oil
¾ cup vinegar
1 teaspoon salt
1 teaspoon pepper
1 teaspoon Worcestershire sauce
1 teaspoon Dijon mustard
¾ cup sugar

DIRECTIONS:

Par boil carrots in salted water for 10 minutes. (It is important that carrots stay very crisp.) Mix thoroughly marinade sauce ingredients. Place vegetables in a large bowl that can be sealed tightly and pour sauce over. Cover and refrigerate for 12 hours.

Serve cold as an hors d'oeuvre or as a cool summer snack. May be kept as long as 2 weeks.

COCKTAIL MEATBALLS

YIELD: 100 meatballs

Meatballs:
3 pounds lean ground
  beef
½ cup seasoned bread
  crumbs
2 onions, minced
4 teaspoons prepared
  horseradish
2 cloves garlic, crushed
1½ cups tomato juice
4 teaspoons salt
½ teaspoon pepper

Sauce:
¼ cup butter
2 onions, chopped
¼ cup flour
3 cups beef broth
1 cup red wine
¼ cup brown sugar
¼ cup catsup
2 tablespoons lemon juice
1 gingersnap, crumbled (optional)
2 teaspoons salt
Pepper to taste

DIRECTIONS: **OVEN TEMPERATURE: 450°**

Meatballs: Combine all ingredients and shape into bite-sized balls. Place on jelly roll pan and brown in 450 degree oven for 10 minutes. Remove and drain.

Sauce: In large skillet melt butter. Add onions and sauté until golden. Blend in flour. Add broth, stirring until smooth. Stir in remaining ingredients and simmer over low heat for 15 minutes. Add meatballs and serve warm.

EGG ROLLS

YIELD: 20-30 Rolls

1 pound ground beef
1 large cabbage, chopped
2 large carrots, grated
3 large slices ginger root, minced
1 bunch green onions, chopped

½ teaspoon Chinese Five-Spices (optional)
Salt and soy sauce to taste
1 tablespoon cornstarch mixed with ½ cup water
1 package egg roll skins

DIRECTIONS:

OVEN TEMPERATURE: 425°

Brown ground beef; add cabbage, carrots, ginger root, and onions and sauté for 1 to 2 minutes, keeping vegetables crisp. Add salt and soy sauce to taste (and Five-Spices if desired.) Stir. Add cornstarch and water; mix quickly. (This helps to hold mixture together.)

Remove from heat immediately and transfer to large bowl to prevent from cooking further. Place a teaspoon of mixture in center of each egg roll skin; bring lower corner of skin up over filling but not clear to top corner; fold over sides to middle and roll up, ending with last corner on outside like an envelope. Moisten tip of this corner with a drop of water and press it onto the roll to seal. As egg rolls are wrapped, place in single layer on cookie sheet until all are wrapped.

To fry, heat oil until very hot, 375-400 degrees. Fry a few at a time very quickly until each is golden brown. Remove and drain on paper towels. Keep warm in oven until all are fried and ready to eat. These may be frozen after they are fried and cooled completely. Wrap well. When ready to use, remove from freezer, place on cookie sheet and heat at 425 degrees for approximately 15 to 20 minutes.

Serve with soy sauce or with hoisin sauce mixed half and half with water. Hot sauce is also very good.

VARIATION:

Pork or shrimp may be used as a filling instead of ground beef.

GLORIOUS MUSHROOMS

SERVES 6-8

2 pounds fresh mushrooms
½ cup butter
2 cups sour cream
1 teaspoon paprika
1 tablespoon chopped parsley

1 tablespoon lemon juice
1 teaspoon Worcestershire sauce
¼ teaspoon salt
⅛ teaspoon pepper
Dash garlic powder (optional)

DIRECTIONS:

Sauté mushrooms in butter. Add sour cream and mix well. Add rest of ingredients. Serve hot.

GREEK CHICKEN SPANAKOPITAS

YIELD: 42 Appetizers

2 tablespoons vegetable or olive oil
1 small onion, diced
1 · 10-ounce package
  frozen chopped spinach,
  thawed and squeezed dry
⅓ cup grated Parmesan cheese

2 cooked chicken breasts, chopped
  in very small pieces or ground
⅛ teaspoon pepper
1 egg
⅓ pound phylo or 12 leaves or sheets
½ cup butter, melted

DIRECTIONS:
OVEN TEMPERATURE: 425°

In 2-quart saucepan, cook onion in oil until tender. Remove from heat and stir in spinach, chicken, cheese, pepper and egg until well mixed.

With knife, cut phylo lengthwise into 2 inch-wide strips. Place strips on waxed paper; cover with slightly damp towel to prevent phylo from drying out. Place one strip of phylo on work surface; brush top lightly with melted butter. Place about 1 teaspoon spinach-chicken mixture at short end of strip. Fold one corner of strip diagonally over filling so that the short edge meets the long edge of the strip. Fold like a flag until you reach the end, forming a triangle. Place seam side down on jelly roll pan and brush with butter. Bake at 425 degrees for 15 minutes or until brown. Serve hot.

GYOZA

YIELD: 60

1 pound ground beef
1 · 4½-ounce can shrimp,
  drained and chopped
1 · 8-ounce can water chestnuts,
  drained and chopped

1 small clove garlic, minced
Salt and pepper to taste
1 teaspoon sesame seed oil
1 package won-ton skins

DIRECTIONS:
OVEN TEMPERATURE: 400°

Mix together ground beef, shrimp, water chestnuts, garlic, seasonings and sesame seed oil. Place a teaspoon of mixture in center of skin. Fold lower corner of skin over filling to top corner. Crimp and crease edges together.

Fry in hot oil (350-400 degrees) 2-inches deep until each is golden. Remove and drain on paper towels.

These may be made in advance, refrigerated and reheated at 400 degrees for 10 minutes.

Good served with a sweet and sour sauce.

TIP:
To turn chicken pieces during frying or sautéing, use tongs rather than a fork to keep juices from escaping.

KOREAN STYLE BARBEQUE BEEF

YIELD: 18-20 Skewers

½ cup soy sauce
2 tablespoons lemon juice
2 tablespoons sugar
1 garlic clove, minced
½ teaspoon ground ginger

2 tablespoons vegetable oil
1 teaspoon sesame seeds
2 green onions, finely chopped
1 pound beef sirloin, thinly sliced
6" bamboo skewers

DIRECTIONS:

OVEN TEMPERATURE: Broil

Combine soy sauce, lemon juice, sugar, garlic, ginger, oil, sesame seeds and onions. Thread meat on bamboo skewers. Place skewered meat in marinade. Turn to coat all sides. Cover and refrigerate 3 to 4 hours, turning occasionally.

Broil meat in oven or on grill 1½ to 2 minutes; turn and broil 1 minute longer.

HINT:

Beef may be easily sliced to wafer thin strips if partially frozen.

LINA'S WON TONS

YIELD: 100 Won Tons

Won Tons
½ pound ground pork
¼ cup chopped mushrooms
1 tablespoon minced green onion
¼ teaspoon pepper
¼ teaspoon salt
1 egg yolk
1 package won ton skins
Peanut or salad oil

Red Sauce
3 tablespoons catsup
3 tablespoons chili sauce
3 tablespoons horseradish
1 teaspoon lemon juice
¼ teaspoon Tabasco
Salt and pepper to
taste

DIRECTIONS:

Won tons: Mix first six ingredients thoroughly. Place ½ teaspoon of pork mixture in center of each won ton skin. Dampen two open edges with water and fold into an uneven triangle; press to seal edges. Fry in hot oil as needed until lightly browned. Drain and serve with Red Sauce, Chinese mustard, soy sauce, sweet and sour sauce, etc.

HINT:

May be made ahead, frozen and reheated in 350 degree oven for 10 to 15 minutes. May also be made earlier in the day and kept covered in the refrigerator until ready for frying.

Red Sauce: Combine all ingredients thoroughly and serve with won tons. This sauce is also good served with any seafood.

MARINATED MUSHROOMS

YIELD: 36

1½ pounds fresh mushrooms
1½ cups cider vinegar
1¼ cups corn oil
5 cloves garlic, pressed

4 tablespoons minced fresh parsley
4 tablespoons minced green onions
1½ teaspoons sugar
1½ teaspoons salt

DIRECTIONS:

Mix all ingredients together and marinate overnight. Serve the following day.

OLIVE CHEESE PUFFS

YIELD: 48 Puffs

2 cups grated sharp Cheddar cheese
½ cup butter, softened
1 cup flour

½ teaspoon salt
Dash Worcestershire sauce
48 pimento stuffed green olives

DIRECTIONS:

OVEN TEMPERATURE: 400°

Blend cheese with butter; add rest of the ingredients except olives. Blend well. Wrap one teaspoon dough around each olive and mold into ball. Place on cookie sheet and freeze. When frozen, place in plastic bag. Freeze until ready to use. Bake frozen at 400 degrees for 15 minutes.

PINEAPPLE WITH LIQUEUR

SERVES 16

1 · 29-ounce can of pineapple chunks *OR* 1 fresh pineapple
½ cup Créme de Menthe *OR* Grand Marnier liqueur

DIRECTIONS:

Drain the canned pineapple chunks or cut the fresh pineapple into cubes. Place in a container and pour liqueur over all. Marinate overnight.

HINT:

If using a fresh pineapple, the shell can be used for an attractive serving container.

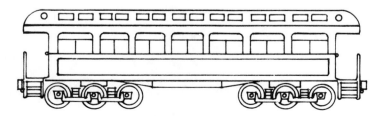

PIZZA IN PHYLO

SERVES 8

"Great as an appetizer or entrée!"

1 pound ground beef
2 · 8-ounce cans tomato sauce
½ teaspoon salt
⅛ teaspoon pepper
1 teaspoon sugar
¾ teaspoon oregano leaves
¼ teaspoon garlic salt
2 teaspoons dehydrated onion
  flakes
1 teaspoon Italian seasoning

1 · 2½-ounce bottle sliced
  mushrooms, drained
½ cup chopped pepperoni
2 cups grated mild Cheddar cheese
1 cup butter, melted
1 · 1-pound package phylo
  pastry sheets
Grated mozzarella cheese
Chopped black olives
Chopped parsley

DIRECTIONS:

OVEN TEMPERATURE: 350°

Crumble ground beef and brown; drain off fat. Combine beef, tomato sauce, salt, pepper, sugar, oregano, garlic salt, onion, Italian seasoning, mushrooms and pepperoni.

For each roll, use 2 phylo sheets. Place one sheet on counter; brush with melted butter. Place second sheet on top of first; brush with melted butter. Place ½ cup filling about 2 inches from end of phylo. Sprinkle filling with Cheddar cheese. Roll two times; fold over sides and continue rolling. Makes about 8 rolls.

Place rolls seam side down on ungreased baking sheet. Bake at 350 degrees for 30 to 40 minutes or until light brown. To serve, garnish with mozzarella cheese, chopped olives and parsley.

HINT:

Place damp cloth over phylo dough to keep it from drying out. Phylo sheets can also be cut into strips to make individual appetizers by folding them like a flag.

SAUSAGE STRUDEL

SERVES 16

1 pound sweet Italian sausage
1 pound mushrooms, finely chopped
¼ cup butter
2 shallots, chopped (optional)
1 · 8-ounce package cream cheese,
  cut into small pieces

1 package frozen strudel
  or phylo dough
Melted butter
Dried fine bread
  crumbs

DIRECTIONS:

OVEN TEMPERATURE: 350°

Remove sausage from casing; scramble and brown. Drain off fat. Sauté mushrooms in butter and cook slowly until all liquid has evaporated. Add shallots if desired.

Spread melted butter and sprinkle crumbs on one sheet of phylo; top with another sheet and spread with the butter and crumbs, using two sheets of phylo for each roll. Repeat for a second roll; recipe makes two rolls.

Spread sausage, mushrooms and cheese over the dough for each roll approximately ⅔ of length; roll up carefully. Bake at 350 degrees for 35 minutes until browned. Cut with sharp knife – 8 pieces per roll.

SAUSAGE STUFFED MUSHROOMS

YIELD: 25 Mushrooms

25 mushrooms, cleaned and stems removed
1 package Jimmy Dean Sausage (regular or hot)
4 ounces cream cheese

DIRECTIONS:

OVEN TEMPERATURE: Broil

Cook sausage until brown and crumbled; drain on paper towel. Mix with cream cheese. Stuff mixture into the mushroom caps. Broil till brown.

SESAME CHICKEN WITH HONEY DIP

SERVES 6

½ cup mayonnaise
1 teaspoon dry mustard
1 teaspoon instant minced
  onion
½ cup fine dry bread crumbs
¼ cup sesame seeds

2 cups cubed cooked chicken
  or turkey

Honey Dip:
1 cup mayonnaise
2 tablespoons honey

DIRECTIONS:

OVEN TEMPERATURE: 425°

Mix together the mayonnaise, mustard and minced onion; set aside. Combine crumbs and sesame seeds together.

Coat each piece of chicken with mayonnaise mixture and then crumb mixture. Place on baking sheet and bake for 12 minutes or until lightly browned. Serve hot with dip.

Honey Dip: Mix mayonnaise and honey together.

SHRIMP PUFFS

YIELD: 28 Medium-Size Cream Puffs

Cream Puffs
1 cup water
½ cup butter
1 cup flour
4 eggs

Filling:
1 · 4½-ounce can shrimp

½ cup finely chopped
  celery
1 · 8-ounce package cream
  cheese
1 teaspoon grated onion
¼ teaspoon lemon juice
¼ teaspoon garlic salt

DIRECTIONS:

OVEN TEMPERATURE: 400°

In a small sauce pan, heat water and butter to a rolling boil. Stir in flour and continue stirring vigorously over low heat to form a ball (1 minute). Remove from heat. Beat eggs into mixture one at a time until it is smooth and glossy.

Drop dough by teaspoons on an ungreased baking sheet. Bake for 25 minutes until brown and dry. Cool away from draft. Cut off tops.

Filling: Mix all ingredients together and fill each puff.

SHRIMP ROLL-UPS

YIELD: 40 Appetizers

1 · 8-ounce package cream cheese, softened
1 · 4½-ounce can shrimp or crab, drained
Dash garlic and onion powder (to taste)

1 teaspoon lemon juice
¼ teaspoon Worcestershire sauce
1-2 teaspoons salad dressing or mayonnaise
20 slices white sandwich bread
Butter

DIRECTIONS:

OVEN TEMPERATURE: Broil

Beat cream cheese until smooth and creamy; add shrimp, garlic powder, onion powder, lemon juice and Worcestershire sauce. Blend in enough salad dressing or mayonnaise to make spreadable.

Trim crusts from bread. Spread each slice with butter; place buttered side down on waxed paper. Spread other side with shrimp mixture and roll up with filling inside. Cut in half. Place seam side down on cookie sheet. Broil until bread looks toasted, 1 to 2 minutes.

SPINACH BALLS

YIELD: Approximately 70

2 · 10-ounce packages frozen chopped spinach, cooked and drained
2 cups herb-seasoned stuffing mix
2 large onions, chopped
5 eggs, beaten

¾ cup margarine, melted
½ cup grated Parmesan cheese
½ tablespoon garlic salt
1 teaspoon black pepper
½ tablespoon thyme

DIRECTIONS:

OVEN TEMPERATURE: 350°

Mix all ingredients and chill for two hours. Roll into small balls. Bake on a cookie sheet for 20 to 30 minutes at 350 degrees.

HINT:

These may be frozen unbaked on a cookie sheet and then packed in freezer bags. Remove spinach balls from freezer and bake as needed.

SPINACH-FILLED MUSHROOMS

YIELD: 16-20

16-20 mushrooms, 1½"-2" in diameter
1 cup finely chopped onion
3 tablespoons butter

1 · 10-ounce package frozen chopped spinach, cooked and drained
½ cup grated Swiss cheese
Grated Parmesan cheese

DIRECTIONS:

OVEN TEMPERATURE: 300°

Remove stems from mushrooms. Chop stems finely and sauté with onions in butter until onion is tender but not brown. Add spinach and stir to mix thoroughly. Add Swiss cheese, stirring lightly. Remove from heat.

Fill mushroom caps with mixture. Sprinkle with Parmesan cheese and place in a buttered shallow pan. Bake at 300 degrees for 15 to 20 minutes. Serve warm.

STUFFED CHERRY TOMATOES

SERVES 12

2 cups marinated artichoke hearts,
  drained and finely chopped
½ cup chopped celery
½ cup chopped green onion
1 cup mayonnaise

Salt and pepper to taste
2 cups cherry tomatoes
12 slices bacon, cooked and crumbled
2 bunches parsley

DIRECTIONS:

Mix artichokes, celery, green onion, mayonnaise, salt and pepper. Set aside. Cut each tomato in half; remove seeds and drain upside down on paper towel. Stuff tomato halves with artichoke mixture and sprinkle with bacon. Serve on bed of parsley.

STUFFED MUSHROOMS

YIELD: 16-20

12 large mushrooms
1 tablespoon minced onion
¼ cup butter
¼ teaspoon salt
1 cup soft wheat bread crumbs
  (1½ slices)

¼ cup grated Parmesan or
  Romano cheese
3 tablespoons chopped walnuts
1 tablespoon A-1 Sauce
1 tablespoon water

DIRECTIONS:

OVEN TEMPERATURE: 400°

Remove stems from mushrooms and chop. Sauté onions and stems in butter until onions are transparent. Mix in salt, crumbs, cheese, walnuts and A-1 Sauce.

Stuff caps with mixture. Place in shallow baking dish. Sprinkle water over mushrooms. Bake at 400 degrees for 20 minutes.

SWEET AND SOUR DOGS

SERVES 10

1 cup currant jelly
1 cup prepared mustard

1 pound hot dogs,
  cut in diagonal pieces

DIRECTIONS:

Heat jelly and mustard together. Add hot dog pieces and simmer for ½ hour. Use as cocktail pick-up food.

TIROPETES
(Cheese Triangles)

YIELD: 75-100

1 cup bechamel sauce
1 pound feta cheese, crumbled
  (or ½ pound feta cheese and
  1 · 8-ounce package cream cheese)
3 egg yolks
1 cup grated Parmesan cheese
2 tablespoons chopped parsley
1 cup melted butter

1 pound phylo leaves (dough)

Bechamel Sauce
¼ cup butter
3 tablespoons flour
2 cups hot milk
Salt and white pepper
  to taste

DIRECTIONS:

OVEN TEMPERATURE: 375°

Bechamel Sauce: Melt butter; add flour and stir until smooth. Lower heat and gradually add the hot milk, stirring constantly until thick. Season with salt and pepper. Cool.

Tiropetes: To 1 cup bechamel sauce, add feta cheese, egg yolks, Parmesan cheese, parsley and 3 tablespoons melted butter and mix well.

Cut phylo sheets into long strips 3 inches wide and brush with melted butter. Place 1 teaspoon of the cheese mixture at the bottom of each strip and fold the corner up to form a triangle. Continue folding in a triangular shape until the entire strip is folded. Continue this method until all the ingredients are used.

Place triangles on cookie sheets. Brush each with remaining melted butter and bake at 375 degrees for 15 to 20 minutes or until golden brown. Serve immediately.

HINT:

Cover unused phylo dough with a slightly damp cloth to prevent it from drying out. Triangles may be prepared ahead of time, frozen and baked when ready to serve.

ZUCCHINI APPETIZERS

YIELD: 4 Dozen

1 cup buttermilk baking mix
4 eggs
½ cup chopped onion
1 cup grated Parmesan cheese
½ teaspoon salt
½ teaspoon seasoned salt

½ teaspoon oregano or
  Italian seasoning
1 clove garlic, pressed
½ cup oil
3 cups thinly sliced zucchini

DIRECTIONS:

OVEN TEMPERATURE: 350°

Mix all ingredients except zucchini in a large bowl. Fold in zucchini. Spread in greased 9 x 13 inch baking pan. Bake at 350 degrees for 20 to 25 minutes until golden brown. Cut into 2 x 1 inch squares.

ALOHA DIP

SERVES 10-12

12 macaroon cookies, crushed into
  small pieces
¼ cup brown sugar, firmly packed
2 cups sour cream

1 large pineapple
Assorted berries
Seedless green grapes
Various fruits and melons, sliced

DIRECTIONS:

Mix together macaroons, sugar and sour cream. Chill several hours to soften crumbs. Do not stir again.

Slice a cap-shaped piece off the top of the pineapple about 1 inch below bottom of leaves. Hollow out center of pineapple. Leave a firm shell to hold macaroon mixture. Cut pineapple fruit into small pieces. Discard hard core. Fill pineapple shell with dip and place in center of large platter or bowl.

Arrange fruit and berries in groups around pineapple. If desired, sprinkle fruit with Kirsh or Brandy.

ARTICHOKE DIP

SERVES 10-12

1½ cups sour cream
1½ cups mayonnaise
1 small package Hidden Valley
  Ranch Style Dressing

1 · 14-ounce can artichoke hearts,
  drained and coarsely chopped

DIRECTIONS:

Mix all ingredients. Refrigerate until ready to serve. Serve with Wheat Thins.

AVOCADO- TOMATO DIP

SERVES 12-18

4-6 avocados, chopped
2 green onions, chopped
1 · 4-ounce can diced green chilies
1 · 12-ounce bottle chili sauce

2 · 7¾-ounce cans salsa
⅛ teaspoon garlic salt
Salt and pepper to taste

DIRECTIONS:

Mix the chopped avocado, green onion and green chilies. Add chili sauce, salsa, garlic salt, salt and pepper. Chill 2 to 4 hours. Serve with corn chips.

CHEESE DIP FOR ROUND-LOAF FRENCH BREAD

YIELD: 2 cups

1 · 8-ounce package cream cheese
¾ teaspoon dry mustard
⅓ cup chopped green onions
1 tablespoon Accent (MSG)
2 teaspoons Worcestershire sauce
1 tablespoon Jalapeño Pepper
   Cheeze Whiz

1 teaspoon lemon juice
1 teaspoon garlic powder
Tabasco sauce to taste
1 loaf round French bread
1 loaf (baguette) French bread
Slivered almonds (optional)
Vegetables for dipping (optional)

DIRECTIONS:

Mix together all ingredients. This can be done quickly in a food processor, eliminating the need to chop the green onions.

Scoop out the middle of the round loaf of bread and reserve the pieces for dipping. Just before serving, fill the hollowed shell with dip. Sprinkle with slivered almonds. Slice the additional loaf of bread in small pieces for dipping. Great dip for vegetables, too.

CLAM COCKTAIL DIP

SERVES 8-10

2 · 3-ounce packages cream cheese
   softened
2 teaspoons lemon juice
2 teaspoons finely grated onion
1 teaspoon Worcestershire sauce

3-4 drops Tabasco sauce
¼ teaspoon salt
1 cup minced clams
1 tablespoon minced parsley

DIRECTIONS:

Beat cream cheese until· smooth and creamy. Add lemon juice, onion, Worcestershire sauce, Tabasco and salt. Beat with beater until light and fluffy. Stir in clams and parsley. Serve with chips or crackers.

VARIATION:

Substitute shrimp or crab for the clams.

DILLY DIP

YIELD: 1 cup

½ cup mayonnaise
½ cup sour cream
1 teaspoon Beau Monde
1 teaspoon dill weed

1 teaspoon parsley
1 teaspoon chives
¼ teaspoon curry powder (optional)

DIRECTIONS:

Mix all ingredients and chill several hours. Serve with favorite vegetables.

FAVORITE SPINACH DIP

YIELD: 2 cups

"So good and so easy!"

1 · 10-ounce package chopped frozen spinach, cooked and drained well
2 cups sour cream
1 · 8-ounce can water chestnuts, chopped
1 package Knorrs vegetable soup mix

DIRECTIONS:

Mix all ingredients together and serve with king-size corn chips.

FRESH FRUIT DIP

SERVES 8

1 · 8-ounce package cream cheese,
   softened
1 · 7-ounce bottle marshmallow cream
Grated rind of 1 orange

1 tablespoon orange juice
Dash ground nutmeg
Dash ground ginger

DIRECTIONS:

Mix all ingredients well and chill until ready to serve. Serve with a variety of fresh cut-up fruits.

HOT CRAB DIP

SERVES 8-10

1 · 8-ounce package cream cheese,
   softened
1 tablespoon milk
1 · 6-ounce can flaked crabmeat
2 tablespoons minced onion

½ teaspoon horseradish
¼ teaspoon salt
⅛ teaspoon pepper
Sliced almonds, toasted

DIRECTIONS:

Mix all ingredients together except the almonds. Put in a small oven-proof dish and bake at 325 degrees for 15 minutes or until bubbly. Top with toasted almonds. Serve with chips.

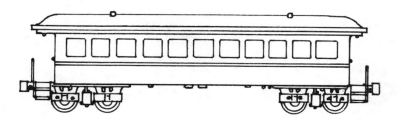

KAHLUA FRUIT DIP

SERVES 35

1 · 8-ounce package cream cheese,
   softened
1 cup non-dairy whipped cream
¾ cup brown sugar

⅓ cup Kahlua liqueur
1 cup sour cream
6 ounces unsalted peanuts,
   chopped fine

DIRECTIONS:

In medium-sized bowl, mix cream cheese and whipped cream together until
smooth. Add brown sugar and Kahlua; blend until brown sugar is melted. Add
sour cream; beat until smooth and creamy. Fold in nuts and refrigerate.

HINT:

This may be made days ahead of serving; the longer it sits, the better it gets.
Recommended fruits include fresh strawberries, fresh pineapple wedges,
Thompson seedless grapes, apple wedges.

LAYERED TACO TREAT

SERVES 20

1 · 31-ounce can refried beans
4 or 5 avocados
2 tablespoons lemon juice
½ cup mayonnaise
¼ teaspoon garlic salt
⅛ teaspoon onion salt

2 cups sour cream
1 · 1¼-ounce package dry taco
   seasoning mix
2 cups Cheddar cheese, grated
Optional: chopped green onions, sliced
   black olives, chopped tomatoes

DIRECTIONS:

Spread refried beans in bottom of a 9 x 13 inch cake pan. Mash avocados and
mix with lemon juice, mayonnaise, garlic salt and onion salt; spread on top of
refried beans. Mix sour cream and taco mix together and spread on top of
avocado mixture. Top with grated cheese and optional ingredients. Serve with
tortilla chips.

HINT:

For a change of pace, try heating for 8 minutes at 350 degrees and serving
warm. Great this way too!

TIP:
Chopped onions may be frozen in a plastic bag and used without
defrosting. To remove onion odor from hands, rub with a slice of
lemon.

MICROWAVE HOT BEEF DIP

YIELD: 2 cups

1 · 3-ounce package smoked sliced beef or chipped beef
½ cup Parmesan cheese
¼ cup chopped green onion

¼ cup sour cream
¼ cup mayonnaise
1 · 8-ounce package cream cheese
1 tablespoon parsley flakes

DIRECTIONS:

Cut beef into bite-size pieces. Combine beef and all other ingredients in a small bowl. Microwave on simmer for 5 to 6 minutes or until hot, stirring once.

Serve with crackers, vegetables or as a topping for baked potatoes.

VARIATION:

Shrimp or clams may be substituted for beef.

SOUR DOUGH BEEF DIP

SERVES 8

1 · 8-ounce package cream cheese
1 cup sour cream
1 · 4-ounce package chipped beef, chopped

¼ cup chopped green onion
2 tablespoons chopped green pepper
Dash Worcestershire sauce
1 · 8-ounce round loaf sour dough bread

DIRECTIONS:

OVEN TEMPERATURE: 300°

Combine all ingredients except bread and mix well. Slice top off bread and hollow out carefully making sure there are no weak places in bread shell. Fill shell with chipped beef mixture and put top back on. Wrap in foil and bake for 1½ hours. Use leftover bread and crackers to dip in hot mixture.

VARIATION:

Also good with chopped pepperoni or pastrami instead of chipped beef.

SOUTHWEST SHRIMP DIP

SERVES 10-12

1 · 8-ounce package cream cheese
1 cup sour cream
1 package dry Italian salad dressing mix

2 teaspoons lemon juice
4 ounces cleaned shrimp
   (2 cans can be used if desired)

DIRECTIONS:

Blend all ingredients together and chill. Serve with chips.

SPINACH VEGETABLE DIP

YIELD: 2½-3 cups

½ package fresh spinach, washed
   and drained
1 · 8-ounce package cream cheese
2 cups mayonnaise

½ cup half-and-half
1 tablespoon minced onion
1 teaspoon chives
1 teaspoon Accent (MSG)

DIRECTIONS:

Blend all ingredients in blender. Store in refrigerator several hours or overnight to blend flavors. Serve with favorite vegetables.

TOMATO DIP

SERVES 8

1 pound sausage, browned
   and crumbled
1 medium onion, chopped
1 large green pepper, chopped

1 · 16-ounce can stewed tomatoes,
   well drained
1 cup sour cream
1 · 8-ounce package cream cheese

DIRECTIONS:

Mix all ingredients well; serve warm with vegetables or tortilla chips. Great microwave recipe.

CHEESE-FILLED ROLL

SERVES 12

1 · 8-ounce package Velveeta cheese, room temperature
1 · 8-ounce package cream cheese, room temperature
1 · 4-ounce can chopped green chilies
1 · 8-ounce can black olives, chopped or sliced

DIRECTIONS:

Roll out Velveeta cheese between waxed paper until ¼ inch thick.

Mix cream cheese, green chilies and black olives together. Spread onto the rolled out Velveeta cheese. Roll up jelly-roll fashion. Refrigerate until ready to serve.

Serve with crackers.

CHEESE MOLD

SERVES 10-12

½ cup butter
1 · 8-ounce carton "Kaukauna" sharp cheese
2 ounces blue cheese, crumbled

1 · 8-ounce package cream cheese
½ package Good Seasons Italian salad dressing mix
Parsley or paprika

DIRECTIONS:

Blend butter, sharp cheese, blue cheese and cream cheese in food processor or mixer. Add Italian salad dressing mix. Line a mold with plastic wrap and fill with cheese mixture. Press to get all areas filled. Chill several hours.

Invert and pull off mold and plastic wrap. Garnish with parsley or paprika. Serve with crackers.

CHEESE TORTA

SERVES 20-30

2 · 8-ounce packages cream cheese, softened
2 cups unsalted butter, room temperature
2½ cups *fresh* basil leaves, lightly packed
1 cup Parmesan or Romano cheese, freshly grated
⅓ cup olive oil
¼ cup pine nuts (substitute walnuts if pine nuts not available)
Cheese cloth

DIRECTIONS:

Beat cream cheese and butter in mixer until fluffy.

Pesto: In food processor, using steel blade, chip basil and cheese. Slowly add olive oil. Add nuts.

Place moist cheese cloth in a deep mixing bowl. Layer cheese and pesto, beginning and ending with the cheese mixture. Refrigerate until firm. Remove cheese cloth carefully and wrap mixture in plastic wrap; otherwise, the mixture will bleed and layers will not be distinct.

Serve with French-type bread, thinly sliced, or plain crackers, unsalted.

HINT:

Pesto can be made ahead when fresh basil is available and frozen for future use.

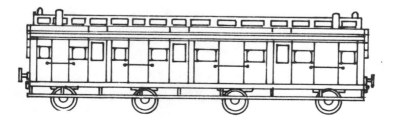

CRAB SPREAD

SERVES 12

1 · 10¾-ounce can cream of mushroom soup
1 package unflavored gelatin
3 tablespoons warm water
1 · 8-ounce package cream cheese
1 cup mayonnaise
1 cup chopped celery
1 cup chopped onion
1 · 6-ounce can flaked crabmeat

DIRECTIONS:

In medium saucepan, warm soup. Dissolve gelatin in warm water and add to soup. Mix in cream cheese until smooth. Remove from stove; add mayonnaise, celery, onion, and crabmeat. Pour into mold and cover. Refrigerate overnight. Serve with crackers.

DEVILED HAM CHEESE BALL

SERVES 15-20

"Devilishly good!"

2 · 8-ounce packages cream cheese
2 cups grated Cheddar cheese
2 tablespoons grated green onion
1 teaspoon lemon juice
1 teaspoon dry mustard
2 tablespoons chopped parsley
2 tablespoons Worcestershire sauce
½ teaspoon paprika
¼ teaspoon salt
½ teaspoon seasoned salt
2 · 2¼-ounce cans deviled ham
1 cup chopped walnuts

DIRECTIONS:

Mix all ingredients except nuts and roll into a ball. Roll cheese ball in the nuts to cover. Serve with crackers.

TIP:

Never peel mushrooms! They need only be washed under running water and quickly dried. Mushrooms will keep for several days in the refrigerator. They may also be frozen and used without defrosting.

EXOTIC EGGPLANT

SERVES 3-4

"Great as an hors d'oeuvre or vegetable"

1½ pounds firm eggplant
1 tablespoon minced fresh garlic
1 tablespoon minced ginger root
3 tablespoons chopped green onion
½ teaspoon red pepper flakes
2 tablespoons salad oil

2 tablespoons soy sauce
1 teaspoon rice vinegar
2 tablespoons brown sugar
1 tablespoon hot water
1 teaspoon sesame oil

DIRECTIONS:

OVEN TEMPERATURE: 475°

Prick eggplant with a fork and bake in 475 degree oven for 30 to 45 minutes until soft. Cool. Remove stems and peel. Tear or cut into very thin strips. Drain if it is watery.

Combine garlic, ginger, green onion and red pepper in small bowl. Combine soy sauce, vinegar, sugar and hot water in another bowl.

In wok or frying pan, add 2 tablespoons oil and heat; add garlic mixture. Stir fry 1 minute. Do not burn! Add soy sauce mixture, stirring. When it simmers, add the eggplant. Turn heat to high and stir fry until the eggplant is hot. Add sesame oil and stir to combine. Serve.

HINT:

This can be served hot, at room temperature, or chilled. Makes a nice hors d'oeuvre when served with crackers or is an excellent vegetable. Reheats well in microwave.

HAM-CLAM SPREAD

YIELD: 40

1 · 7½-ounce can minced clams, drained
½ pound cooked ham, minced
1 cup sour cream
1 cup mayonnaise
1 cup grated Parmesan cheese

⅓ cup finely chopped onion
2 teaspoons anchovy paste, no substitute
½ teaspoon pepper
¼ cup chopped parsley

DIRECTIONS:

Combine all ingredients and mix well. Spread on crackers, use as a dip or fill pastry puffs.

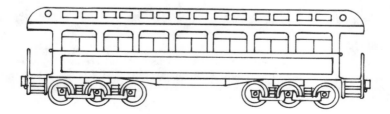

MOLDED AVOCADO PINWHEEL

SERVES: 10-12

1 envelope unflavored gelatin
¼ cup cold water
1 cup mashed avocado
  (2-3 avocados)
1 tablespoon lemon juice

1 · 0.7-ounce package dry Italian
  dressing mix
2 cups sour cream
3 tablespoons chopped parsley
Dash of Tabasco sauce
2-3 drops green food coloring

Assorted garnishes such as cooked baby shrimp, chopped green onions, chopped
black olives, chopped cucumbers, chopped tomatoes.

DIRECTIONS:

In a saucepan, sprinkle gelatin over cold water. Let stand 5 minutes to soften.
Cook over medium heat until mixture comes to a boil and gelatin is dissolved.

In large mixing bowl, blend avocado, lemon juice, salad dressing mix, sour
cream, parsley and Tabasco sauce. Add dissolved gelatin and mix thoroughly. Stir
in food coloring.

Pour mixture into oiled flan pan. Cover with plastic wrap and refrigerate until
firm. Unmold and decorate with garnishes (varied to suit personal taste)
arranged in concentric circles. Serve with cocktail bread or crackers.

OYSTER ROLL

SERVES: 12-15

1 clove garlic, pressed
1 tablespoon minced onion
¼ teaspoon cayenne pepper
2 · 8-ounce packages cream cheese
2 tablespoons mayonnaise

1 tablespoon horseradish sauce
1 teaspoon Worcestershire sauce
2 · 3¾ ounce cans smoked oysters,
  drained
Paprika or parsley

DIRECTIONS:

Blend thoroughly all ingredients except oysters and spread on waxed paper about
¼ inch thick. Place the drained oysters evenly on top of the cheese spread. Roll
up with a cold, wet knife. Garnish with paprika or parsley. Serve with a variety
of crackers.

PECAN SPREAD

YIELD: 1½ cups

½ cup finely chopped pecans
2 tablespoons butter
2 teaspoons minced green onions

¼ cup sour cream
2 · 3-ounce packages cream
  cheese

DIRECTIONS:

Sauté pecans in butter for one minute. Add green onions and remove from heat.
Add remaining ingredients and stir until well mixed. Serve with snack crackers.

PINEAPPLE-PECAN CHEESE BALL

YIELD: 15-20 Servings

2 · 8-ounce packages cream cheese, softened
1 · 15¼-ounce can crushed pineapple, drained
2 cups chopped pecans

¼ cup diced green pepper
2 tablespoons chopped onion
1 tablespoon seasoned salt
1 teaspoon lemon juice

DIRECTIONS:

Mix cream cheese, pineapple, *1 cup* pecans, green pepper, onion, seasoned salt and lemon juice. Form into a ball and roll in the remaining 1 cup of pecans. Chill. Serve with crackers or vegetables.

RED APPLE CHEESE BALL

YIELD: 3 cups

"A favorite Fall treat when apples are so plentiful!"

4 cups grated sharp Cheddar cheese (approximately 1 pound of cheese)
1 · 3-ounce package cream cheese, softened
½ cup apple cider
1 teaspoon Worcestershire sauce

1 teaspoon dry mustard
½ teaspoon onion salt
¼ teaspoon cayenne pepper
2 teaspoons caraway seeds
Paprika
Cinnamon stick

DIRECTIONS:

Combine cheeses, cider, seasonings and seeds; beat until smooth. Refrigerate 2 to 3 hours. Shape into a round, apple shaped ball. Roll all sides in paprika to create a "red apple." Insert cinnamon stick for stem. Refrigerate until served.

Serve as a spread with an assortment of sliced red and golden delicious apples and crackers.

SHRIMP APPETIZER

YIELD: 12-16 Servings

2 · 8-ounce packages cream cheese
2 tablespoons Worcestershire sauce
¼ teaspoon grated lemon peel
1 tablespoon lemon juice
⅓ cup sliced green onions
⅛ teaspoon Tabasco

1 · 12-ounce bottle tomato based chili sauce
1 tablespoon horseradish
1 pound small cooked shrimp (or 2 cans)

DIRECTIONS:

Beat together cream cheese, Worcestershire sauce, lemon peel, lemon juice, green onions and hot pepper seasoning. Spread onto a 10 x 12 inch rimmed platter. Cover and chill if made ahead.

To serve, stir together chili sauce and horseradish. Spread over cheese and top with shrimp. Garnish with parsley. Serve with crackers.

SHRIMP BUTTER

YIELD: Approximately 20 Servings

1 · 8-ounce package cream cheese, softened
½ cup butter, softened
2 cans shrimp, drained well

2 tablespoons mayonnaise
Squirt of lemon juice
1 tablespoon minced onion
Dash garlic powder

DIRECTIONS:

With electric mixer, beat cream cheese and butter together. Add remaining ingredients and beat well. Chill and serve with crackers.

SHRIMP MOUSSE

SERVES 8

1 · 10¾-ounce can tomato soup
3 · 3-ounce packages cream cheese
2 tablespoons unflavored gelatin
1 cup water
¾ cup chopped parsley
¾ cup chopped green pepper

2 tablespoons grated onion
1 cup mayonnaise
1 pound shrimp, cleaned and cooked
¼ teaspoon Worcestershire sauce
2 dashes Tabasco sauce

DIRECTIONS:

Mash cream cheese in the soup and heat in double boiler until very hot. Soak gelatin for 5 minutes in the cup of water and add to soup mixture. When slightly thickened, add vegetables, shrimp, and mayonnaise. Salt to taste. Add Tabasco and Worcestershire sauces. Place in mold and chill until firm.

Delicious served on crackers or as a side dish.

SMOKED SALMON PATÉ

YIELD: 16-20 Servings

1 · 1- pound can salmon
1 · 8-ounce package cream cheese
2 tablespoons grated or finely chopped onion
¼ teaspoon salt
1 tablespoon lemon juice

¼ teaspoon pepper
1 teaspoon liquid smoke
1 teaspoon prepared horseradish
Garnish: chopped nuts, parsley, paprika

DIRECTIONS:

Drain salmon and remove skin and bones. Flake and combine with next seven ingredients. Place in mold and chill several hours. Decorate with chopped nuts and parsley or paprika. Serve with crackers.

BIRDY NUM-NUM PUNCH

YIELD: 2 Gallons

1 · 6-ounce can frozen orange juice
  concentrate
5 cups sugar
2 gallons water

2 tablespoons citric acid
  (may be purchased at a pharmacy)
2 tablespoons lemon juice
1 teaspoon vanilla extract
1 teaspoon almond extract

DIRECTIONS:

Combine all ingredients and refrigerate. Bourbon or Brandy may be added for more punch!

HINT:

1 tray of ice cubes is approximately 2 cups of water. If using ice cubes, reduce the water proportionately.

BRANDY SLUSH

SERVES 30

2 cups sugar
7 cups boiling water
2 cups strong tea
12 ounces frozen orange juice
  concentrate

12 ounces frozen lemonade
  concentrate
1 · 46-ounce can pineapple juice
2 cups Brandy
2 liters Sprite

DIRECTIONS:

Dissolve sugar in boiling water. Add remaining ingredients except Sprite. Freeze overnight. When ready to serve, scrape frozen mixture into a punch bowl. Add Sprite gradually as needed.

TIP:

Packages of frozen melon balls, mixed fruit, raspberries or strawberries can be floated in fruit punches instead of an ice ring. As the fruit thaws, it becomes a garnish for the punch.

EVER READY DAIQUIRIS

SERVES 18-20

2 · 6-ounce cans frozen lemonade concentrate
2 · 6-ounce cans frozen limeade concentrate
2 · 46-ounce cans pineapple juice
1 quart light rum
Optional garnishes: mint sprigs, lemon slices, lime slices.

DIRECTIONS:

Combine all ingredients in a 1½-gallon freezer container and mix until slushy. Store in freezer. (Mixture will never freeze completely.) When ready to serve, ladle into glasses and garnish with one of the above suggestions.

HINT:

Refreshing with a splash of Sprite added just before serving.

FROSTY LIME FLOATS

SERVES 6

1½ cups pineapple juice, chilled
½ cup lime juice
1 quart lime sherbet

1 · 28-ounce bottle lemon-lime soda, chilled
Maraschino cherries

DIRECTIONS:

Pour pineapple and lime juices in blender jar. Spoon half the lime sherbet into the juices. Cover and blend until smooth. Pour mixture into six glasses.

Add a scoop of lime sherbet to each glass. Fill with lemon-lime soda. Garnish with a marachino cherry.

FROSTY TEA AND TONIC

SERVES 4

3 tablespoons powdered sugar
⅓ cup fresh lime juice
3 cups iced tea

1 · 10-ounce bottle tonic water
ice cubes
lime slices

DIRECTIONS:

In 1½-quart pitcher, combine sugar with lime juice to dissolve. Stir in iced tea. When ready to serve, add tonic water, ice cubes and lime slices.

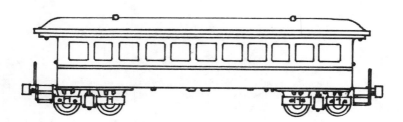

HOT BUTTERED BEVERAGE MIX

YIELD: 24 portions

6 cups packed brown sugar
1 cup butter, room temperature
2 tablespoons honey
1 tablespoon vanilla
1 tablespoon rum flavoring

1 tablespoon brandy flavoring
1 teaspoon cinnamon
½ teaspoon ground cloves
½ teaspoon allspice
¼ teaspoon nutmeg

DIRECTIONS:

In large mixing bowl, combine all ingredients and beat with an electric mixer until well blended.

To serve, stir about 1 teaspoon of mix into each 6 to 8 ounce mug of hot apple or orange juice, hot milk, coffee (with cream and a cinnamon stick), or hot water with rum. Mound the mix in a serving bowl and invite guests to serve themselves.

To store, cover and chill up to 3 months.

HOT BUTTERED RUM BATTER

SERVES 20

1 pint vanilla ice cream
2 cups butter, room temperature
1 pound brown sugar
½ teaspoon nutmeg

½ teaspoon cinnamon
½ teaspoon allspice
Rum

DIRECTIONS:

Combine all ingredients except rum and store in freezer. To serve place 1 tablespoon of batter in a mug with 1 jigger of rum and boiling water. Stir vigorously.

MOCK MARGARITA

SERVES 4

1 · 6-ounce can frozen limeade
6 ounces Tequila
6 ounces beer

Ice
Salted glasses
Sliced lime

DIRECTIONS:

Pour limeade, Tequila and beer into a blender; fill blender near to the top with ice and blend until ice is well chopped and mixture is frothy. Pour into salted glasses and garnish with lime slice.

HINT:

To salt glasses, wet rim of glass with lime juice and dip into salt.

MRS. DIGGINS' HOT CHOCOLATE

YIELD: 2 Quarts

2 tablespoons Hershey's Cocoa
⅓ cup sugar
1 cup water
4 cups milk

1 · cup evaporated milk
Pinch of salt
1 teaspoon vanilla
Sweetened whipped cream

DIRECTIONS:

In saucepan, bring to a boil cocoa, sugar and water; boil one minute. Add milk, salt and vanilla. Serve hot with whipped cream.

NOTE:

Mrs. Diggins is a prominent citizen of San Francisco and Hawaii. Her family owns the famous Parker Ranch on the Big Island of Hawaii. This hot chocolate was served to many famous movie stars when she entertained.

ORANGE-ALMOND PUNCH

SERVES 25

2 . 6-ounce cans frozen lemonade
concentrate
2 · 6-ounce cans frozen orange juice
concentrate
2 cups water

2 cups sugar
1 teaspoon almond flavoring
1 teaspoon vanilla
1 quart Sprite
Ice

DIRECTIONS:

Mix juices as directed on cans. Mix water and sugar together and boil until sugar dissolves. Cool well and add to juices. Just prior to serving, add the almond and vanilla flavorings, Sprite and ice.

ORANGE-BANANA FRUIT DRINK

SERVES 6-8

3-4 ripe bananas
1 · 6-ounce can frozen orange juice
1 · 6-ounce can lemonade concentrate

3 ounces pineapple juice
1 · 16-ounce bottle of Sprite or 7-UP
Lime slices as garnish

DIRECTIONS:

Combine bananas and fruit juices in blender and blend until quite smooth. Pour 3 ounces of juice into 8-ounce glass and fill the rest of the way with Sprite or 7-Up. Stir carefully and garnish with lime slice.

ORANGE JULIUS

SERVES 4-5

1 · 6-ounce can frozen orange juice
   concentrate
4 cups milk
1 teaspoon vanilla
5-6 tablespoons sugar (or to taste)

2 eggs or 1 pint vanilla ice cream
8-9 ice cubes
A peeled orange may be added
   for flavor

DIRECTIONS:

Place all ingredients in blender and blend until smooth and creamy.

PARTY HOT CHOCOLATE

SERVES 16

3 cups whipping cream
2 tablespoons powdered sugar
1½ teaspoons vanilla
3 teaspoons granulated sugar
2 teaspoons nutmeg

2 teaspoons cinnamon
Dash of cloves
3 quarts chocolate low-fat milk
1½ teaspoons vanilla

DIRECTIONS:

Beat whipping cream until foamy. Gradually add powdered sugar and vanilla and beat until soft peaks form.

In large sauce pan, combine granulated sugar, nutmeg, cinnamon, and cloves. Blend in chocolate milk and heat, but do not boil. Remove from heat and stir in vanilla. Blend half of whipped cream into chocolate milk mixture. Garnish with remaining whipped cream. Serve hot.

PIÑA COLADA DRINK

SERVES 4-6

"Delightful and festive with or without liquor."

1 · 15-ounce can Lopez Cream
   of Coconut
⅓ cup whipping cream
1 cup unsweetened pineapple juice

8-10 drops almond flavoring
10-15 ice cubes
   (or more to make desired thickness)

DIRECTIONS:

Put all ingredients in blender and crush. Serve at once.

HINT:

If made ahead, chill all but ice and add ice when ready to serve. Rum may be added for alcoholic Piña Colada.

PARTY PUNCH

SERVES 30-40

1½ cups sugar
3 cups water
3 bananas
1 · 6-ounce can frozen fruit punch
1 · 12-ounce can frozen orange juice
  concentrate

1 · 6-ounce can lemonade concentrate
3 · 5½-ounce cans pineapple juice
1 quart fresh strawberries or
  1 package frozen
4 · 2-liter bottles Squirt
2 oranges, sliced

DIRECTIONS:

Bring sugar and water to a boil. Let cool. Blend fruit (except orange slices) and juices in a blender. Mix fruit and sugar mixtures. In punch bowl, place 2 cups of fruit mixture with one bottle of Squirt. Garnish with orange slices.

SEAFOOD COCKTAIL DRINK

YIELD: 2 Quarts

1 · 46-ounce can tomato juice
2 · 6½-ounce cans broken shrimp
  or crab (or 1 of each)
1 cup catsup
1 tablespoon
  horseradish

1 cup finely chopped celery
½ teaspoon garlic salt
3 teaspoons Worcestershire sauce
3 tablespoons sugar
juice of ½ lemon

DIRECTIONS:

Mix all ingredients together and chill. Great served with crackers and cheeses or just by itself.

SPICED APPLE CIDER

YIELD: 1 Gallon

1 gallon apple cider
1 cup sugar
12 whole cloves
½ teaspoon salt

4 cinnamon sticks
4 teaspoons grated lemon rind
1 teaspoon grated orange rind

DIRECTIONS:

Mix all ingredients and simmer two hours (DO NOT BOIL). Serve warm.

SUMMER RELIEF

YIELD: 1 Gallon

"Ah-h-h"

1 gallon water
Juice of 3 oranges

Juice of 2 lemons
1½ cups sugar

DIRECTIONS:

Combine all ingredients in a gallon container. Serve in ice-filled glasses.

BROCCOLI CHEESE SOUP

SERVES 10-12

¾ cup chopped onion
3 tablespoons oil or margarine
6 cups water
6 chicken bouillon cubes
8 ounces uncooked egg or corkscrew
  noodles
1 teaspoon salt

2 · 10-ounce packages frozen
  broccoli
¼ teaspoon garlic powder
6 cups milk ·
1 pound Velveeta cheese, grated
  or chopped
pepper to taste

DIRECTIONS:

Sauté onion in oil for 3 minutes. Add water and bouillon cubes and heat to
boiling. Stir until dissolved. Gradually add noodles and salt and cook 3 minutes.
Stir in broccoli and garlic powder and cook for 4 minutes. Add milk and cheese,
stirring constantly. Add pepper to taste.

HINT:

May substitute Cheddar cheese for more Cheddar flavor.

CHEESY CHICKEN SOUP

YIELD: 32 Servings or 8 quarts (party size)

6 to 8 chicken breasts
6 carrots, diced small
6 stalks celery, chopped fine
2 onions, diced
1 package frozen peas
1½ gallons water

6 ounces chicken soup base or
  chicken boullion
1 pound butter
3 cups flour
1 · 16-ounce bottle Cheese Whiz
pepper to taste

DIRECTIONS:

Boil chicken until tender or wrap and bake chicken in oven for 40 minutes at
350 degrees. Remove meat from bones and cut into small pieces. Par boil and
drain raw vegetables. Set aside.

Boil 1½ gallons water and chicken soup base.

In another pan melt butter then add flour until thickened. Add the butter and
flour mixture to the soup base. Add all the vegetables and chicken. Add the
cheese whiz (warm in microwave to make it easier to pour out). Add more water
if the soup is too thick.

Heat and serve.

HINT:

This recipe may easily be cut in half for a smaller family.

CANADIAN CHEDDAR CHEESE SOUP

YIELD: 10 Large or 15 Small Servings

1 pound medium Cheddar cheese, shredded
2 tablespoons corn starch
2 cups water
1 teaspoon salt
¼ teaspoon pepper
1 teaspoon Worcestershire sauce
dash garlic powder

8 tablespoons butter (½ cup)
¾ cup diced, cooked cauliflower
1 cup sliced mushrooms
½ cup finely chopped carrots
1 cup finely chopped onion
¾ cup diced ham
2 cups half and half or evaporated milk, undiluted

DIRECTIONS:

Mix corn starch with cheese. Heat water to boiling in 6 quart saucepan. Add cheese mixture to boiling water a little at a time stirring constantly.

Continue to cook over medium heat stirring constantly until cheese is melted and mixture is smooth. Add salt and pepper, Worcestershire sauce and garlic powder.

Sauté each vegetable separately in two tablespoons butter each until tender. Add to soup along with the ham.

Heat, stirring constantly, adding half and half until desired thickness is reached.

This recipe comes from Darrell W. Hardy, chef at Big Sky Ski Lodge in Montana.

CHEESY CAULIFLOWER SOUP

SERVES 4-6

1 · 2 pound head cauliflower
¼ cup margarine
¼ cup flour
4 cups chicken stock

1 small onion, chopped
1 large stalk celery, chopped
1½ cups grated Cheddar cheese

DIRECTIONS:

Break cauliflower head into pieces and steam in boiling water until barely soft. Drain. Chop cauliflower into small pieces.

Melt margarine in large saucepan. Add flour and cook, stirring until a smooth paste is formed. Gradually add chicken stock, stirring until sauce is smooth and thickened. Add onion and celery and simmer for 20 minutes. Add cauliflower and grated cheese. Serve as soon as cheese melts.

HINT:

May be reheated slowly, but do not boil.

CHEYENNE CHILI

SERVES 12

⅓ cup diced salt pork or bacon
 (about 2 ounces)
1 cup water
4 cups chopped onion (1½ pounds)
3 tablespoons minced garlic
3 to 5 pounds cubed beef chuck,
 trimmed of excess fat (can use more
 or less meat) Sirloin may be
 substituted.
¼ cup ground cumin
¼ cup chili powder (or less)
1 tablespoon crushed red pepper
 flakes
1 teaspoon salt
1 teaspoon Tabasco sauce
1 · 15-ounce can tomato sauce

2 · 14½-ounce cans stewed
 tomatoes
1 · 12-ounce can beer
2 · 13¾ or 14½-ounce cans beef
 broth
¼ cup masa harina (ground corn
 meal)
¼ cup water

Condiments:
4 · 15½-ounce cans pinto beans,
 heated
2 cups chopped onions
2 cups grated cheddar cheese
2 cups sour cream

DIRECTIONS:

In large Dutch oven cook salt pork or bacon. Add water and cook over medium heat until all water has evaporated. Add onions and garlic and sauté until tender, about 15 minutes. Add beef chuck and continue cooking over medium heat until lightly browned. Add seasonings, tomato sauce and stewed tomatoes and mix well. Stir in beer and beef broth. Simmer 2¼ hours over low heat being careful not to scorch.

In a small bowl mix masa harina with water, stirring until smooth. Add the masa harina mixture to the soup and simmer another 30 minutes. If desired, add pinto beans to chili instead of serving as a condiment.

Serve chili topped with condiments.

HINT:

May substitute cubed sirloin for the chuck if a leaner meat is preferred.

TIP:

Stock may be frozen, but because freezing causes ingredients to separate, it should be brought to a boil before using.

STEVIE'S CHILI

SERVES 8-10

1 pound green peppers, seeded, and
  coarsely chopped
2 cloves garlic, peeled and crushed
2 large onions, chopped
2 · 28-ounce cans tomatoes, undrained
½ cup finely chopped parsley
¼ cup butter
2½ pounds lean ground beef

1 pound lean ground pork
¼ cup chili powder (less if desired)
1 tablespoon salt (or salt to taste)
1½ teaspoons pepper
1½ teaspoons cumin seed
1½ teaspoons MSG (optional)
1 · 15-ounce can chili beans

DIRECTIONS:

In Dutch oven slowly sauté green pepper in small amount of oil for 5 mintues.
Add garlic and onion and cook until tender, stirring frrequently. Add tomatoes
and parsley; simmer five minutes.

In large skillet melt butter and sauté beef and pork until cooked. Combine meat
and onion mixture. Stir in chili powder, salt, pepper, cumin seed and optional
MSG and cook ten mintues. Simmer covered one hour. Remove cover and cook
ten more minutes.

Before serving add chili beans and heat through.

HINT:

May use less meat and more chili beans.

QUICKIE CHILI CON CARNE

SERVES 6

2 tablespoons oil
½ cup chopped green pepper
½ cup chopped onion
1 pound lean ground beef
2 cups canned tomatoes
1 · 10-ounce can tomato soup
½ teaspoon paprika

⅛ teaspoon cayenne pepper
1 bay leaf
1 tablespoon chili powder
1 clove garlic, mashed
1 · 16-ounce can red beans, chili
  beans or kidney beans with liquid
Salt to taste

DIRECTIONS:

Heat oil in a 10 inch skillet. Brown the green pepper, onion and ground beef in
the oil, stirring occasionally. Add the tomatoes, tomato soup, paprika, cayenne
pepper, bay leaf and chili powder.

Cover and simmer over low heat for about 1 hour, stirring occasionally. Add
more water if the mixture becomes too thick.

Add the garlic and beans with liquid and heat thoroughly. Salt to taste.

BEEF CHOWDER

SERVES 8-10

1½ pounds ground beef
½ cup chopped celery
½ cup chopped onion
⅓ cup chopped green pepper
½ teaspoon salt

2 · 10½-ounce cans condensed cream of celery soup
2 · 16-ounce cans tomatoes, cut up
1 · 17-ounce can whole kernel corn
¼ cup snipped parsley

DIRECTIONS:

Cook beef, celery, onion and green pepper until meat is browned. Drain and add remaining ingredients. Simmer covered for 30 minutes. Pour into containers; freeze.

Before serving, cover and heat soup about 30 minutes or until bubbly, stirring often. Add salt to taste.

CORN CHOWDER

SERVES 4-6

"A hearty and unique corn chowder.!"

¼ pound bacon slices, chopped
1 cup chopped onion
½ cup chopped celery
¼ cup chopped celery leaves
1 · 4-ounce can diced green chilies, drained
dash cumin

2 tablespoons flour
1 · 16-ounce can whole-kernel corn, undrained
3 cups milk
1 teaspoon salt
⅛ teaspoon pepper
1½ cups shredded Monterey Jack cheese

DIRECTIONS:

Fry bacon in saucepan. Remove, drain and set aside. Pour off all but 3 tablespoons fat. Add onion, celery, celery leaves and chilies. Cook until vegetables are tender, about 8 mintues. Add cumin and flour and stir until blended. Add undrained corn, milk, salt and pepper. Cook and stir until soup comes to a boil and is slightly thickened.

Just before serving, stir in 1 cup cheese. Garnish with remaining cheese and crumbled bacon. Serve soup as soon as possible.

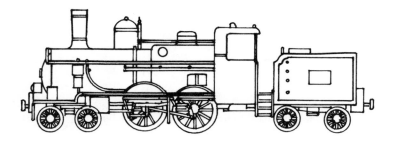

CREAMY CLAM CHOWDER

YIELD: 10-12 Servings (1 cup)

6 slices bacon
1 large onion, chopped
4 to 5 cups diced potatoes
2 cups water
1 teaspoon salt

3 · 6½-ounce cans clams
3 cups sour cream
1 cup evaporated milk
salt and pepper to taste

DIRECTIONS:

Fry bacon until crisp. Remove from pan and set aside. Cook onion in bacon drippings. Drain and set aside.

Boil the potatoes in salted water until tender . Drain and wash the clams. Add clams and cooked onion to the undrained potatoes. Add sour cream, evaporated milk, salt and pepper. Stir and heat to hot but do not boil. When serving, add bacon crumbled on top.

LEEK CHOWDER

SERVES 6-8

3 cups sliced fresh mushrooms
3 large leeks, sliced
10-ounces fresh asparagus cut in
  2 inch lengths, blanched or 10-ounce
  package frozen asparagus, thawed
  and drained
6 tablespoons butter
3 tablespoons flour

½ teaspoon salt
¼ teaspoon pepper
2 cups chicken broth
2 cups light cream
1 · 12-ounce can whole kernel
  white corn
dash saffron threads, crushed
  (optional)

DIRECTIONS:

Sauté mushrooms, leeks and asparagus in butter until tender but not brown. Stir in flour, salt and pepper. Add chicken broth and light cream. Cook until thick and bubbly. Reduce heat; add corn and saffron. Heat but do not boil.

TIP:

Simmer meat trimmings, celery tops and 1 or 2 boullion cubes to make a good soup stock.

MARKET STREET CLAM CHOWDER

SERVES 12

1 cup potatoes, diced ½ inch
1 cup celery, diced ½ inch
1 cup onion, diced ½ inch
1 cup green pepper, diced ½ inch
1 cup leeks (tops and bottoms)
   diced ½ inch
¾ cup chopped clams (canned or fresh)
¾ tablespoon coarse ground black
   pepper
1½ tablespoons salt

¾ tablespoon whole thyme
6 bay leaves
1 teaspoon Tabasco
¾ cup sherry wine (optional)
2 cups water
¾ cup clam juice (drained from canned
   clams or purchased separately in can
¾ cup (1½ sticks) butter, melted
1 cup flour
2 quarts half & half

DIRECTIONS:

In large saucepan combine all ingredients except butter, flour and half & half; simmer together until potatoes are thoroughly cooked. In meantime, combine melted butter and flour in ovenproof container, and bake at 325 degrees for 30 minutes (to eliminate raw flour flavor and stabilize chowder.) Stir roux (butter-flour mixture) into chowder and cook and stir until thick. Mixture will be slightly less thick than cookie dough. Remove chowder from heat; stir in half & half until blended. Heat to serving temperature, stirring occasionally, and serve immediately.

RECIPE PROVIDED BY:

Market Street Grill
50 Post Office Place
Salt Lake City, Utah

Market Street Broiler
258 South 1300 East
Salt Lake City, Utah

SALMON CHOWDER

SERVES 8-10

"Easy but elegant!"

1 bunch of green onions
½ cup butter
1 · 16-ounce can salmon, red or pink
1 · 16-ounce can cream style corn

2 · 10½-ounce cans cream of
   potato soup
1 quart half and half cream

DIRECTIONS:

Chop green onions, using part of the green. Sauté the onions in butter until soft. Add all other ingredients. Heat to boiling and serve.

COLD SHRIMP SOUP

SERVES 6-8

1 quart tomato juice
1 · 8-ounce bottle shrimp sauce
   (gourmet section of grocery)
2 small cans shrimp
2 cups diced celery
½ cup diced green pepper
½ cup sugar (scant)

2 tablespoons lemon juice
1 tablespoon Worcestershire
   sauce
1½ teaspoon horseradish
¼ teaspoon garlic salt
1 minced onion
salt to taste

DIRECTIONS:

Combine all ingredients and chill overnight.

HINT:

Wonderful summer party soup or appetizer.

SOUPER SUMMER SOUP

YIELD: 6 Large or 10 Small Servings

"Elegant and refreshing soup!"

½ Honeydew melon
2 peaches, peeled
⅓ cup sugar
juice of one lemon

½ cup orange juice
1-ounce Grand Marnier liqueur
½ cup cream

DIRECTIONS:

Mix all the ingredients in a blender or food processor until of desired consistency. Chill. Garnish with mint leaves.

DUTCH APPLE SOUP

SERVES 8

2 pounds firm, ripe apples
4 cloves (whole)
½ teaspoon cinnamon
juice of one lemon
⅔ cup sugar

1 cup dry white wine
4 cups milk
1 cup heavy cream
4 tablespoons flour

DIRECTIONS:

Peel and core apples and place in saucepan. Add water to cover. Add cloves, cinnamon, lemon juice and sugar. Simmer until tender, about 30 minutes. Remove cloves. Run through a sieve or purée in a blender until smooth. Return to boil.

Stirring constantly, add wine and milk. Remove from heat.

Combine the cream and flour and stir into soup. Return soup to a boil and simmer five minutes. Chill.

ZUCCHINI SOUP

SERVES 8-10

2 medium zucchini, sliced
3 stalks celery, sliced
3 green onions chopped
2 tablespoons butter
1 tablespoon chicken stock (dry)

1 · 14½-ounce can Swansons
   chicken broth
2 tablespoons flour
1½ cups half and half
1 cup chopped parsley

DIRECTIONS:

Sauté zucchini, celery and onions for 5 minutes in butter. Stir in chicken broth and cook 5 mintues more. Combine flour and cream. Add to vegetable, broth mixture, cooking another 5 minutes. Add parsley, and remove from heat. Place soup in blender and purée. Chill and serve.

GAZPACHO

SERVES 10-12

1 · 46-ounce can tomato juice
2 large tomatoes, chopped
1 cucumber, chopped
1 large green pepper, chopped

1 Bermuda onion, chopped
½ cup oil
3 green onions, thinly sliced

DIRECTIONS:

Put all the tomato juice, ½ of the tomatoes, ½ of the cucumber, ½ of the green pepper, ½ of the Bermuda onion and the oil in a blender and blend well. Stir in remaining tomato, cucumber, green pepper and onion.

Refrigerate until chilled. It is best if chilled for 24 hours. When serving, garnish with green onion.

CREAM OF BROCCOLI SOUP

SERVES 8-10

1½ pounds fresh broccoli
5 cups chicken stock
¼ cup butter
2 tablespoons chopped onion
3 celery stalks, minced
¼ cup flour

2 cups cream or half and half,
   scalded
¼ teaspoon nutmeg
salt to taste
paprika
Parmesan cheese

DIRECTIONS:

Wash broccoli and cut off flowerettes. Set flowerettes aside. Peel stems and chop coarsely. Place stems in large saucepan and cover with chicken stock. Bring to a boil and simmer for ½ hour. Drain and reserve the stock.

Purée broccoli stems in blender with 1 cup of the stock. Set purée aside.

Put the flowerettes in the stock and simmer until tender.

Melt the butter in a saucepan and sauté the onion and celery for 5 minutes. Stir in flour and cook for 3 to 4 minutes. Slowly stir in the stock with the flowerettes and bring to a boil. Add the purée and the scalded cream. Bring to a boil; add the nutmeg, salt and paprika to taste.

Remove from the heat. Sprinkle with Parmesan cheese and serve.

NOTE:

May add Cheddar, Swiss or Velveeta cheese to taste.

CREAM OF CARROT SOUP

SERVES 4

1 pound carrots, thinly sliced
1 small onion, finely chopped
4 tablespoons butter
1/3 cup water
1/2 teaspoon sugar
1 teaspoon salt

1/8 teaspoon pepper
2 tablespoons flour
3 cups milk
1/8 teaspoon nutmeg
1 tablespoon fresh lemon juice

DIRECTIONS:

In a large saucepan, combine carrots, onion, 2 tablespoons butter, water, sugar, salt and pepper. Place over low heat, cover and cook 25 to 30 minutes or until carrots are tender. Purée mixture in blender, 1/3 at a time until smooth.

In another saucepan melt remaining butter over low heat and blend in flour, mixing until smooth. Cook, stirring constantly for 5 minutes. Add milk and nutmeg and continue cooking, stirring constantly until mixture is slightly thickened.

Stir in carrot mixture and continue cooking, covered for 30 minutes. Stir occasionally.

Just before serving, add lemon juice. Serve hot, garnished with freshly grated parsley or chopped watercress.

CREAM OF CUCUMBER SOUP

SERVES 6

"Quick, easy and nutritious."

2 pounds cucumber, peeled
2 tablespoons butter
1/3 cup chopped onion or shallot
5 cups chicken broth
1 tablespoon wine vinegar
1/2 cup chopped dill or watercress

1/4 cup quick cooking farina
   (or Cream of Wheat)
salt and pepper to taste
1 cup creme fraiche, sour cream
   or yogurt

DIRECTIONS:

Seed cucumber and chop. Melt butter, cook onion 2 to 3 minutes. Add cucumber, broth, vinegar and 1/3 cup dill. Boil, then whisk in farina. Simmer 20 minutes. Cool and purée. Before serving whisk in most of cremes or yogurt. Serve remaining as garnish along with sprigs of dill, or watercress. May be served hot or cold.

CIOPPINO-ITALIAN FISH SOUP

SERVES 5

⅓ cup oil
1 large or 2 small onions, chopped into bite-sized pieces
1 large green pepper, chopped into bite-sized pieces
1 stalk celery, sliced in chunks
3 cloves garlic
¼ cup chopped fresh parsley
1 · 28-ounce can tomatoes, drained and cut into pieces
2 · 8-ounce cans tomato sauce
12 ounces water

1 cup red wine
3 teaspoons salt
¼ teaspoon pepper
1 teaspoon crushed oregano leaves
¼ teaspoon thyme
¼ teaspoon basil
½ teaspoon garlic powder
1 pound white fish, cut into cubes (halibut is the best)
1 pound shrimp, small size or large shrimp cut into pieces

DIRECTIONS:

Heat oil in kettle and sauté onion, green pepper, celery, whole garlic and parsley over medium heat for 15 minutes, stirring occasionally. Add tomatoes, tomato sauce, water, wine, salt, pepper, oregano, thyme, basil and garlic powder. Cover and simmer 1 hour or more. Remove garlic cloves. (This can be done at any time during the simmering.)

Bring mixture to a boil and add shrimp and white fish. Cook until fish is opaque and done. (Time depends on the variety of fish and size of fish chunks.)

CRAB LEGS SOUP

SERVES 8

1 tablespoon butter
1 tablespoon flour
½ to 1 teaspoon curry powder, depending on taste
4 · 10½-ounce cans beef consommé

1 small onion, chopped
1 small apple, chopped
1 cup cream
salt and pepper to taste
½ pound crab legs or crab meat

DIRECTIONS:

In a 3 quart saucepan, melt butter. Add the flour and cook until it is thick and brown. Add the curry powder and consommé, a little at a time.

Boil the apple and onion together in water until soft. When soft, put them through a sieve and add to the consommé mixture. Season with salt and pepper.

Before serving, add the cream and crab legs or crab meat.

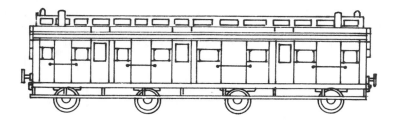

MEATBALL MINESTRONE SOUP

SERVES 8-10

1½ to 2 pounds lean ground beef
2 cups chopped onion
5 tablespoons beef bouillon
8 cups water
2 · 16-ounce cans stewed tomatoes
1½ teaspoons thyme leaves
¼ teaspoon pepper
2 cups chopped cabbage

1 · 16-ounce can garbanzo beans,
   drained
4-ounces thin spaghetti, broken
chopped parsley or green pepper
   (optional)
Parmesan and/or Romano cheese,
   grated

DIRECTIONS:

In a large bowl combine beef, 1 cup onion and 2 tablespoons bouillon. Mix well. Shape into ½ to ¾ inch meatballs.

In large Dutch oven, brown meatballs, ⅓ at a time. Remove from pan, reserving 2 tablespoons drippings. Pour off excess. Cook remaining onion until tender. Add meatballs, water, tomatoes, remaining bouillon, thyme and pepper. Cover and bring to a boil. Reduce heat; simmer for 1 hour.

Add cabbage, garbanzo beans, spaghetti and parsley or green pepper. Cook 15 minutes or until spaghetti is tender.

Serve with cheeses sprinkled over soup.

HINT:

If less meat is preferred, cut the ground beef and ground beef mixings in half.

MEXICAN POTATO– CHICKEN SOUP

SERVES 6-8

1 chicken
2 pounds potatoes
½ cup diced onion
½ cup butter
1 large tomato, skinned and diced

1 · 13-ounce can chopped green
   chilies
½ pound grated Longhorn cheese
½ pound grated Monterey Jack
   cheese

DIRECTIONS:

Cover chicken with water and cook until tender. Remove skin and bones and tear chicken into bite-size pieces. Reserve 2 cups broth.

Dice potatoes and sauté with onions in butter until transparent. Add reserved broth and tomato and cook until tender. Add chicken, diced chilies and cheeses. Stir just until cheese has melted. Serve immediately.

HINT:

Serve with salad and warm flour tortillas.

EASTERN CANTONESE CORN CHICKEN SOUP

SERVES 4

2 cups chicken broth
(homemade is best)
1 · 16-ounce can creamed corn
½ teaspoon salt
1 cup cooked shredded chicken

1 tablespoon cornstarch
3 tablespoons water
2 egg whites, beaten slightly
3 green onions, sliced

DIRECTIONS:

Bring broth to a boil; reduce heat to medium. Add corn and cook approximately 10 minutes, stirring often. Add salt and chicken and bring to a boil.

In a small bowl, mix cornstarch with the water. Add cornstarch mixture to the broth slowly. Allow soup to thicken. Add egg whites slowly and heat until egg whites are cooked.

Serve with thinly sliced green onions on top (use the green of the onion also).

HINT:

This soup can be made in a wok or on the stove top.

PASTA E FAGIOLI

SERVES 8

4 cups link sausage (about 2 pounds)
1 large onion, chopped
1 small clove garlic, minced
2 tablespoons oil
4 cups water
2 envelopes (soup base only, not
noodles) Lipton Chicken Noodle Soup

1 · 8-ounce package macaroni shells
1 · 16-ounce can tomatoes
1 · 16-ounce can red kidney beans
1 bay leaf
½ teaspoon pepper
Parmesan cheese

DIRECTIONS:

Brown and dice link sausage and set aside. In oil, sauté onion and garlic until softened.

In a large kettle add soup base and water. Cover and heat to boiling. Stir in macaroni and cook 10 minutes or until almost tender. Stir in remaining ingredients. Heat to boiling and then simmer slowly for 30 to 40 minutes.

Ladle into soup bowls and sprinkle with Parmesan cheese.

HINT:

The amount of sausage can be reduced according to individual taste. The amount of tomatoes and beans can also be changed according to personal preference. Pinto beans or red beans are great for a change.

PORK POSOLE SOUP

SERVES 10-12

1 · 8-ounce package posole
(dry cooked corn)
1 · 4-ounce package dried red chili
pods (medium hot)
1 · 3 or 4 pound pork roast (with bone)
2 large onions
2 cloves garlic
2 tablespoons oregano leaves
2 tablespoons cumin seeds
1 tablespoon dried chili flakes
1 · 6-ounce can tomato paste

1 · 16-ounce can tomatoes
2½ quarts water
6 tablespoons butter

Garnishes:
chopped green onion
radishes, chopped or shredded
avocado, chopped or guacamole
sour cream
cheese, shredded Monterey Jack
or Cheddar

DIRECTIONS:

Soak posole overnight in tap water. Drain and reserve posole. Soak chili pods overnight in boiling water, making sure all are submerged. A weighted dish on top is sometimes necessary. The next day wearing gloves, drain and remove stems and seeds. Place in blender and add 2 cups water and purée. Strain mixture well and set aside.

Brown pork roast well in a large stock pot and cover with 2½ quarts water. Add one coarsely chopped onion, one clove garlic, minced, and one tablespoon each of oregano leaves, cumin seeds and chili flakes. Simmer for about 3 hours or until meat slips from bone easily. Broth will be reduced approximately one-half. Remove meat from stock and cool; set aside. Strain broth and return to pot adding drained soaked posole and one-half of puréed chili. Simmer for 4 hours or until posole is tender and the kernels pop.

The last hour of cooking time add the shredded pork to the posole broth.

In a large fry pan sauté remaining garlic and onion in butter. Combine tomatoes and tomato paste and the remaining tablespoons of oregano and cumin. Add this mixture to posole broth. Continue to cook last hour.

ITALIAN HAMBURGER SOUP

SERVES 8

1 pound ground beef
1 cup chopped onions
1 cup cubed raw potatoes
1 cup sliced raw carrots
½ cup diced celery
1 · 20-ounce can whole tomatoes
(2½ cups)

1 crushed bay leaf
½ teaspoon dried thyme
¼ teaspoon dried basil
2 teaspoons salt
⅛ teaspoon pepper
1½ quarts water
1 · 8-ounce package noodles

DIRECTIONS:

Sauté beef and onion until slightly brown. Add all other ingredients except noodles. Cover and simmer one hour. Add 8 ounce package of noodles the last 15 minutes. Sprinkle with grated cheese if desired.

VARIATION:

Substitute 1 cup of shredded cabbage for the noodles. Use only ½ instead of 1½ quarts water. Add the cabbage when all the other vegetables are added.

SPICY BEEF AND VEGETABLE STEW

SERVES 8-10

2 pounds boneless beef chuck,
  cut in 1 inch cubes
½ cup flour
1 tablespoon salt
½ teaspoon pepper
½ teaspoon paprika
2 tablespoons shortening or vegetable
  oil
1 cup chopped onion
6 cups water
Garni (1 clove and 1 teaspoon pickling
  spice in cloth)

3 cups drained canned tomatoes, or
  2 · 16-ounce cans, undrained
  stewed tomatoes
2 cups diced carrots
1 cup sliced celery
3 cups diced potatoes
1 cup green peas
1 teaspoon sugar
2 teaspoons salt
¼ teaspoon pepper
3 tablespoons cornstarch blended with
  ¼ cup water

DIRECTIONS:

Dredge beef cubes in mixture of flour, salt, pepper and paprika. Brown in oil on all sides in large heavy kettle. Add onion and brown lightly. Add water and garni. Simmer, covered for 30 minutes. Add vegetables and seasonings. Simmer, uncovered for 50 minutes or until done. Blend some of the hot gravy into the cornstarch mixture and stir into stew until thick.

OVEN STEW

SERVES 4-6

1 pound stew meat, hamburger or
  round steak
2 teaspoons salt
1 · 10½ can tomato soup
¾ can water (tomato soup can)
⅛ teaspoon pepper

1 tablespoon Worcestershire sauce
2 cups sliced carrots
2 cups sliced celery
2 cups cubed potatoes
2 medium onions, chopped

DIRECTIONS:

Put raw meat and vegetables in roaster. Add all other ingredients and stir together. Bake at 350 degrees for 1 hour or 300 degrees for 3 hours or 250 degrees for 4 to 5 hours (a favorite).

TIP:

Salt should be added after the soup boils.

BROCCOLI-CAULIFLOWER SOUP

SERVES 12-15

2 cups chopped cauliflower
3 cups chopped broccoli
2 cups chopped celery
1½ cups chopped onion
½ cup butter
½ cup flour

4 cups milk *or* 2 cups milk
  and 2 cups half and half
1 teaspoon salt (or to taste)
1 teaspoon pepper
2 cups grated Cheddar cheese

DIRECTIONS:

Simmer cauliflower, broccoli and celery in 4 cups water until tender. Drain and set aside.

In large heavy Dutch oven, melt butter. Add onions and cook until tender and golden. Add flour and stir until smooth. While stirring, pour in milk slowly. Add salt, pepper and cooked vegetables. Add cheese and stir until melted. Season to taste.

Ready to serve.

SPLIT PEA SOUP

SERVES 6

"Good meal after a day outdoors!"

1 ham bone or ham hock
1 pound smoked sausage
1 pound split peas, or ½ pound each
  of yellow and green dry peas
6 cups water
1 onion, diced
1 carrot, diced
1 stalk celery, diced
¼ teaspoon thyme

¼ teaspoon savory, summer savory
  or Season All
1 teaspoon salt
¼ teaspoon pepper
1 cup milk or cream
1 tablespoon butter
1 tablespoon flour
grated cheese (Cheddar or Parmesan
  is best)

DIRECTIONS:

Place all ingredients except cream, butter, flour and cheese in crock pot cooker. Cover and cook for 8 to 10 hours on low. When cooked, remove ham bone and sausage and dice the meat. Put soup through a sieve or mash it and return it to the crock pot along with the meat. Turn the heat to high and add milk or cream.

Melt the butter. Add the flour and cook for 1 minute while stirring. Add this mixture to the soup and stir until it thickens.

Serve garnished with grated cheese.

HINT:

This soup is delicious served with crusty warm bread, a green salad and white or rosé wine.

SAUERKRAUT SOUP

SERVES 8

3 pounds pork spareribs
1 · 20-ounce can sauerkraut
4 medium onions, chopped
3 tablespoons shortening
3 tablespoons flour

1 pound mushrooms, chopped
1 bay leaf
1 teaspoon salt
½ teaspoon caraway seed
pepper to taste

DIRECTIONS:

Cover ribs with water, add sauerkraut and simmer 1½ hours. Remove ribs from pot. Remove all but 4 cups of liquid.

In frying pan, brown onions in the shortening. Add flour, then 1 cup of cold water. Add onion mixture to pot and add remaining ingredients. Simmer 1 hour. The ribs may be left in the soup or taken out and served separately.

PORTUGUESE KALE SOUP

SERVES 8-10

6 cups water
⅔ cup dry red kidney beans
1 pound beef shank cross-cuts
8-ounces chavrico or chorizo or
   bulk Italian sausage
⅔ cup dry split peas

2½ teaspoons salt
6 cups torn kale (8 ounces)
2 cups peeled and chopped potatoes
   (2 medium)
2 cups coarsely chopped cabbage

DIRECTIONS:

In a Dutch oven combine water and kidney beans. Bring to a boil and simmer uncovered for 2 minutes. Remove from heat; cover. Let stand for 1 hour. (Or, mix beans and water, cover and let stand overnight.)

In a skillet brown beef shanks and sausage and drain well. Stir into undrained beans along with the peas and salt. Bring to a boil and reduce heat. Simmer covered 2 hours.

Remove beef shanks. When cool enough to handle, remove meat from bones and cube. Discard bones and return meat to pan. Add kale, potatoes and cabbage. Simmer covered 25-30 minutes.

HINT:

May substitute 16-ounce can kidney beans for dry kidney beans.

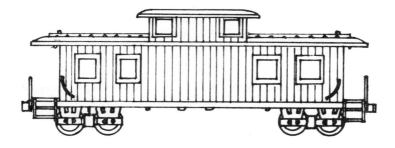

POTATO LEEK SOUP

SERVES 8-10

4 medium potatoes
4 large leeks (white part only)
4 large onions

2 · 24-ounce cans chicken broth
1 pint whipping cream
¼ cup butter

DIRECTIONS:

Chop vegetables and place in large pot with chicken broth. Boil vegetables until tender (about 20 minutes). Mash or mix in blender until smooth. Add whipping cream and butter and refrigerate or serve. May serve hot or cold.

MINESTRONE SOUP

SERVES 10

"A good hearty soup made in minutes!"

1 small onion, chopped or sliced
2 medium zucchini, sliced
2 tablespoons butter
8 cups beef broth
1 · 28-ounce can chopped tomatoes
1 · 10-ounce package frozen baby
  lima beans
¾ cup broken pieces of vermicelli
  or spaghetti, uncooked

3 tablespoons Parmesan cheese
1 · 15½-ounce can garbanzo beans,
  drained
½ teaspoon whole peppercorns
¼ teaspoon basil, crushed
¼ teaspoon garlic salt
dash cayenne pepper
Parmesan or Romano cheese

DIRECTIONS:

In large saucepan, sauté onion and zucchini in butter until onion is tender. Stir in beef broth and tomatoes. Add remaining ingredients. Simmer about 15 minutes, stirring occasionally, or until lima beans are tender. Serve with additional grated Parmesan or Romano cheese.

LOW CALORIE VEGETABLE SOUP

SERVES 6

1½ cups tomato juice
2 cups water
3 cups shredded cabbage
½ cup dehydrated onion flakes
2 tablespoons parsley flakes
2 beef bouillon cubes or 2 packets
  instant beef broth
2 onion cubes or 2 packets instant
  onion broth

dash artificial sweetener
½ teaspoon garlic salt
dash Tabasco
1 · 4-ounce can sliced mushrooms
  and liquid
1 · 16-ounce can French-style green
  beans and liquid
1 teaspoon salt

DIRECTIONS:

Combine tomato juice, water and cabbage in heavy saucepan. Bring to boil and simmer uncovered until cabbage is tender. Add remaining ingredients and heat. Keeps for a week in refrigerator.

FRENCH ONION SOUP

SERVES 4

3 large onions, thinly sliced
½ cup butter
6 cups beef broth or instant bouillon
1 teaspoon Worcestershire sauce

½ teaspoon salt
4 slices toasted French bread
4 slices Monterey Jack cheese
¼ cup grated fresh Parmesan cheese

DIRECTIONS:

In large skillet, sauté onions in butter until browned.

In pot combine browned onions, broth, worcestershire sauce and salt. Cover and cook on low heat for 1 hour.

Top each bowl of soup with French bread and cheeses.

SOUP IN A PUMPKIN

SERVES 8

3 cups French bread, torn in pieces
1 · 9 inch diameter pumpkin
1 tablespoon butter
1 teaspoon salt
1½ cups chopped onion (1 medium)
¾ cup butter
1 teaspoon salt
1 teaspoon nutmeg

½ teaspoon pepper
1 teaspoon sage
1 cup grated Swiss cheese
5 cups chicken broth
2 bay leaves
1 cup heavy cream
chopped parsley for garnish

DIRECTIONS:

OVEN TEMPERATURE: 375°

Spread the bread pieces on a cookie sheet. Bake them in a 300 degree oven for 15 minutes or until they are dry.

Cut a crown in the pumpkin and clean it out. Rub insides with butter and salt.

Sauté onion in ¾ cup butter for 10 minutes over low heat until transparent. Stir in bread pieces. Cook 2 minutes for bread to absorb butter Stir in salt, nutmeg, pepper and sage. Remove from heat and stir in cheese. Spoon mixture into pumpkin and pour in broth. Lay bay leaves on top and replace pumpkin top. Place pumpkin in greased baking pan. Bake at 375 degrees for 2 hours.

Just before serving, stir in cream and garnish with parsley. Spoon out some pulp with each serving if you wish.

DELI HAM SANDWICHES

YIELD: 12 Large Sandwiches

12 Poorboy or Hoagie sandwich rolls
mayonnaise
sweet mustard sauce (recipe below)
1½ pounds thinly sliced honey
   cured ham

1½ pounds thinly sliced
   Provolone cheese
sandwich onions (recipe below)
2 large tomatoes
½ head shredded lettuce

DIRECTIONS:

Split sandwich rolls. Spread mayonnaise on one side and mustard on the other side of each roll. Divide the ham and cheese equally among the 12 rolls. Top each roll with ham, cheese, thin tomato slices, sandwich onions and lettuce. Use toothpicks to secure until serving time.

Additional serving suggestions: Spread rolls with mashed avocado or add thin slices of cucumber, pickles or sprouts.

SANDWICH ONIONS

YIELD: 10-12 Sandwiches

1½ pounds red onions, peeled and
   sliced thin
½ cup oil
½ cup red wine vinegar
½ cup water

½ teaspoon pepper
2 teaspoons salt (or less
   if preferred)
2 tablespoons sugar
4 drops Tabasco sauce

DIRECTIONS:

Slice onions in crockery or bowl. Mix the rest of ingredients together in a saucepan and bring to a boil. Pour over onions. Let cool; refrigerate overnight.

Drain the onions and use on sandwiches made on French, Hoagie or Poorboy rolls, with any meat and cheese combination, lettuce and tomatoes. The onions keep for 1 to 2 weeks in a covered container in the refrigerator.

SWEET MUSTARD SAUCE

YIELD: 2 Cups

¼ cup butter
2 eggs
½ cup sugar
½ cup condensed tomato soup

½ cup prepared mustard
¼ cup vinegar
¼ cup water

DIRECTIONS:

Melt butter in top of double boiler. In a mixing bowl beat eggs. Gradually beat in sugar, soup, mustard, vinegar and water. Add to butter and cook over hot water until thick, stirring constantly.

Serve hot or cold. The sauce keeps well in the refrigerator.

HINT:

This sauce may be used on any meat and cheese sandwich combination. It is delicious with ham loaf and other pork dishes.

BROILED CRAB OPENFACERS

YIELD: 6-8 Muffin Halves

1 · 7-ounce can crab meat, drained
¼ cup mayonnaise
1 · 3-ounce package cream cheese
1 egg yolk
1 teaspoon chopped onion

¼ teaspoon prepared mustard
dash salt
dash pepper
3 muffins, rolls or Bagels

DIRECTIONS:
OVEN TEMPERATURE: Broil

Stir together the crab meat and mayonnaise. Set aside. Beat the cream cheese, egg yolk, onion, mustard, salt and pepper until smooth and creamy.

Spread toasted (optional) bread halves with butter and crab mixture. Top with cream cheese mixture. Put on a baking sheet and broil 5 to 6 inches from heat for 2 to 3 minutes or until the top is bubbly and golden.

GREENWICH CRABWICHES

SERVES 48

½ cup butter, softened
1 jar Old English Cheese Spread
1½ teaspoons mayonnaise

dash garlic salt
1 · 7-ounce can crab meat
6 English muffins, split

DIRECTIONS:
OVEN TEMPERATURE: Broil

Combine butter and cheese spread. Add mayonnaise, garlic salt and crab meat. Spread on muffins. Freeze 10 minutes. Cut in fourths and broil. Serve hot.

HINT:
These may be made ahead of time and frozen.

BEEF DIP SANDWICH

SERVES 6-8

2½ to 4 pound chuck roast
salt
pepper
2 · 10½-ounce cans beef consommé
2 cans water

1 onion, chopped
¼ to ½ teaspoon cayenne pepper
    (depending on hotness desired)
1 dozen French rolls

DIRECTIONS:
OVEN TEMPERATURE: 250-275°

Place meat in roasting dish. Salt and pepper it to taste. Pour remaining ingredients in with roast. Bake for 5 hours at 250 to 275 degrees.

Thinly slice roast and serve on French rolls with au jus from roast pan.

HINT:
This can also be done in a crock pot for 5 hours on high or 6 to 7 hours on low.

ITALIAN ROAST BEEF SANDWICHES

YIELD: 6-8 Sandwiches

3 to 4 pound Chuck or Arm roast
1 large onion, chopped
¾ cup chopped celery
½ teaspoon oregano
2 teaspoons rosemary
1 tablespoon dry parsley leaves
½ teaspoon garlic salt

2 bay leaves
1 · 8-ounce can tomato sauce
1½ cups water
6 Pepperocinis (peppers in a jar in the gourmet food section)
salt and pepper to taste
6 to 8 Italian rolls

DIRECTIONS:

OVEN TEMPERATURE: 350°

Brown roast in small amount of margarine. Mix together all ingredients except rolls and place in roast pan. Bake, covered, at 350 degrees for 2 hours. Let cool and shred apart.

Add a small amount of the Pepperocini juice (more if desired) from the jar to the existing meat juice in the pan. Use this when serving the meat on the rolls to make them fairly moist.

PICNIC LOAF

SERVES 6

1½ cups chopped pimento stuffed olives
1 cup chopped black olives
⅔ cup olive oil
⅓ cup minced fresh parsley
1 · 4-ounce jar chopped pimentos
3 anchovy fillets, minced into paste
2 tablespoons capers

1 tablespoon minced garlic
1 teaspoon oregano
pepper to taste
1 · 9 inch round loaf of French or Italian bread
¼ pound Italian hard salami
¼ pound Provolone cheese
¼ pound mortadella (Italian Sausage)

DIRECTIONS:

Combine all ingredients except bread, salami, Provolone and mortadella and refrigerate overnight. The next morning drain this salad mixture and set it aside. Save the liquid.

Split the loaf of bread horizontally. Remove the soft bread inside, leaving a ½ inch thick shell. Brush the inside of the shell with the liquid reserved from the salad mixture.

Mound half the salad in the bottom shell. Layer the salami, Provolone and mortadella on top of the salad. Top with the remaining salad. Cover the salad with the top shell of bread. Cover completely with foil and refrigerate 30 minutes, covered with a 3 to 5 pound weight.

HINT:

This sandwich is wonderful to take on a picnic or to a game. It can easily be prepared ahead of time.

PIROSHKI

YIELD: 6-8 Servings or 20 Small sandwich rolls

1½ pounds hamburger
1 medium onion, chopped
3 hard-boiled eggs
¼ pound mushrooms, chopped
(optional)

salt and pepper to taste
2 packages refrigerator biscuits
(10 biscuits each)
oil for frying

DIRECTIONS:

Sauté hamburger and onion and drain. Add mushrooms. Allow to cool and add eggs, mashing them in with a fork. Add salt and pepper to taste.

Roll out biscuits to a 4 to 5 inch diameter. Put 2 tablespoons of the meat mixture in the center, fold biscuit in half and crimp edges shut carefully. Fry in oil until golden brown. Or, you may put the filling in a pastry crust and bake in the oven at 400 degrees for 30 minutes.

HINT:

These sandwiches may be dipped in sauces such as catsup, mustard, sweet and sour sauce, honey or a mayonnaise and catsup mixture.

PIZZA BY-THE-YARD

SERVES 6-8

"Great for a party!"

1 unsliced loaf French bread
1 · 6-ounce can tomato paste
⅓ cup Parmesan cheese
¼ cup finely chopped green onion
¼ cup chopped black olives
½ teaspoon crushed dried oregano
¾ teaspoon salt

pepper to taste
1 pound ground beef, browned
2 tomatoes, sliced
1 green pepper, cut in thin rings
1 cup shredded sharp processed
American cheese

DIRECTIONS:

OVEN TEMPERATURE: 400°

Cut loaf in half lengthwise. Combine tomato paste, Parmesan cheese, onion, olives, oregano, salt and pepper. Add meat and mix well. Spread atop loaf halves. Place on baking sheet. Bake in 400 degree oven for 20 minutes.

Remove from oven. Top with tomato slices and green pepper rings. Sprinkle shredded cheese on top. Return to oven and bake for 5 more minutes. Cut in slices and serve.

HINT:

This can be served as a meal or an appetizer.

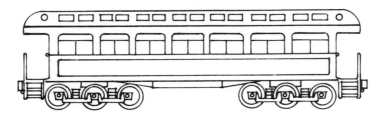

NAVAJO TACOS

SERVES 20

2 pounds lean hamburger
2 teaspoons garlic powder
2 teaspoons oregano
2 teaspoons cumin
1 teaspoon MSG
3 tablespoons sugar
2 tablespoons catsup

2 tablespoons chili powder
1 teaspoon salt
1 small green pepper – diced
1 · 4-ounce can green chilies
1½ cups of water
1 package 'Bake & Serve' rolls

DIRECTIONS:

OIL: 350°

Mix all ingredients except rolls together in a Dutch oven or crock pot. Cook over *low* heat for 3 to 4 hours.

Thaw the rolls while the hamburger mixture is cooking. Stretch the rolls into flat circles and deep fry in 350 degree oil until golden.

Place the hamburger mixture on top of each scone and cover with your choice of toppings.

Toppings: Lettuce, avocados, tomatoes, sour cream, salsa, or tortilla chips.

CHICKEN SALAD IN A BOAT

SERVES 6-8

Boat
⅔ cup water
5 tablespoons butter
¼ teaspoon salt
⅔ cup flour
3 eggs

Chicken Salad
3 cups cooked, cut up chicken
1 · 8-ounce can sliced water
  chestnuts, drained
½ cup sliced green onions

2 hard boiled eggs
¼ pound green peas, blanched

Dressing
1 cup sour cream
½ to 1 cup mayonnaise
1 teaspoon lime juice
1 to 2 teaspoons garlic salt
½ teaspoon ginger
2 teaspoons sugar
½ to 1 teaspoon curry powder
  (to taste)

DIRECTIONS:

OVEN TEMPERATURE: 400°

Boat: In saucepan combine water, butter and salt. Bring to a boil, stirring to melt butter. Remove from heat and add flour all at once and beat until smooth. Add eggs one at a time and beat until glossy. Pour into greased 9 inch cheesecake pan (springform). Spread evenly on sides and bottom. Bake crust for 40 minutes at 400 degrees.

Combine all dressing ingredients in a small bowl. Combine salad ingredients and add dressing. Salt and pepper to taste. Chill until ready to use.

Fill boat with salad mixture just before serving.

SAUCY BEAN SALAD

SERVES 12-14

1 · 16-ounce can green beans
1 · 16-ounce can wax beans
1 · 15½-ounce can red kidney beans
1 · 8-ounce can garbanzo beans
   (optional)
½ cup sugar
⅓ cup salad oil

⅔ cup vinegar
1⁄16 teaspoon pepper
½ tablespoon finely chopped
   parsley
¼ cup diced onion
¼ cup diced green pepper

DIRECTIONS:

Drain all beans well in collander. In medium to large bowl mix the sugar, oil, vinegar, pepper, parsley, onion and green pepper. Add beans to mixture and mix well. Let stand in refrigerator several hours or overnight.

SIEMISALAATH- MUSHROOM SALAD

SERVES 8-10

4 cups water
4 tablespoons lemon juice
2 pounds fresh mushrooms, cleaned and
   sliced crosswise
1 cup heavy cream

4 tablespoons grated onion
1 teaspoon sugar
2 teaspoons salt
1 teaspoon white pepper

DIRECTIONS:

Bring water and lemon juice to a boil in a large heavy pan with lid. Add mushrooms and cook in covered pan, gently simmering for 2 to 3 minutes. Drain mushrooms and pat dry with paper towel. Mix remaining ingredients in large bowl. Add mushrooms to cream mixture; mix gently to coat. Refrigerate.

TANGY HOT POTATO SALAD

SERVES 10

8 large potatoes
4 slices bacon, diced
2 large celery stalks, diced
1 medium onion, sliced
⅓ cup salad or olive oil

¼ cup red wine vinegar
2 tablespoons chopped parsley
1½ teaspoons salt
1¼ teaspoons sugar
2 teaspoons prepared mustard

DIRECTIONS:

One hour before serving, in 5-quart saucepan, boil unpeeled potatoes until fork tender (approximately 30 minutes); drain. Cut potatoes into bite-size cubes (do not peel). Return to saucepan.

In a 2-quart saucepan, fry bacon until crisp. Remove bacon, leaving bacon drippings in pan and crumble; set aside. In drippings, cook celery and onion until tender, stirring occasionally. With slotted spoon, remove vegetables to potato saucepan.

In same 2-quart saucepan, mix oil and remaining ingredients. Heat over medium heat to boiling. Reduce heat to low; simmer dressing 5 minutes to blend flavors.

Pour hot dressing over potato mixture in saucepan and add bacon. Toss gently and serve.

SPINACH SALAD
SERVES 6-8

1 · 10-ounce package spinach
3 cups shredded red cabbage
1 pound bacon, fried and crumbled

6 hard boiled eggs, chopped
1 bottle "Little Chalet Italian Dressing"
or any regular Italian dressing

DIRECTIONS:

Clean spinach and tear into bite size pieces. Toss with rest of ingredients (add dressing to taste). Serve immediately.

TOMATO BOATS SALAD
SERVES 8

2 large tomatoes
1 small eggplant (½ pound)
1 small onion
1 small green pepper
1 small zucchini
¼ cup salad oil

1½ teaspoons salt
1 teaspoon oregano leaves
¾ teaspoon sugar
spinach leaves for garnish
small slices garlic toast

DIRECTIONS:

About 2 hours before serving or early in the day: Cut each tomato into 4 wedges. With spoon, scoop out pulp from tomato wedges, leaving a ¼-inch thick shell. Cover and refrigerate tomato shells. Chop tomato pulp.

Cut eggplant into ½-inch cubes. Dice onion and green pepper. Cut zucchini crosswise into ¼-inch thick slices. Cut slices into thin strips.

In a 4-quart saucepan over medium heat in hot salad oil, cook eggplant, onion and chopped tomato pulp until vegetables are tender (about 20 minutes) stirring occasionally. Stir in green pepper, zucchini, salt, oregano and sugar. Cook 5 minutes or until green pepper and zucchini are tender crisp, stirring occasionally. Spoon mixture into medium bowl. Cover and refrigerate until mixture is chilled.

To serve, fill each tomato shell with some eggplant mixture. Garnish each serving with spinach leaves and bread.

WHOLE TOMATO SALAD
SERVES 4-6

Dressing:
½ teaspoon paprika
1 clove garlic, minced
1 teaspoon salt
2 tablespoons lemon juice
½ teaspoon celery seed
¼ teaspoon sugar
¼ teaspoon pepper
5 tablespoons salad oil

Salad:
4 large tomatoes, thickly
sliced
1 cup grated carrots
1 cup chopped celery
3 tablespoons chopped
parsley
¼ cup diced chives

DIRECTIONS:

Combine dressing ingredients and mix thoroughly. Chill several hours or ovenight to let flavors blend.

Toss together carrots, celery, parsley, and chives. Mound on top of tomato, slices. Pour dressing over top of mounds and serve.

CRANBERRY SALAD

SERVES 8-10

1 · 16-ounce package cranberries
2 cups water
1 cup sugar
1 · 6-ounce package black cherry
  gelatin

¼ cup lemon juice
1¾ cups orange juice
¾ cup diced celery
½ cup chopped nuts

DIRECTIONS:

Cook cranberries in 2 cups water until soft and popping. Add sugar and cook 5 minutes more. Add to gelatin and stir until gelatin dissolves. Add remaining ingredients; mix well. Refrigerate until set.

LEMON PUDDING FRUIT SALAD

SERVES 16

1 · 3-ounce package lemon pudding and pie filling
1 · 3-ounce package lemon gelatin
1½ cups hot water
1 cup heavy cream, whipped
2 · 11-ounce cans mandarin oranges, drained
1 · 17-ounce can fruit cocktail, drained
1 · 13-ounce can pineapple tidbits, drained
3 bananas, sliced
½ package (10½-ounce) miniature marshmallows

DIRECTIONS:

Cook pudding according to package directions. Cool. Dissolve gelatin in hot water. Refrigerate until partially set.

Combine pudding, gelatin and whipped cream. Fold in fruit and marshmallows. Refrigerate until set (approximately 5 hours).

PINK FROZEN FRUIT SALAD

SERVES 8-10

2 · 3-ounce packages cream cheese
⅛ teaspoon salt
1 · 8½-ounce can crushed pineapple,
  undrained
¼ cup chopped maraschino cherries

3 tablespoons cherry syrup
2 bananas, sliced
¼ cup halved grapes
1 cup miniature marshmallows
½ cup heavy cream, whipped

DIRECTIONS:

Blend cheese, salt and pineapple. Stir in cherries and syrup. Fold in bananas, grapes, marshmallows and whipped cream. Place in desired mold and freeze until set.

FROZEN FRUIT SALAD

SERVES 12-16

1 · 8-ounce package cream cheese, softened
1 cup mayonnaise
½ cup sugar
2 tablespoons orange juice
1 tablespoon lemon juice
2 cups heavy cream, whipped

2 · 30-ounce cans fruit cocktail
1 · 20-ounce can pineapple tidbits
1 · 4-ounce bottle maraschino cherries chopped
1 cup miniature marshmallows
3 bananas, sliced
1 · 11-ounce can mandarin oranges

DIRECTIONS:

Cream together cream cheese, mayonnaise and sugar then add juices. Fold in rest of ingredients and pour into 9 x 13 inch casserole dish. Freeze. Cut into squares to serve.

MANDARIN TOSSED SALAD

SERVES 4-6

½ cup sliced almonds
3 tablespoons sugar
½ head iceberg lettuce
½ head romaine lettuce
1 cup chopped celery
2 whole green onions, chopped
1 · 11-ounce can mandarin oranges, drained

Dressing:
½ teaspoon salt
dash of pepper
¼ cup vegetable oil
1 tablespoon chopped parsley
2 tablespoons sugar
2 tablespoons vinegar
dash of Tabasco sauce

DIRECTIONS:

In a small pan over medium heat cook almonds and sugar, stirring constantly until almonds are coated and sugar is dissolved (watch carefully as they will burn easily). Cool and store in air tight container.

Mix all dressing ingredients and chill.

Mix lettuces, celery and onions. Just before serving, add almonds and oranges. Toss with the dressing.

ORANGE APRICOT FREEZE SALAD

SERVES 8-10

2 · 8-ounce cartons orange yogurt
½ cup sugar
1 · 17-ounce can unpeeled apricot halves, drained

⅓ cup coarsely chopped pecans
lettuce
2 oranges, sliced thin

DIRECTIONS:

In mixing bowl, stir together yogurt and sugar until blended. Cut up apricots and fold with nuts into yogurt mixture. Spoon into 8 to 10 paper bake cup lined muffin pans. Cover and freeze until firm. Peel off paper from salads. Serve on lettuce-lined plates with slice of orange.

APPLE PINEAPPLE SALAD

SERVES 12

1 · 3-ounce package strawberry gelatin
1 scant cup boiling water
⅓ cup sugar
½ cup orange juice
Grated rind of ½ orange

1 · 8-ounce can crushed pineapple, drained
3 large red delicious apples, peeled and grated

DIRECTIONS:

Pour boiling water over gelatin and sugar. Dissolve completely and let set until cool. Combine pineapple, orange juice, rind, and shredded apples. Stir well into gelatin mixture. Pour into 8 x 8 inch pan and chill until set.

CRANBERRY SUPREME SALAD

SERVES 8-10

"A delightful holiday salad"

4 cups fresh cranberries
2¼ cups sugar
2 cups red grapes, seeded and halved
½ cup chopped pecans

1 · 8-ounce can crushed pineapple, well drained
1½ cups heavy cream, whipped

DIRECTIONS:

Grind cranberries, sprinkle with sugar and let drain overnight.

Add grapes, pecans, and pineapple to well drained cranberry mixture. Fold in whipped cream. To serve, mound in lettuce cups.

HINT:

Leftover cranberry juice can be used for fruit punch.

LEMONADE SALAD

SERVES 8

1 · 3-ounce package lemon gelatin
1 cup boiling water
½ cup sugar
⅛ teaspoon salt

1 · 6-ounce can frozen lemonade concentrate
1 cup heavy cream, whipped

DIRECTIONS:

Dissolve gelatin in boiling water. Add sugar, salt and lemonade concentrate. Refrigerate until mixture is thickened but not set. Fold in whipped cream. Set in a 9 x 9 inch pan or a 4-cup mold. Garnish with chunks of fresh fruit; strawberries, melons, green grapes and sprigs of mint.

Recipe can be doubled for a 9 x 13 inch pan or a larger ring mold.

FAVORITE BLUEBERRY SALAD

SERVES 12

1 · 6-ounce package raspberry
  gelatin
2 cups boiling water
cold water
1 · 15-ounce can blueberries, drained
  (reserve juice)

1 · 8-ounce can crushed pineapple,
  drained (reserve juice)
1 cup chopped pecans
1 cup heavy cream, whipped
1 cup miniature marshmallows
  (optional)

DIRECTIONS:

Dissolve gelatin in the boiling water. Add enough cold water to the reserved blueberry and pineapple juice to measure 2 cups. Add this juice to gelatin and stir. Remove 1 cup of gelatin and set aside. Do not chill. Chill remaining gelatin until syrupy; then add fruit and pecans. Pour into an 11 x 7 inch dish; chill until firm.

Combine reserved 1 cup gelatin with whipped cream and marshmallows. Spread over gelatin layer. Chill 3 to 4 hours.

GAZPACHO SALAD

SERVES 4-6

1 envelope unflavored gelatin
½ cup cold water
1 · 10¾-ounce can tomato soup
1 tablespoon vinegar
⅛ teaspoon salt

⅛ teaspoon hot pepper sauce
½ cup chopped cucumber
½ cup minced green pepper
¼ cup minced onion
Optional garnish: Salad greens

DIRECTIONS:

In saucepan, sprinkle gelatin into water. Stir over low heat until gelatin dissolves.

Blend next four ingredients together. Stir in gelatin mixture and chill until thickened.

Fold in cucumber, pepper and onion. Pour into a 3-cup mold and chill until set. Unmold and serve on greens.

TIP:

To set an aspic or gelatin dish quickly, put it into the freezer for 20 minutes — no longer!

ORANGE SALAD SUPREME

SERVES 10

1 · 3¼-ounce package tapioca pudding mix
1 · 3-ounce package orange gelatin
1 · 3-ounce package instant vanilla pudding mix
3 cups hot water
1 envelope whipped topping mix
1 · 11-ounce can mandarin oranges, drained

DIRECTIONS:

In large saucepan combine tapioca pudding mix, gelatin and instant pudding. Stir in hot water. Cook over medium heat until thick and bubbly, stirring constantly as it will scorch easily. Let cool completely and fold in whipped topping mix, prepared according to package directions. Fold in drained oranges. Chill in a bowl or mold until set.

RAINBOW SALAD

SERVES 10-12

"Especially attractive when served during Christmas holidays"

1 · 3-ounce package strawberry gelatin
1 cup crushed pineapple
1 · 3-ounce package lemon gelatin
1 · 10½-ounce package miniature marshmallows

1 · 8-ounce package cream cheese, softened and cut into chunks
1 cup heavy cream, whipped
1 · 3-ounce package lime gelatin

DIRECTIONS:

Prepare strawberry gelatin according to package directions. Pour into 9 x 13-inch pan and refrigerate until set.

Drain crushed pineapple reserving juice. Add enough water to pineapple juice to make 2 cups. Bring juice to a boil and pour over lemon gelatin; stir until dissolved. Add marshmallows and stir until melted. Add cream cheese and beat until smooth. Cool mixture until partially set. Fold in pineapple; then whipped cream and pour over strawberry gelatin layer. Chill until set.

Prepare lime gelatin according to package directions. Cool until slightly thickened and pour over lemon layer. Chill several hours until firmly set (preferably overnight).

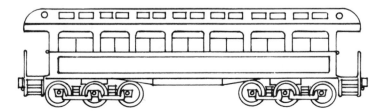

SHRIMP GELATIN SALAD

SERVES 8-12

"Superb luncheon salad"

2 · 3-ounce packages lemon flavored
gelatin
2 cups boiling water
1 · 8-ounce package cream cheese,
softened
¼ cup half-and-half
1 cup chopped celery
¼ green pepper, chopped
1 teaspoon grated onion
½ · 6-ounce can black olives,
chopped

2 tablespoons diced pimento
1 cup heavy cream, whipped

Dressing
4 · 4¼-ounce cans shrimp, rinsed and
drained
1 teaspoon grated onion
2 cups mayonnaise
2 tablespoons lemon juice
1 tablespoon diced pimento

DIRECTIONS:

Dissolve gelatin in boiling water. Add cream cheese and stir until smooth and creamy; add half-and-half. Chill until partially set and mix in celery, green pepper, onion, olives and pimento. Fold in whipped cream. Pour into mold and refrigerate until set.

To make dressing combine all ingredients and refrigerate overnight. Serve over gelatin mold.

SPRITE PARTY SALAD

SERVES 16

7-ounces Sprite
¼ pound marshmallows
1 · 3-ounce package lemon gelatin
2 · 3-ounce packages cream cheese,

softened
1 · 20-ounce can crushed pineapple
(undrained 2½ cups)
1 cup heavy cream, whipped

DIRECTIONS:

Combine Sprite and marshmallows in saucepan. Cook over medium heat until marshmallows are melted. Add gelatin, stirring until dissolved.

Add hot mixture slowly to cream cheese and beat until smooth. Add pineapple and mix well. Chill until partially set. Fold in the whipped cream. Pour into a 9 x 13 inch pan. Chill until set.

AVOCADO LOUIS

SERVES 4

1 egg yolk
2 teaspoons prepared imported mustard
½ teaspoon Worcestershire sauce
2 teaspoons red wine vinegar
½ cup peanut, vegetable or corn oil
1 tablespoon chili sauce
¼ cup finely chopped scallions,
  including green part, or green onions
4 large stuffed green olives, chopped
  (about ¼ cup)

salt and pepper
1 pound lump crab, all traces of shell
  and cartilage removed, or 1 pound
  shrimp
2 large ripe avocados
lettuce leaves
2 eggs, hard boiled, sliced
4 parsley sprigs
4 lemon wedges

DIRECTIONS:

Put yolk in a mixing bowl or blender and add mustard, Worcestershire sauce and vinegar. Beat with a wire whisk. Add oil gradually, beating rapidly. When thickened and smooth, add chili sauce, scallions and olives. Mix well and season to taste with salt and pepper. Add crab and mix gently so as not to break up the crab lumps more than necessary. Split the avocados in half and discard the pits. Pile equal portions of the crab into the avocado halves. Serve on a bed of lettuce leaves, and garnish dish with sliced eggs, parsley sprig and lemon wedge.

CHINESE CHICKEN SALAD

SERVES 10

½ pound teriyaki chicken
  (use breast)
1 head lettuce, shredded
4 stalks green onion, chopped
2 tablespoons chopped almonds
2 tablespoons sesame seeds, toasted
2 ounces won ton skins, cut
  in strips, or rice sticks
  (Mai Fun), or both

Dressing:
2 tablespoons sugar
2 teaspoons salt
1 teaspoon MSG (Ajinomoto)
½ teaspoon pepper
¼ cup salad oil
1 tablespoon sesame seed oil
  (do not substitute this ingredient)
3 tablespoons Japanese vinegar

DIRECTIONS:

To make teriyaki chicken, bake chicken breasts in teriyaki sauce until tender, or grill chicken that has been marinated in teriyaki. Cool and shred.

Deep fry won ton skins until golden brown or, if using rice sticks, prepare according to package directions.

To make dressing, combine all ingredients and mix well.

Toss all salad ingredients together; add dressing and toss again. Serve immediately.

HINT:

To successfully fry rice sticks, be sure oil is to temperature 375 to 400 degrees. They should puff almost immediately when placed in oil.

CHICKEN SALAD

SERVES 12

2 tablespoons salad oil
2 tablespoons orange juice
2 tablespoons cider vinegar
1 teaspoon salt
4 cups cubed, cooked chicken
4 cups diced celery

1 cup chopped water chestnuts
1 cup cashews
1 teaspoon chopped onions
1 teaspoon salt
2 cups mayonnaise

DIRECTIONS:

Mix together the salad oil, orange juice, vinegar, and salt. Add chicken and marinate for two to three hours. Add remaining ingredients to the chicken and mix well.

Serve on a bed of lettuce or put in a cream puff shell or on a small roll for sandwiches.

CURRIED CHICKEN SALAD

SERVES 6

2 to 3 cups cooked chicken breast, cubed
1 · 8-ounce can water chestnuts, drained and sliced
½ pound seedless grapes, halved or
1 · 11-ounce can mandarin oranges

1 cup finely chopped celery
1 cup mayonnaise
1 teaspoon curry powder
2 teaspoons soy sauce
2 teaspoons lemon juice
salt to taste

DIRECTIONS:

Combine chicken, water chestnuts, grapes or oranges and celery. Mix all remaining ingredients together and add to chicken. Toss well. Chill several hours. Serve on Bibb lettuce.

HOT CHICKEN SALAD

SERVES 6

"Good light dinner or luncheon."

2 cups cooked chicken, cubed
2 cups chopped celery
½ cup chopped onion
2 tablespoons lemon juice

¾ cup mayonnaise
1 cup grated cheddar cheese
1 cup crushed potato chips

DIRECTIONS:

OVEN TEMPERATURE: 450°

In a 2 quart casserole, mix together all ingredients, except cheese and chips. Top with chips, then cheese. Bake uncovered 15 minutes in a preheated 450 degree oven.

May serve with fruit salad and rolls.

HINT:

This may be made ahead or frozen. Add chips and cheese just prior to baking.

ITALIAN MACARONI SALAD

SERVES 12

2 cups macaroni
1 red onion, chopped
1 green pepper, chopped
1 · 6-ounce can black olives, sliced
1 · 6-ounce can green olives, sliced
  (less if desired)

2 stalks celery, chopped
chopped ham or salami
grated cheese
Italian dressing

DIRECTIONS:

Cook macaroni in boiling water and drain. Add all other ingredients to macaroni and toss with Italian dressing. (Use as much ham and cheese as desired.)

ITALIAN STYLE PASTA SALAD

SERVES 8-10

4-ounces spaghetti or vermicelli
1 · 16-ounce jar marinated artichoke
  hearts
½ small zucchini, sliced
1 carrot, shredded
2-ounces sliced salami, cut into strips
1 cup shredded mozzarella cheese

2 tablespoons grated Parmesan cheese
2 tablespoons salad oil
2 tablespoons white wine vinegar
¾ teaspoon dry mustard
½ teaspoon dried oregano, crushed
¼ teaspoon dried basil, crushed
1 clove garlic, crushed

DIRECTIONS:

Break pasta in half and cook according to package directions. Drain and set aside.

Drain artichokes, reserving marinate. Coarsely chop artichoke hearts. Halve the zucchini slices. In a large bowl combine the cooked pasta, artichokes, zucchini, carrot, salami, mozzarella, and Parmesan cheeses.

In a screw top jar combine the reserved artichoke marinate, salad oil, vinegar, mustard, oregano, basil and garlic. Shake well. Pour dressing over pasta mixture. Toss to coat evenly. Transfer salad to a covered container. Chill several hours.

TIP:

To test for doneness of pasta, boil it "al dente". In Italian this means "to the tooth" — tender but firm to bite — and that's the way pasta tastes best.

To estimate pasta quantities, use this general guideline: 2 ounces dried pasta makes about 1 cup cooked pasta or 1 serving.

RED CHILI PASTA SALAD

SERVES 8-10

Red Chili Pasta:
3 tablespoons pure ground medium hot red chilies or chili powder
2¼ to 2½ cups unbleached flour
1½ teaspoons salt
1 teaspoon cumin
½ teaspoon garlic powder
3 large eggs
1 tablespoon vegetable oil

Salad Dressing:
1 clove garlic, minced
4 to 5 sprigs cilantro or parsley
¼ cup white wine vinegar
1 teaspoon salt

¼ teaspoon cayenne pepper
½ cup salad oil
2 teaspoons fresh lime juice
½ teaspoon dry mustard

Salad
½ recipe Red Chili Pasta
1 tablespoon salad oil
1 tablespoon salad dressing
⅓ cup pine nuts
1 medium zucchini, grated or julienned
12 to 14 spinach leaves, cut into strips
8-ounces feta, crumbled

DIRECTIONS:

Combine flour, chili powder, salt, cumin, and garlic powder. (If using commercial chili powder, omit cumin and garlic.) Add oil and eggs and process in a food processor 60 seconds. Let sit at room temperature 20 minutes; then make into fettuccine.

Cook pasta in boiling water. Drain and combine with ½ tablespoon oil; refrigerate.

To prepare salad dressing, in food processor, process garlic and cilantro a few seconds and then add all other ingredients and process until blended.

Shell and sauté pine nuts in a pan with ½ tablespoon oil and 1 tablespoon salad dressing until lightly browned. Drain and reserve.

To serve, combine pasta, zucchini, spinach and cheese. Toss with dressing and sprinkle with pine nuts.

SPAGHETTI SALAD

SERVES 6-8

1 pound thin spaghetti
3 tablespoons salt
1 green pepper, chopped
3 small tomatoes, chopped
1 bunch radishes, sliced
1 red onion, sliced

½ cup sliced black olives
2 tablespoons Salad Supreme Seasoning
1 teaspoon coarse black pepper
3 teaspoons paprika
1 cup Italian salad dressing

DIRECTIONS:

Cook spaghetti in boiling water with salt. Drain and rinse. Mix the remaining ingredients with the spaghetti. Let chill several hours before serving.

BUTTERMILK DRESSING

YIELD: 1 Quart

2 cups mayonnaise
2 cups buttermilk
½ teaspoon onion salt
1 teaspoon Accent
¼ teaspoon garlic powder

½ teaspoon coarse pepper
1¼ teaspoons salt
1 teaspoon dried parsley flakes
⅛ teaspoon celery seeds

DIRECTIONS:

Combine all ingredients and refrigerate for several hours to let flavors blend.

HINT:

This is excellent base for Blue Cheese dressing. Simply add Blue Cheese to taste.

CELERY SEED DRESSING

SERVES 8-10

1 teaspoon dry mustard
½ cup sugar
1 teaspoon poppy seed
½ teaspoon celery seed
¼ teaspoon salt
1 teaspoon paprika

1 teaspoon onion salt
⅔ cup honey
1 cup oil
1 tablespoon lemon juice
5 tablespoons vinegar

DIRECTIONS:

Combine dry ingredients. Add honey, oil, lemon juice and vinegar. Mix well. Serve over fresh fruit.

CRAB DRESSING

SERVES 24-30

"Wonderful for Luncheons"

2 cups mayonnaise
1 cup chili sauce
2 tablespoons catsup
few drops Tabasco sauce

lemon juice to taste
2 · 6-ounce cans crab, drained
6 hard boiled eggs, chopped fine
salt to taste

DIRECTIONS:

Combine all ingredients and chill. Serve over tossed salad using iceburg lettuce.

ITALIAN BLUE CHEESE DRESSING

YIELD: ½ Pint

1½ cups oil
½ cup red wine vinegar
2 small tomatoes
12 cloves garlic (less if desired)
1 teaspoon thyme
1 teaspoon sweet basil
1 teaspoon oregano

½ teaspoon garlic salt
1 teaspoon salt
1 teaspoon freshly ground pepper
4-ounces gorgonzolla or blue cheese, crumbled
2-ounces capers, drained

DIRECTIONS:

Place all ingredients except the cheese and capers in a food processor and purée. Stir in the cheese and capers.

MINT DRESSING

YIELD: 2 Cups

1¼ cup salad oil
⅓ cup white vinegar
½ cup lemon juice
2½ teaspoons seasoned salt

⅛ teaspoon pepper
3 tablespoons sugar
¼ cup fresh mint, finely chopped

DIRECTIONS:

Combine oil with remaining ingredients in jar with tight fitting lid. Shake to mix well. Refrigerate until ready to use.

NANA'S FRENCH DRESSING

YIELD: 1 Quart

1 · 10¾-ounce can tomato soup
1½ cups vegetable or corn oil
½ cup sugar
⅔ cup vinegar
1 tablespoon horseradish

1 tablespoon Worcestershire sauce
1 tablespoon pepper
1 tablespoon salt
1 tablespoon paprika
1 tablespoon dry mustard

DIRECTIONS:

Mix all ingredients until well blended. Chill.

RUSSIAN SALAD DRESSING

YIELD: 1¾ Cups

⅔ cup salad oil
½ cup catsup
¼ cup sugar
3 tablespoons lemon juice
2 tablespoons Worcestershire sauce

2 tablespoons vinegar
2 tablespoons water
1 tablespoon grated onion
½ teaspoon salt
½ teaspoon paprika

DIRECTIONS:

In screw-top jar combine all ingredients. Cover and shake well; chill. Shake again just before serving.

CHILI BEER POT ROAST

SERVES 10

1 · 3½-pound beef chuck roast
2 tablespoons cooking oil
1 · 7½-ounce can chopped tomatoes
1 · 4-ounce can diced green chilies
½ cup beef broth or beer

2 teaspoons chili powder
2 teaspoons instant beef boullion
　granules
¼ cup beef broth or beer
2 tablespoons all purpose flour

DIRECTIONS:

Trim excess fat from the meat. Heat the oil in a dutch oven and brown the meat on all sides. Combine the undrained tomatoes, undrained chili peppers, ½ cup of beef broth or beer, chili powder and dry boullion. Pour this over the meat, bring to a boil, reduce the heat and simmer 2 to 2½ hours.

Remove the meat to an ovenproof platter and keep warm. For gravy, pour the pan juices into a measuring cup, skim off the fat and add water, if necessary to make ¾ cup. Pour the liquid into a saucepan. Combine the remaining beef broth or beer and the flour and add to the liquid in the saucepan. Cook and stir until thickened and bubbly. Cook and stir 1 minute more. Serve the meat with the gravy.

MARINATED CHUCK ROAST

SERVES 6-8

1 · 2 to 3 pound boneless chuck roast
　or sirloin
2 teaspoons cooking oil
2 teaspoons soy sauce
1 teaspoon Worcestershire sauce
1 teaspoon prepared mustard

1 teaspoon salt or Accent
¼ teaspoon pepper
¼ teaspoon garlic powder
⅓ cup wine vinegar
¼ cup catsup

DIRECTIONS:

Combine all the marinade ingredients and pour over the roast. Marinate the meat all day, turning it every now and then, and poking with a fork so that the marinade can seep into the meat.

Grill over charcoal or broil to desired doneness. Cooking time will depend upon meat thickness. A 1½ inch thick piece of meat may take 30 minutes to cook.

NO WORK STANDING RIB

SERVES 6-8

1 standing rib roast, (5 pounds)
salt and pepper to taste

Mushroom topping:
1 medium onion, chopped

1 pound mushrooms, sliced
½ cup butter
½ package au jus seasoning

DIRECTIONS:　　　　　　　　OVEN TEMPERATURE: 350°

In the morning remove roast from refrigerator until roast is room temperature. Then rub salt and pepper all over roast and bake at 350 degrees for 1 hour. Turn the oven off for at least 1 hour. DO NOT OPEN THE OVEN. Before serving, reheat the roast at 350 degrees for 45 minutes. Serve with mushroom topping if desired.

Mushroom topping: Sauté the onion and mushrooms in the butter until limp. Add the seasoning mix and simmer 15 minutes.

HINT:

A roast at room temperature helps the tenderizing process.

SAUCEY OVEN ROAST

SERVES 6-8

1 · 3 to 4 pound pot roast
1 · 10¾-ounce can cream of mushroom
   soup
1 · 10¾-ounce can cream of chicken
   soup

1 package onion soup mix
1 · 10¾-ounce can tomato soup
6 potatoes, peeled and halved
6 carrots, peeled and cut in chunks

DIRECTIONS:

OVEN TEMPERATURE: 250° for 8 hours or
300° for 6 hours

Combine all the soups in a large roasting pan and stir well. Add the roast, potatoes, and carrots and cook for 8 hours at 250 degrees or 6 hours at 300 degrees.

TERIYAKI TENDERLOIN

SERVES 10

1 beef tenderloin roast,
   about 2 pounds

1 bottle teriyaki sauce
salt and pepper to taste

DIRECTIONS:

OVEN TEMPERATURE: 500°

Marinate the tenderloin roast overnight in the teriyaki sauce.

When ready to serve, preheat the oven to 500 degrees. Drain the excess teriyaki sauce from the tenderloin, sprinkle with salt and pepper if desired, place in a roasting pan and bake for 15 minutes at 500 degrees. Turn the oven off and leave the roast in the oven for 1 hour more. DO NOT OPEN THE OVEN DOOR. Meat will be medium to medium-rare.

WHOLE FILLET OF BEEF

SERVES 6-8

1 whole beef fillet or tenderloin
   (2 to 2½ pounds)
6 tablespoons butter
3 to 4 teaspoons Worcestershire
   sauce

2 teaspoons dry mustard
½ teaspoon salt
¼ teaspoon freshly ground
   pepper

DIRECTIONS:

OVEN TEMPERATURE: 450°

Preheat the oven to 450 degrees. Place the filet in a large, shallow roasting pan and bake 35 minutes for medium rare. DO NOT OPEN THE OVEN.

When done, remove from the oven and cover gently with tin foil; let the meat sit for 10 minutes.

Combine the butter, Worcestershire sauce, dry mustard, salt and pepper; melt over low heat. To serve: Slice the steak and pour the sauce over the meat.

HINT:

This recipe can also be done with a whole boneless New York strip. Just increase the cooking time to 45 minutes.

BEEF PARMESAN

SERVES 6

1½ pounds round steak, ⅜ inch thick
1 egg, beaten
⅓ cup grated Parmesan cheese
⅓ cup fine dry bread crumbs
⅓ cup vegetable oil
1 medium onion, minced
1 teaspoon salt

¼ teaspoon pepper
½ teaspoon sugar
½ teaspoon marjoram
1 · 6-ounce can tomato paste
2 cups hot water
½ pound mozzarella cheese,
    sliced

DIRECTIONS:

OVEN TEMPERATURE: 350°

Place the meat on a board between sheets of waxed paper and pound with a rolling pin until it is ¼ inch thick. Trim off the fat and cut into 6 to 8 pieces. Dip the meat in beaten egg, roll in a mixture of the Parmesan cheese and bread crumbs. In a large skillet heat the oil and brown the meat over medium heat until golden brown. Lay the meat in a shallow baking dish.

In the same skillet, cook the onion until soft. Stir in the salt, pepper, sugar, marjoram, and tomato paste. Gradually add the hot water, stirring constantly. Boil 5 minutes scraping the browned bits from the sides of the pan.

Pour most of the sauce over the meat. Top with slices of mozzarella cheese and the remaining sauce. Bake in a preheated 350 degree oven for 60 minutes or until tender.

HINT:

This recipe is also excellent made with veal.

STEAK DIANE

SERVES 4

1-1½ pound New York steak
1 to 2 tablespoons green peppercorns
1 tablespoon soy sauce
1 tablespoon olive oil
3 tablespoons butter
1 tablespoon shallots, finely chopped

2 tablespoons parsley, finely chopped
½ cup beef boullion
1 to 2 teaspoons lemon juice
1 tablespoon Madeira
1 tablespoon Worcestershire sauce
1 teaspoon dry mustard

DIRECTIONS:

Trim all the fat and gristle from 1 or 2 half inch thick New York steaks. Pound the steaks to ¼ inch thick. Rub them with fresh, mashed green peppercorns, soy sauce, and olive oil.

Heat the butter in a large frying pan and fry the steaks quickly, 1 to 2 minutes per side. Remove when done and roll up to keep warm.

Add the shallots and parsley to the pan and fry 2 minutes. Add the beef boullion, lemon juice, Madeira, Worcestershire and dry mustard. Cook until reduced and slightly thickened. Pour over the steak and serve.

ESTERHAZY STEAK

SERVES 6

2 pounds round steak,
   ¾ to 1 inch thick
½ cup flour
1 teaspoon salt
½ teaspoon pepper
¼ cup oil or butter
3 carrots, thinly sliced
2 small onions, sliced
1 stalk of celery, sliced

1 cup beef boullion
1 tablespoon oil
1 tablespoon flour
¼ teaspoon salt
¼ teaspoon pepper
¼ cup dry wine
1 cup sour cream (optional)
1 teaspoon paprika (optional)

DIRECTIONS:

OVEN TEMPERATURE: 350°

Pound the round steak on one side using ¼ of the seasoned flour. Turn over and repeat, pounding the meat to no more than ¼ inch in thickness. Cut into serving size pieces and coat with any remaining flour.

Heat oil in a skillet and slowly brown meat on both sides. Remove and reserve. Add vegetables and cook slowly for about 10 minutes. Remove and reserve.

Prepare and set aside the beef boullion. Heat 1 tablespoon of oil in the skillet. Add the flour, salt and pepper; heat all until it bubbles and is light brown. Remove from the heat and gradually add the beef boullion. Return to the heat and cook, stirring constantly, until thickened. Blend in the white wine.

Grease an 11 x 13 inch baking dish. Place the browned meat and vegetables in the dish. Pour the sauce over the meat, cover with tin foil and bake in a preheated 350 degree oven for 1¼ hours.

OPTIONAL:

After 1¼ hours, remove the meat from the oven, spread the sour cream and paprika over the top, and return to the oven for an additional 15 minutes.

STEAK WITH BORDELAISE SAUCE

SERVES 4

"Also excellent made with game."

4 steaks, whatever kind you wish
1½ tablespoons flour
2½ tablespoons butter
¼ cup minced green onions,
   including tops
1¼ cups beef stock or canned
   boullion

1 cup dry red wine
2 tablespoons minced fresh parsley
¾ teaspoon thyme
¼ cup chopped mushrooms
1½ tablespoons fresh lemon juice
salt and pepper to taste

DIRECTIONS:

Trim all the fat from the steaks and broil or barbecue.

Bordelaise sauce: Brown the flour in a dry iron skillet, set aside. In a saucepan, melt the butter and sauté the onions until light brown. Add the boullion, wine, parsley, thyme and mushrooms. Simmer over low heat. Remove from the heat and add the flour. Return to the heat and stir until smooth and thickened.

MARINATED FLANK STEAK

SERVES 6

"Spicy and Good!"

1 · 2 to 3 pound flank steak
¼ cup cooking oil
¼ cup red wine vinegar
¼ cup soy sauce
½ cup onion, chopped

1 teaspoon salt
1 teaspoon pepper
1 tablespoon basil
½ teaspoon ginger
1 teaspoon to 1 tablespoon
   garlic powder

DIRECTIONS:

Charcoal Grill

Combine all the ingredients and pour over the flank steak. Cover tightly and place in refrigerator overnight.

Grill the flank steak over hot coals for 5 to 7 minutes on each side. Slice against the grain and serve.

ROLLED FLANK STEAK

SERVES 10-12

2 large flank steaks
  (1½ to 2 pounds each)
4 tablespoons grated Parmesan
  cheese
10 slices bacon
16 slices hard salami
12 slices Provolone cheese

Neopolitan Gravy:
2 · 29-ounce cans tomato purée

2 cloves garlic, minced
½ cup parsley, chopped
½ pound mushrooms, sliced
¾ cup dry red wine
2 tablespoons dry basil
1 tablespoon oregano leaves
2 teaspoons salt
1 teaspoon sugar
½ teaspoon pepper
1½ cups water

DIRECTIONS:

Butterfly each steak by splitting it horizontally through the center, leaving one edge attached. Open and place between sheets of plastic wrap. Pound each with a mallet until flattened, especially the center ridge. Discard the top piece of wrap and evenly sprinkle the meat with the Parmesan cheese.

Partially cook the bacon to render the excess fat. The bacon should be limp. Arrange 5 slices across each steak. Cover with 6 slices of Provolone cheese and 8 slices of salami.

Using the plastic wrap to help, lift and roll up the meat as tightly as possible to enclose the filling. With a cord, tie each roll lengthwise, tucking in the ends; then tie around each roll in 6 to 8 places.

Heat the oil in an 8 quart kettle over medium heat and brown the meat rolls on all sides, one at a time.

Neopolitan gravy: Combine all ingredients and pour over the meat. Bring it to a boil, cover and reduce the heat to low. Simmer 2 hours or until the meat is fork tender.

Lift out the meat and skim off the fat from the cooking liquid. Slice the rolls into ½ inch thick slices and serve either hot or cold. If served hot, it is very good with pasta.

LONDON BROIL WITH GREEN PEPPERCORNS

SERVES 10

"Wonderful for a summer evening."

1 · 2 inch thick top round steak
  (4) pounds
1 cup dry red wine
½ cup olive oil
1 scallion, minced
3 cloves garlic, minced
1 teaspoon salt
½ teaspoon black pepper
½ teaspoon dry mustard
½ teaspoon thyme
6 parsley sprigs

1 bay leaf
1½ tablespoons black
  peppercorns

Green Peppercorn Butter:
½ cup unsalted butter
¼ cup fresh parsley, chopped
1 tablespoon green peppercorns
1 teaspoon fresh lemon juice
1 teaspoon Dijon mustard
1 teaspoon Worcestershire sauce

DIRECTIONS:

Charcoal Grill

Mix together the red wine, olive oil, scallion, garlic, salt, pepper, mustard, thyme, parsley sprigs and bay leaf. Marinate the meat in this mixture, covered, overnight in the refrigerator.

Drain the meat, pat it dry; crush the black peppercorns and press them into the meat. Grill the meat 15 to 20 minutes per side for rare meat. Serve with green peppercorn butter.

Prepare the green peppercorn butter by combining the butter, parsley, green peppercorns, lemon juice, mustard, and Worcestershire in a food processor and blending together.

BEEF STEW

SERVES 6-8

2 pounds beef, cubed
¼ cup Brandy
2 tablespoons bacon grease
½ cup seasoned flour
2 cloves garlic, minced
1 onion sliced
½ cup celery, sliced
½ cup carrots, sliced
2 tomatoes

¼ pound mushrooms, sliced
½ cup beef boullion
2 cups dry red wine
1 teaspoon salt
½ teaspoon thyme
½ teaspoon marjoram
1 bay leaf
½ teaspoon pepper

DIRECTIONS:

Rub the beef with Brandy and set aside. Heat the bacon grease in a dutch oven. Fry the beef until browned on all sides. When brown, sprinkle the meat with seasoned flour, pour any remaining Brandy over the top and ignite. Stand back when lighting. Cover the dutch oven to put out the flames.

When the fire has gone out, add all the remaining ingredients and simmer slowly 2 to 3 hours. Add more liquid if needed.

HINT:

Add any vegetables you like for the last hour of cooking; potatoes, corn or peas are good. This recipe is also good if made with game such as venison or elk.

CARBONNADE OF BEEF

SERVES 8

6 pounds beef chuck, cut into
  2 inch cubes
¾ cups oil
1½ cups flour
4 teaspoons salt
½ teaspoon pepper
8 cups sliced onions
6 cloves garlic, peeled and halved

⅓ cup Brandy
3 · 12-ounce cans of beer

Bouquet Garni: (in cheesecloth)
2 bay leaves
2 celery ribs, sliced
1 leek, cleaned and chopped
¼ teaspoon peppercorns

DIRECTIONS:

OVEN TEMPERATURE: 350°

Mix ½ cup of flour with the salt and pepper and set aside.

Preheat the oven to 350 degrees. Pour a thick flim of oil into a large heavy skillet and heat over moderate heat. Dredge the meat in seasoned flour and brown on all sides in batches, adding more oil as necessary. When the meat is dark crusty brown, transfer to a large casserole.

After all the meat has been browned, pour any remaining oil into the skillet; cook the onions and garlic over medium heat until limp. Add to the meat in the casserole.

Pour the Brandy into the skillet and stir over moderate heat to dissolve any crusty bits in the pan. Pour over the meat. Add the remaining flour and mix very well. Add the bouquet garni (tied in cheesecloth) and the beer. Bring the meat to a simmer, cover and place in the preheated at 350 degrees oven.

Bake for 2½ hours or until the meat is tender but not falling apart. Stir occasionally. Remove the bouquet garni. Cool the carbonnade, then refrigerate.

To reheat the casserole, place it in a preheated 325 degree oven for 1 hour or until heated through. Stir and serve.

SHORTRIBS

SERVES 6-8

4 to 5 pounds lean shortribs
¼ cup oil for frying
1 teaspoon salt
¼ teaspoon sugar
⅛ teaspoon tumeric
⅛ teaspoon paprika
⅛ teaspoon celery salt
⅛ teaspoon black pepper
1 cup catsup
¾ cup water
½ cup finely chopped onion

½ cup finely chopper green pepper
⅓ cup cider vinegar
¼ cup firmly packed brown sugar
1 tablespoon Worcestershrie sauce
1½ teaspoons minced garlic
1 teaspoon dry mustard
½ teaspoon Tabasco sauce
½ teaspoon salt
¼ teaspoon basil
¼ teaspoon black pepper

DIRECTIONS:

OVEN TEMPERATURE: 350°

Heat the oil in a large fry pan. Brown the shortribs in the oil and place them in a roasting pan. Combine the salt, sugar, tumeric, paprika, celery salt and pepper; sprinkle over the ribs. Bake in a preheated 350 degree oven, covered, for 1 hour. Drain off any fat.

Combine remaining ingredients and spoon over ribs. Reduce oven temperature to 275 degrees and bake for 2 hours more, basting every 30 minutes.

BAKED HAMBURGER MOUSSAKA

SERVES 10-12

"Worth the effort."

2½ pounds hamburger
3 medium eggplants
1½ cups flour
1 cup olive oil
1 cup butter
½ cup butter
3 large onions, chopped
¼ cup chopped parsley
3 tablespoons tomato paste
1 cup dry red wine
1 tablespoon salt
¼ teaspoon pepper
¼ teaspoon cinnamon

1 cup grated Parmesan cheese
3 tablespoons bread crumbs

Bechamel Sauce:
7 tablespoons butter
6 tablespoons flour
3 cups hot milk
1 tablespoon salt
¼ teaspoon white pepper
dash nutmeg
4 egg yolks, slightly beaten
½ cup grated Parmesan
   cheese

DIRECTIONS:

OVEN TEMPERATURE: 350°

Slice eggplant into ¼ inch slices and sprinkle with salt. Cover and set aside for 2 hours. Drain dry, dredge with flour and fry in oil and 1 cup butter. Drain on paper towel.

Heat ½ cup butter and sauté onions 5 minutes. Add hamburger and sauté 15 minutes. Add parsley, tomato paste, red wine, salt, pepper and cinnamon. Mix well. Cool and drain off fat. Mix in Parmesan cheese and 3 tablespoons bread crumbs.

Bechamel sauce: Melt the butter, add flour and cook 1 minute. Add hot milk, salt, pepper and nutmeg. Cook until thick. Cool and stir in egg yolks.

Assemble in buttered 10 x 16 inch pan. Layer some eggplant, meat, eggplant, meat, and eggplant. Pour the sauce over the top, sprinkle with ½ cup of Parmesan cheese and bake in a preheated 350 degree oven for 1 hour or until golden brown. Let the moussaka sit for 15 minutes before serving.

HINT:

Great with lamb, too.

ENCHILADA CASSEROLE

SERVES 6-8

1 pound hamburger
1 medium onion, chopped
1 green pepper, chopped
3 · 8-ounce cans tomato
   sauce

2 · 3-ounce cans of green chilies or
   jalapenos, chopped
1 dozen corn tortillas
¼ cup oil
1 pound sharp Cheddar cheese, grated

DIRECTIONS:

OVEN TEMPERATURE: 350°

Brown onion, green pepper, and hamburger. Drain any fat and set aside.

In a sauce pan simmer the tomato sauce and chili peppers 20 minutes. Fry the tortillas in heated oil 15 seconds on each side. Drain on paper towels. Dip the tortillas in tomato sauce and layer in a casserole: tortillas, hamburger mixture, cheese; repeat until ingredients are gone. Pour any remaining sauce over the top. Top with cheese and bake 15 minutes at 350 degrees.

FIESTA OLIVA NACHOS

SERVES 4-6

1 pound lean ground beef
1 large onion, chopped
1 teaspoon seasoned salt
½ teaspoon ground cumin
2 · 17-ounce cans refried beans
1 package taco seasoning mix
2 cups grated Monterey Jack cheese
1 · 4-ounce can chopped green chilies
1 cup grated Cheddar cheese
½ cup taco sauce or salsa

1 · 16-ounce package taco flavored
   corn chips

Garnishes
1 cup sliced ripe olives
1 cup guacamole
½ cup sour cream
½ cup chopped green onions
½ head lettuce, shredded

DIRECTIONS: OVEN TEMPERATURE: 400°

Brown the meat and onion and drain off any fat. Stir in the cumin and seasoned salt.

Combine the beans, taco seasoning and Monterey Jack cheese. Mix well and spread the beans in a shallow baking dish. Cover with the meat mixture. Sprinkle the chilies over the meat. Top this with the cheddar cheese and pour the taco sauce over this.

Bake in a preheated 400 degree oven for 20 to 25 minutes or until thoroughly heated. Tuck the corn chips around the edge of the baking dish and garnish as suggested.

HINT:

This is also good rolled up in a soft tortilla or as an appetizer.

SALISBURY STEAK

SERVES 6

2 pounds lean hamburger
1 medium onion, minced
½ green pepper, minced
1 stalk of celery, minced
1 clove garlic, minced
2 tablespoons parsley, minced
½ teaspoon dry mustard
½ teaspoon each marjoram, thyme,
   paprika, salt and pepper
1 tablespoon olive oil

Sauce: (Optional)
3 tablespoons butter
¼ pound mushrooms, sliced
½ tablespoon flour
1 teaspoon lemon juice
1 teaspoon Worcestershire sauce
dash of Tabasco
¼ cup dry red wine
⅓ cup chili sauce

DIRECTIONS:

Mince the onion, green pepper, celery, garlic and parsley in a food processor. Add this to the hamburger along with the mustard marjoram, thyme, paprika, salt and pepper. When completely blended, shape the meat into patties about ¾ inch thick. Brush them with olive oil and broil 2 to 3 minutes per side. Barbecue the steaks if you prefer.

Sauce: Melt the butter in a pan and sauté the mushrooms for 5 minutes. Sprinkle them with ½ tablespoon flour and cook 1 minute. Add all the remaining ingredients, bring almost to the boiling point and serve.

MEAT LOAF

SERVES 10-12

3 pounds hamburger
1 pound sausage
1 onion
½ green pepper
½ pound mushrooms
1 cup celery leaves
1 tablespoon parsley
1 cup bread crumbs
¼ cup Madeira
2 eggs, lightly beaten
¼ cup beef boullion
¼ cup dry red wine
1 clove garlic, minced
2 teaspoons Worcestershire sauce
⅛ teaspoon allspice

⅛ teaspoon thyme
½ teaspoon paprika
1 teaspoon salt
¼ teaspoon pepper

Tomato Sauce: (Optional)
¼ cup water
½ teaspoon chili sauce
1 clove garlic minced
1 · 15-ounce can tomatoes
¼ cup red wine
½ teaspoon chili powder
½ onion, chopped
2 teaspoons Worcestershire sauce

DIRECTIONS:

OVEN TEMPERATURE: 375°

Place the onion, green pepper, mushrooms, celery leaves and parsley in a food processor and mince.

In a large bowl combine the hamburger and sausage. Add the vegetables from the food processor.

Soak the bread crumbs in Madeira. Then add them to the meat mixture along with the eggs, beef boullion, red wine, garlic, Worcestershire and all the spices. Blend all together, cover and let sit in a cool spot for 30 minutes.

Shape the meat loaf, place in a roasting pan, and place in a preheated 375 degree oven. Bake the meat loaf 30 minutes at 375 degrees and 1 hour at 350 degrees. Skim the fat from the pan as needed during cooking.

Tomato Sauce: While meat is baking, combine all the ingredients and simmer for 30 minutes. Serve with meat loaf.

STUFFED CABBAGE

SERVES 10-12

1 pound hamburger
1 medium onion, chopped
¾ cup cooked rice
¾ teaspoon salt
½ teaspoon pepper
1 egg, slightly beaten
1 large head cabbage

2 cups canned tomatoes
1 onion, sliced
½ cup raisins
¼ cup brown sugar
⅛ cup vinegar
1 teaspoon salt

DIRECTIONS:

Mix the hamburger, onion, rice, salt, pepper and egg and set aside.

Steam the cabbage leaves gently to soften them. Stuff equal amounts of the meat mixture into the cabbage leaves. It should make 10 to 12.

Put any cabbage scraps in the bottom of a large pot. Add the cabbage rolls. In a bowl, combine the tomatoes, onion, raisins, brown sugar, vinegar and salt. Pour the sauce over the top. Cover and simmer 2 hours.

HINT:

If you are not ambitious enough to make the cabbage rolls, you can simply combine all the ingredients in a large pot and serve it as soup.

GRILLED PORK WITH PEACH-CHUTNEY GLAZE

SERVES 4

4 pork chops 1 inch thick
½ cup peach chutney
½ cup peach preserves
1 tablespoon lemon juice
2 teaspoons red wine vinegar

1 teaspoon minced fresh ginger
¼ teaspoon dry mustard
⅛ teaspoon ground cloves
⅛ teaspoon anise seeds
1 tablespoon catsup

DIRECTIONS:
CHARCOAL GRILLED

Combine all the ingredients except the porkchops, in a bowl and mix well.

Grill the pork chops for 15 minutes, turning once. Brush the pork with the chutney mixture and cook 1 minute. Turn, baste again and grill another 1 minute. Serve with any remaining sauce.

PECAN PORK CHOP CASSEROLE

SERVES 4-6

6 pork loin chops
1 cup sliced celery
1 tablespoon oil
1 cup dry onion-mushroom rice
  mix
2 cups water
½ cup pecan pieces
2 tablespoon soy sauce

½ teaspoon paprika

Onion-mushroom Rice Mix:
3 cups long grain rice
1 envelope onion-mushroom
  soup mix
¼ cup parsley flakes
2 teaspoons dry basil

DIRECTIONS:
OVEN TEMPERATURE: 350°

Rice mix: Combine all ingredients. Store in plastic container and use as needed.

Trim excess fat from the pork chops and set aside. In a saucepan fry celery in oil until tender. Stir in rice mixture and water. Bring to a boil, remove from the heat and stir in the nuts. Turn the mixture into a 13 x 9 x 2 inch pan.

Arrange the pork chops over the rice. Brush the chops with soy sauce, sprinkle with paprika and bake, covered, in a 350 degree oven for 25 minutes or until the chops are tender and the rice is fluffy.

SPARE RIBS IN BARBECUE SAUCE

SERVES 8

4 pounds spare ribs
½ cup cider vinegar
¼ cup brown sugar
1 cup catsup
⅓ cup Worcestershire sauce

1 teaspoon celery seed
1 large onion, chopped
1 teaspoon paprika
2 cups water
1 teaspoon chili powder

DIRECTIONS:
OVEN TEMPERATURE: 350°

Brown the spare ribs under the broiler and drain off any excess fat.

Combine all the remaining ingredients, pour over the ribs in a large roasting pan and bake in a preheated 350 degree oven for 1½ hours.

STUFFED LOIN OF PORK

SERVES 6-8

"Looks pretty and tastes even better"

1 · 4 pound boned pork loin	2 tablespoons unsalted butter
1 cup dry white wine	2 tablespoons oil
2 teaspoons sage	1½ cups beef broth
1 teaspoon thyme	½ cup water
1 large garlic clove, minced	2 tablespoons Dijon mustard
1 bay leaf, crumbled	½ cup dark brown sugar, packed
salt and pepper to taste	1½ tablespoons cornstarch
12 pitted prunes	3 tablespoons water
12 dried apricots	3 tablespoons unsalted butter

DIRECTIONS:

OVEN TEMPERATURE: 350°

Tie a 4 pound boned loin of pork at 1 inch intervals. Make a hole through the center of the pork loin with a sharpening steel or larding needle. The hole should be about 1 inch in diameter.

In a pan large enough to hold the pork, combine the white wine, sage, thyme, garlic, bay leaf and salt and pepper to taste. Marinate the pork, covered in the refrigerator, overnight.

Remove the pork from the marinade and pat it dry. Stuff the pork through the center with a mixture of the prunes and apricots. In a large, heavy pan heat the butter and oil and brown the pork over high heat. Remove the pork to a plate and add the marinade ingredients to the pan. Cook until reduced to ½ cup. Add the pork back to the pan plus 1½ cups beef broth and ½ cup water. Cover the pork tightly with foil and bake in a 350 degree oven for 1 hour or until the meat registers 160 degrees on a meat thermometer.

Transfer the pork to an ovenproof dish, remove the string, brush the pork with mustard, coat it with brown sugar and roast it in a 450 degree oven for 15 minutes or until the meat registers 165 degrees and the coating is crisp and bubbly. Remove and let stand 15 minutes.

Strain the cooking liquid from the roasting pan, skim the fat and bring to a boil. Add the cornstarch mixed with water and the butter. Heat over high heat until the butter is incorporated. Add salt and pepper if necessary. Serve with the pork.

TIP:

For a different taste, try smoking a pork loin in an electric smoker. Place the pork in a smoker for 1½ hours and then cook as desired.

CHICAGO PIZZA

SERVES 8-10

"A great deep-dish pizza."

Crust:
1 tablespoon yeast dissolved in
  ¼ cup tepid water
3¾ cup bread flour
2¼ teaspoons salt
1¼ cups tepid water
1 tablespoon olive oil

Sausage Topping:
1 pound Italian sausage
1 clove garlic, minced

1 · 1 pound can Italian tomatoes
1 tablespoon tomato paste
2 teaspoons oregano
2 teaspoons thyme
2 teaspoons basil
2 to 3 mushrooms, sliced
½ onion sliced and marinated in 1
  tablespoon olive oil with mushrooms
4 cups grated cheeses:
  Mozzarella, Swiss, and Cheddar

DIRECTIONS: OVEN TEMPERATURE: 450°

Crust: Dissolve the yeast in the tepid water. Combine the flour, salt and tepid water. Add the yeast mixture and knead in a mixer or by hand. Let the dough rest 5 minutes; add the oil and knead again. Place the dough in a covered bowl and let it rise until triple in volume, about 3 hours. Deflate and let it rise again 1½ hours more. If it is rising too quickly, cover, wait and refrigerate until ready to use.

Sausage topping: Brown the sausage slowly and drain off the fat. Add the garlic, tomatoes, tomato paste and herbs. Simmer uncovered 30 minutes.

When ready to cook, preheat the oven to 450 degrees. Lightly oil and sprinkle with cornmeal a 2 x 13 inch heavy, iron fry pan. Line the bottom with the dough, cover with meat, mushrooms, onions and cheese. Bake to 15 to 20 minutes.

CROCKPOT SPAGHETTI SAUCE

SERVES 8

1 pound German sausage
1 pound hamburger
1 teaspoon salt
¼ teaspoon oregano
¼ cup Parmesan cheese
1 egg, beaten
1 · 32 ounce can tomatoes
1 · 32 ounce can tomato sauce

1 clove garlic, minced
½ medium onion, chopped
⅓ cup parsley, minced
2 bay leaves
¼ teaspoon thyme
⅛ teaspoon pepper
1½ teaspoons oregano
spaghetti noodles

DIRECTIONS:

Cut and brown the German sausage. Remove the meat and retain the oil.

In a medium bowl combine the hamburger, salt, oregano, Parmesan cheese and egg. Mix well and form into quarter-sized meat balls. Brown in the sausage oil. Place the meatballs and sausage in a crockpot. Combine the tomatoes, tomato sauce, garlic, onion, parsley and spices and add to the crockpot. Cook uncovered for 4 hours. Add more water or red wine if needed.

Serve over cooked spaghetti noodles.

SWEET AND SOUR PORK

SERVES 8-10

2 to 3 pounds lean pork, cut in cubes
¼ cup oil
¼ cup brown sugar
3 tablespoons soy sauce
½ teaspoon salt
⅛ cup vinegar
2 tablespoons cornstarch
2 tablespoons or more water

1 green pepper, cut in thin strips
1 onion, sliced and separated
  into rings
½ bunch celery, sliced into
  diagonal strips
1 · 8-ounce can pineapple tidbits,
  undrained
Rice

DIRECTIONS:

Heat the oil in a frying pan and brown the pork. Drain.

Combine the brown sugar, soy sauce, salt and vinegar. Mix the cornstarch with enough water to make a thin paste and add it to the brown sugar mixture. Then add all this to the browned pork in a frying pan. Simmer over low heat for 1 hour.

Add the pepper, onion, celery and pineapple during the last 15 minutes and heat through until just slightly tender, yet a little crispy.

Serve over rice.

YAKI SOBA

SERVES 4

"Looking for something unique?"

½ pound pork, sliced into bite
  sized pieces
1 package yaki soba, steamed noodles
¼ cup oil
1 inch piece fresh ginger, minced
1 large onion, sliced
½ cup mushrooms, sliced

¼ head cabbage, sliced
1 cup bean sprouts

Sauce:
¼ cup tonkatsu sauce
2 tablespoons soy sauce
MSG or salt to taste

DIRECTIONS:

Yaki soba and tonkatsu sauce must be purchased at an Oriental market but the result will be worth the effort.

Soak the noodles in hot water to separate. Drain when ready to use them.

In a large pan heat the oil with the fresh ginger in it. Add the pork and fry. Add the onion, mushrooms and cabbage and fry briefly. Add the noodles, bean sprouts and sauce. Stir and serve.

NOTE:

You may substitute ingredients as you like, i.e. chicken, peapods, water chestnuts, etc.

DELUXE HAM CREPES

YIELD: 24 Crepes

Crepes:
3 eggs
½ teaspoon salt
2 tablespoons melted butter
1¼ cups flour
2 cups milk

Sauce:
6 tablespoons butter
½ cup flour
2½ cups hot milk
2 egg yolks
1½ cups cream

1 teaspoon salt
¼ teaspoon white pepper
1 teaspoon lemon juice

Filling:
2 cups chopped ham
1 cup grated Cheddar cheese
½ cup grated Parmesan cheese
2 tablespoon chopped parsley
½ teaspoon salt
½ teaspoon pepper
1 · 4-ounce can chopped green chilies
1 · 4-ounce can sliced mushrooms

DIRECTIONS:

OVEN TEMPERATURE: 325°

Crepes: Pour all the ingredients into a blender and process 40 seconds. Refrigerate at least 2 hours. To make the crepes, melt a little butter in a small heavy skillet and pour in about 2 tablespoons of the crepe batter. Swirl the batter around to make a 5½ to 6 inch circle and cook over medium heat until slightly brown. Turn and brown on the other side. Crepes may be stacked with waxed paper between until ready to use. They may be frozen. Makes 24 crepes.

Sauce: In a saucepan melt the butter; add the flour and cook 1 minute. Beat in the hot milk with a whisk, bring to a boil over moderate heat and cook 1 minute stirring constantly. Remove the sauce from the heat. In a bowl beat the egg yolks and cream. Add ½ cup of the hot sauce to it and pour the egg yolk mixture into the remaining sauce. Cook over moderate heat until it comes to a boil. Add the salt, pepper and lemon juice.

Filling: Mix all the ingredients together and add enough sauce to bind.

Assembly: Put 1 tablespoon of filling in the center of each crepe, roll it up and place the crepe in a baking dish that has a thin coating of sauce on the bottom. Pour the remaining sauce over the crepes, sprinkle with Parmesan cheese and bake in a preheated 325 degree oven for 15 to 20 minutes.

ORANGE-CRANBERRY HAM

SERVES 10

3 to 4 pound cooked ham
½ cup sugar
3 tablespoons cornstarch

1 · 12-ounce jar orange marmalade
2 cups fresh cranberries, ground

DIRECTIONS:

OVEN TEMPERATURE: 350°

Cut ham into ¼ inch slices – do not slice all the way through. In a saucepan, blend the sugar, cornstarch, marmalade and cranberries. Cook until sugar dissolves and mixture thickens. Cool.

Spread 1 tablespoon of the marmalade mixture on every other slice of ham. Tie the ham together and bake in a preheated 350 degree oven for 30 minutes.

Remove string and serve with any extra sauce.

HAM-ASPARAGUS CASEROLE

SERVES 8-10

6 hard boiled eggs
1 teaspoon prepared mustard
3 tablespoons sour cream
salt and pepper to taste
2 tablespoons butter
½ cup chopped green pepper
⅓ cup onion, chopped

¼ cup chopped pimento
1 · 10¾ ounce can cream of
  mushroom soup
¾ cup sour cream
1 pound fresh asparagus, cooked
½ cup Cheddar cheese, grated
10 slices of ham, ¼ inch thick

DIRECTIONS:

OVEN TEMPERATURE: 350°

Cut peeled eggs in half lengthwise. Scoop out the yolk, mash it, and mix with mustard, sour cream, salt and pepper. Put the mixture back into the whites and set aside.

Melt the butter and sauté the pepper and onions until tender but not brown. Remove from the heat and stir in the pimento, soup and sour cream.

Layer the ingredients in a greased 9 x 13 inch pan. First, half of the sauce, all of the asparagus, ham, eggs and the other half of the sauce. Top with the cheese. Bake in a preheated 350 degree oven for 30 minutes.

SHERRY GLAZED HAM

SERVES 24

14 pound Virginia ham
3 cups medium dry Sherry
1 cup packed light brown sugar

1 cup cornmeal
⅓ cup cooking juices
cloves

DIRECTIONS:

OVEN TEMPERATURE: 325°

Soak a 14 pound ham in cold water in a bathtub or pail for 24 hours. Scrub off any mold and put the ham in a large kettle with enough water to cover it. Bring the water to a boil, reduce the heat and simmer the ham 20 minutes per pound. For a 14 pound ham, this may take 4 hours and 40 minutes. When done, transfer the ham to a cutting board and trim off all but ½ inch of fat.

In a large baking pan, place the ham fat side down. Add 3 cups of Sherry, cover with foil and bake the ham at 325 degrees for 1 hour. Remove the ham and turn it fat side up. Score the fat in diamond shapes and dot with cloves.

Mix together the brown sugar, cornmeal and pan juices to make a thick paste. Spread over the ham and bake another 30 minutes or until the ham is brown and crusty.

BARBECUED LEG OF LAMB
SERVES 8-10

1 · 3 to 5 pound leg of lamb, butterflied
½ cup soy sauce
½ cup water
½ cup dry white wine

3 tablespoons catsup
1 tablespoon ground or 1 teaspoon
   fresh ginger
juice of 1 lemon

DIRECTIONS:
Charcoal Grilled

Mix all the marinade ingredients together and pour over the butterflied leg of lamb in a dish. Marinate 24 hours.

Heat the coals in a barbecue and barbecue the lamb 20 to 25 minutes per side. Since a butterflied leg of lamb varies in thickness, some of the meat will be rare and some will be well-done.

HINT:
This is also an excellent marinade for a venison roast.

BRAISED LAMB SHANKS
SERVES 4

4 lamb shanks
2 onions, thinly sliced
½ cup butter
½ cup white wine
½ cup tomato juice
1 teaspoon paprika

1 teaspoon ground ginger
1 cup chicken broth
salt and pepper to taste

Roux: 2 tablespoon butter
      2 tablespoons flour

DIRECTIONS:
OVEN TEMPERATURE: 250°

Preheat the oven to 250 degrees. Fill a large pot with water and bring it to a boil. Drop the lamb shanks into the boiling water for 8 to 10 minutes. Remove the lamb shanks and peel off the skin and most of the fat from the shanks. Rinse them in cold water and dry.

In a large pan heat the butter and brown the lamb shanks. When brown, remove them to a casserole. Add the onions to the skillet and cook until limp. Add the rest of the ingredients, bring to a boil, pour over the lamb, bake at 250 degrees for 2½ hours.,

After 2½ hours, remove the lamb, skim off the fat and add more wine or stock to make 2½ cups, if necessary. Make a roux of the flour and butter in a small bowl. Add 3 to 4 tablespoons of the hot liquid from the lamb and beat until smooth. Add this roux mixture back to the liquid in the casserole and boil for 2 minutes or until slightly thickened. Check seasonings.

Return the lamb shanks to the casserole and cook an additonal 30 minutes at 300 degrees before serving.

HINT:
These lamb shanks are even better reheated. Make all ahead of time and reheat when desired.

EASY LAMB CURRY

SERVES 4

1 pound lamb stew meat
2 · 10¾ ounce cans cream of celery
  soup
½ cup milk
1 · 4-ounce can of mushrooms

1 teaspoon curry powder
¼ teaspoon salt
¼ teaspoon pepper
4 cups cooked brown or white rice

Optional condiments to sprinkle over the curry: raisins, shredded coconut, chopped cooked bacon, chutney, chopped peanuts

DIRECTIONS:

Brown the lamb in a frying pan. Add all the other ingredients and simmer until the lamb is tender, about 30 minutes. Serve over rice. Sprinkle condiments over the top.

IRISH STEW

SERVES 6-8

1 shoulder of lamb, boned and cubed
1 teaspoon salt
pinch of cayenne
3 medium potatoes, peeled and sliced
2 leeks, white part only, chopped
3 stalks of celery, chopped
2 onions, chopped
2 pounds small potatoes, cut into
  1 inch cubes

Creme Anglaise:
2 tablespoons butter
2½ tablespoons flour
1 cup white veal or chicken
  stock
2 tablespoons mushroom juice
⅓ cup creme fraiche or whipping
  cream
1 tablespoon parsley for garnish

DIRECTIONS:

Put the lamb in a kettle, add water to cover and season with salt and cayenne. Add the potatoes, leeks, celery and onions. Bring to a boil, skimming the foam as needed. Reduce heat and simmer covered for 45 to 50 minutes or until the lamb is tender. Remove the lamb with a slotted spoon to a large heatproof casserole and keep warm.

Press the vegetables and cooking juices through a seive or process in a food processor. The sauce should be naturally bound by the vegetables. Simmer this over gentle heat for several minutes.

Trim the 2 pounds of small potatoes into pieces about the size of large olives and cook in boiling, salted water until tender. Drain and add to the stew. Top both with creme Anglaise and serve garnished with parsley.

Creme Anglaise: Melt the butter and add the flour. Cook a few minutes. Blend in the stock and mushroom liquid, stirring until smooth. Add the creme fraiche and blend well.

HINT:

Make creme fraiche by combining 1 cup of cream with 1 tablespoon buttermilk. Cover and refrigerate.

LAMB SHISHKABOB
SERVES 6

3 pounds boneless lamb – cut into
   1¼ inch pieces
12 pickling onions
6 slices bacon
12 whole cloves
4 medium green tomatoes,
   quartered

Marinade:
3 tablespoons fresh mint leaves

1 teaspoon dry tarragon
3 tablespoons wine vinegar
½ cup light brown sugar
1 teaspoon dry mustard
1 teaspoon salt
½ cup salad oil
¼ cup lemon juice
1 teaspoon lemon peel grated

6 bamboo skewers

DIRECTIONS:

Combine all the marinade ingredients together in a saucepan and bring to a boil. Simmer 5 minutes. Cool. The day before cooking, pour the marinade ingredients over the lamb and refrigerate overnight.

If the onions are fresh, boil 10 minutes. Cool. Wrap ½ a bacon strip around each onion and secure it with a clove. Alternate the lamb, onions, and tomatoes on the skewers. Grill 6 inches from the coals for 15 minutes, turning and brushing with marinade as the meat cooks. These may be broiled if you prefer.

RACK OF LAMB
SERVES 2

"Superb!"

1 · 2½ pound rack of lamb
2 teaspoons Dijon mustard
1 teaspoons olive oil
1 clove garlic, minced
½ teaspoon thyme
½ teaspoon rosemary
salt and pepper to taste

1 tablespoon shallot, minced
1 clove garlic, minced
3 tablespoons butter
½ cup stale, fresh bread crumbs
1 tablespoon parsley, minced
¼ teaspoon each thyme and rosemary
salt and pepper to taste

DIRECTIONS:
OVEN TEMPERATURE: 500°

Trim the fat from the rack of lamb. Combine the mustard, olive oil, garlic, thyme, rosemary, salt and pepper in a small bowl. Rub the mixture into the lamb and marinate in the refrigerator, covered, overnight.

In a fry pan cook the shallot and garlic in butter until soft. Add the bread crumbs and seasonings and cook 2 minutes. Remove from heat and refrigerate overnight.

Arrange the lamb fat side up in a roasting pan and bake in a preheated 500 degree oven for 10 minutes. Remove the lamb and pat the crumb mixture onto the fat side, reduce the oven to 400 degrees and bake the lamb an additional 40 to 45 minutes or until desired doneness.

OSSO BUCCO

SERVES 4

4 pounds veal shanks, cut into 2 inch
   thick pieces
⅓ cup olive oil
¼ cup seasoned flour
1 large onion, chopped
4 carrots, peeled and chopped
salt and pepper to taste
1 cup dry white wine

1 cup chicken stock
1 · 1 pound can Italian tomatoes
1 bay leaf
½ teaspoon thyme
4 sprigs of parsley
2 · ½ x 3 inch strips of lemon peel
rice

DIRECTIONS:

OVEN TEMPERATURE: 325°

In a large ovenproof casserole, heat the olive oil. Dredge the lamb in flour and
brown over medium high heat. Remove and reserve. Add the onion and carrots
and cook over medium heat until limp. Return the veal to the casserole. Add the
white wine, chicken stock, tomatoes, bay leaf, thyme, parsley and lemon peel.
Bring to a boil, stirring constantly. Cover and bake in a 325 degree oven for 2
hours.

When done, discard the bay leaf, parsley and lemon peel. Serve with rice.

VEAL PAPRIKA

SERVES 4

1 pound veal cutlets, sliced ¼ inch thick
   in ¼ pound portions, pound until
   ⅛ inch thick
¼ cup tissue thin sliced onions
3 tablespoons butter
¼ cup flour
1 teaspoon salt

⅛ teaspoon pepper
1½ cups chicken stock or chicken
   broth
¾ cup sour cream
1 teaspoon paprika
buttered noodles or rice

DIRECTIONS:

Sauté the onions in butter, remove and brown cutlets that have been rolled in
seasoned flour. Add stock or broth and onions and simmer covered for 1 hour.
Add sour cream and paprika. Cook slowly until well blended.

Serve with buttered noodles or rice. (Fettucine is good.)

TIP:

Quality veal should be light grayish-pink in color with a firm texture
and fine grain.

VEAL PICCATA

SERVES 6

1½ pounds of veal, thinly sliced
salt and pepper
¼ cup flour
6 tablespoons butter
2 tablespoons oil

2 shallots, finely chopped
3 to 4 mushrooms, sliced
¼ cup dry white wine
2 to 3 tablespoons lemon juice
lemon wedges and parsley for garnish

DIRECTIONS:

Pound the veal scallops between sheets of waxed paper, season with salt and pepper and dust lightly with flour. Heat half the butter and oil in a large skillet. Add the shallots and mushrooms and cook for 1 minute. Add the veal and brown gently, adding more butter and oil as needed.

When the veal is done, remove from skillet. Add the wine to deglaze the pan. Return the veal to the pan and sprinkle with lemon juice, stirring and scraping the glaze from the bottom of the pan. Garnish with lemon wedges and parsley.

VEAL WITH CHAMPAGNE

SERVES 4

"Wonderful!"

1 pound veal scallopine, ¼ inch thick
¼ cup flour
¼ teaspoon salt
¼ teaspoon pepper
½ cup unsalted butter
2 tablespoons oil

¼ pound mushrooms, thinly sliced
¼ cup minced prosciutto
½ cup beef broth
½ cup Champagne or other sparkling
wine

DIRECTIONS:

Mix together the flour, salt, and pepper. Gently pound the veal and coat with the seasoned flour, shaking off any excess.

In a large frying pan melt 2 tablespoons each butter and oil over medium high heat. Add the veal and brown lightly. Remove to a heated platter and keep warm.

Add 2 more tablespoons of butter, the mushrooms, and the prosciutto. Cook, stirring, until the liquid evaporates and pour over the veal.

Add the broth and ½ cup of Champagne to the frying pan and cook until it is reduced to ½ cup. Add the remaining butter, stirring constantly, pour over the veal and serve.

VEAL ROULADE

SERVES 10-12

"Elegant and delicious."

1 breast of veal, 4 pounds boned
2 tablespoons butter
5 to 6 hard boiled eggs
1 teaspoon salt
¼ teaspoon pepper
4 cups beef boullion
Stuffing (recipe follows)
Mustard sauce (recipe follows)

Mustard Sauce:
½ cup mayonnaise
3 tablespoons Dijon
   mustard
½ teaspoon dry mustard
½ cup sour cream

Stuffing
1 egg
3 tablespoons milk
1 cup fresh bread cubes, about 2 slices
½ cup grated Parmesan cheese
¾ teaspoon marjoram
½ teaspoon thyme
¼ teaspoon each salt and pepper
1 · 10-ounce package chopped spinach,
   thawed
4 carrots, finely diced
1 large onion, chopped
2 cloves garlic, minced
2 tablespoons butter
1 · 10-ounce package frozen peas,
   thawed

DIRECTIONS:

OVEN TEMPERATURE: 350°

Prepare the stuffing. In a large bowl beat 1 egg with 3 tablespoons of milk. Add the bread cubes. Stir in the Parmesan cheese, marjoram, thyme, salt and pepper. Squeeze the moisture from the thawed spinach and add it along with 1 pound of sausage. Cook the carrots in boiling salted water until just tender, then drain and cool. In a small pan sauté the onions and garlic in 2 tablespoons butter until the onions are limp. Add the thawed peas, carrots and onions to the sausage mixture.

Lay the boned breast of veal on a cutting board and separate the meat at the natural membrane, cutting with a knife, until there is one flat piece of meat. Spread half of the stuffing down the center of the meat. Place the peeled hard boiled eggs down the middle, end to end, and cover with the rest of the stuffing. Roll the meat over the stuffing, sewing around the edges to seal.

Place the veal rib side down in a buttered roasting pan. Brush with 1 tablespoon of butter and sprinkle with salt and pepper. Pour the beef broth over, cover with foil and bake at 350 degrees for 1 hour. After 1 hour, remove the foil and broil the veal to brown the outside, turning as needed. Remove the veal from the oven and cool 20 minutes in the broth. Remove the veal from pan and refrigerate overnight.

To serve: Cut the chilled veal into thin slices and serve with mustard sauce. This is an excellent dish for a summer party.

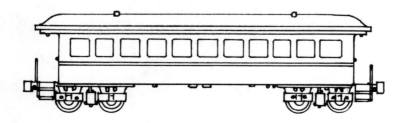

ANTELOPE AU POIVRE
SERVES 4

8 thin slices of antelope,
　tenderloin is best
¼ cup clarified butter
1 clove garlic, minced

¼ cup dry white wine
1 tablespoon capers
1 teaspoon freshly cracked pepper
1 lemon

DIRECTIONS:

Pound the antelope slices between sheets of waxed paper until ⅛ thick. Reserve.

Heat the clarified butter in a large pan. Add the minced garlic and fry for a few minutes. Add the antelope and wine. Fry for 2 minutes on each side. Add the capers and pepper. Garnish with lemon slices.

HINT:

This recipe is also excellent if made with veal scallops.

ANTELOPE RAGOUT
SERVES 4

1½ pounds antelope, cut in
　1 inch cubes
1 small clove garlic, minced
2 shallots, chopped
6 large mushrooms, sliced
2 tablespoons butter
3 tablespoons brandy
salt and pepper to taste

½ teaspoon thyme
1½ cups chicken broth
1 small package dry instant onion
　soup mix
2 cups sliced carrots
½ cup fresh or frozen peas
1 tablespoon cornstarch mixed with
　2 tablespoons water

DIRECTIONS:

Brown the antelope, garlic, shallots and mushrooms in butter for 3 minutes. Add the brandy and flame. Add salt and pepper to taste, thyme, chicken broth and onion soup. Cover and simmer 1½ hours. Add carrots and peas the last 30 minutes of cooking time. Serve over rice or noodles. Thicken with cornstarch mixed with water, if desired.

HINT:

This is also excellent if made with veal instead of antelope.

TIP:

A dressed antelope is half the dressed weight of a large deer.

BAKED RABBIT BURGUNDY

SERVES 6-8

2 · 2½ to 3 pound rabbits
½ cup flour
salt and pepper to taste
¼ pound bacon, cut in small pieces
¼ cup butter
2 cups carrots, sliced
1 cup onion, chopped
1 tablespoon parsley, chopped

¼ cup flour
1½ cups beef boullion
1 cup dry red wine
1 bay leaf, crushed
¼ teaspoon thyme
¼ teaspoon marjoram
1½ teaspoons salt
¼ teaspoon pepper

DIRECTIONS:

OVEN TEMPERATURE: 350°

Disjoint the rabbits and shake in a bag of seasoned flour.

In a large skillet cook the bacon until crisp and golden brown. Remove and reserve. Add the butter to the pan and brown the rabbit pieces. As the rabbit browns, remove it to a large casserole. Add the carrots, onion, parsley and bacon to the rabbit pieces.

To the drippings in the skillet, add ¼ cup of flour and blend well. Then add the beef boullion and red wine, preferably a Burgundy. Cook, stirring constantly, until the mixture boils and thickens. Then add the bay leaf, thyme, marjoram, salt and pepper. Pour over the rabbit, cover and bake in a preheated 350 degree oven 1½ to 2 hours. Baste occasionally. Add more wine during cooking to thin the gravy if needed.

HINT:

This is also excellent made with chicken, if you don't care for rabbit.

ELKMEAT TOSTADOS

SERVES 12

1 pound elkmeat hamburger
½ pound sausage
1 large onion, finely chopped
1 clove garlic, minced
2 teaspoons chili powder
2 teaspoons oregano
1 teaspoon cumin
¼ teaspoon cinnamon
3 tablespoons vinegar
1 · 10½-ounce can red chili sauce

2 ounces chopped green chilies
12 corn tortillas
½ cup oil for frying

Garnishes:
2 cups grated Cheddar cheese
2 cups shredded lettuce
3 to 4 seeded, diced tomatoes
guacamole (optional)
taco sauce or salsa

DIRECTIONS:

OVEN TEMPERATURE: 350°

Brown the meat, sausage, onion and garlic slowly. Drain off the fat. Add all the other ingredients for the meat filling and simmer for 30 minutes or until most of the liquid has been absorbed.

Fry the tortillas in heated oil until crisp. Drain. When ready to serve, spread 2 tablespoons of the meat mixture on each tortilla and bake in a 350 degree oven for 15 minutes. Garnish with cheese, lettuce, guacamole and salsa.

HINT:

This tostado filling can be made with any kind of hamburger and is also an excellent taco or enchilada filling.

STIR FRIED VENISON

SERVES 6

1½ to 2 pounds of venison, cut in strips
¼ cup soy sauce
¼ cup sherry
¼ teaspoon accent or MSG (optional)
1 tablespoon fresh ginger, grated
1 teaspoon sugar

1 onion, sliced
¼ pound mushrooms, sliced
½ pound broccoli or asparagus, sliced
¼ to ½ cup of oil
1 tablespoon cornstarch

DIRECTIONS:

Cut the venison in strips and marinate in the soy sauce, sherry, MSG, ginger and sugar for 1 hour. Remove and save the marinade.

Slice the vegetables and reserve.

Heat ¼ cup of oil in a frying pan over medium high heat. Add the venison, reserving the soy sauce mixture. When the venison is done, remove it to a platter. Add the vegetables and fry them quickly in oil. When the vegetables are done, add the meat from the platter.

Mix the cornstarch with the marinade and add to the vegetables and meat. Serve with rice.

HINT:

Use any vegetables you like. This dish is also excellent if made with beef. An interesting variation is to add 1 tablespoon of schezun hot chili sauce.

VENISON CHILI

SERVES 6

1½ pounds venison, ground or diced
½ pound pork, ground or diced
1 pound dry kidney beans or
    1 · 27-ounce can
1 large onion, chopped
1 clove garlic, minced
½ cup oil
1 bay leaf

2 tablespoons chili powder
½ teaspoon oregano
1½ cups enchilada sauce
1 small jar of taco sauce or salsa
1 red chili, chopped
1 teaspoon MSG
2 teaspoons salt
¼ cup cornmeal (optional)

DIRECTIONS:

If using dry beans, soak them overnight. In a large, heavy pot heat the oil and sauté the meat, onion and garlic in oil. Add the beans, dry or soaked, and enough water to cover 3 inches above the beans. Add the bay leaf, chili powder, oregano, enchilada sauce, salsa, red chili and MSG. Cover and let simmer 1½ hours, stirring occasionally.

Add the salt and cornmeal to thicken the chili (if desired) and cook 30 minutes more.

HINT:

This chili is good garnished with onion, sour cream or shredded Cheddar cheese.

VENISON BEURRE ROUGE

SERVES 4

"Worth the cholesterol!"

4 venison steaks, about 1 inch thick
2 tablespoons butter
1 cup Champagne
1 tablespoon shallots

¼ tablespoon salt
⅛ teaspoon pepper
¼ cup Balsamac vinegar
1½ cup butter

DIRECTIONS:

Fry the venison in 2 tablespoons butter. Remove and keep warm

Make the beurre rouge by boiling the Champagne with the shallots until it is reduced to 1½ tablespoons of liquid. It is best to do this in the pan in which the meat was cooked to capture all the flavors of the meat. Add the Balsamac vinegar, salt and pepper and reduce again to 1½ tablespoons. Add the butter, a small piece at a time, stirring constantly until thick and creamy. Remove from heat and serve immediately. (Sauce will separate if cooled and reheated.)

HINT:

This sauce is excellent with any red meat.

VENISON BOURGUIGNON

SERVES 8

2 pounds venison or lean beef
10 small or 5 medium onions
2 tablespoons bacon grease or oil
1½ tablespoons flour
½ teaspoon marjoram

½ teaspoon thyme
salt and pepper to taste
½ cup beef boullion
1 cup red wine, Burgundy is best
½ pound mushrooms, sliced

DIRECTIONS:

Peel and slice the onions. Heat the bacon grease or oil in a Dutch oven and fry the onions until limp. Remove and reserve.

Cut the venison into 1 inch cubes and sauté in the dutch oven, adding more oil if necessary. When brown, sprinkle the meat with flour, marjoram, thyme, salt and pepper and stir. Add the boullion and red wine and simmer slowly 2 hours.

The meat should be barely covered when cooking. It may be necessary to add more liquid during cooking. If so, keep the boullion and wine in the same proportions of half as much boullion as wine.

After 2 hours, add the mushrooms and onions and cook ¾ to 1 hour more.

AUNT KAY'S SESAME CHICKEN

SERVES 4

"Very tasty"

5 whole chicken breasts, boned,
   skinned, and cut into bite sized
   pieces
¼ cup flour
salt and pepper
½ cup peanut oil

¼ cup sugar
¼ cup soy sauce (preferably Japanese
   style)
2 tablespoons sesame seeds
¼ cup chopped green onions

DIRECTIONS:

Dredge chicken pieces in flour seasoned with salt and pepper. In a frying pan
heat oil and cook chicken chunks until done. Keep warm and set aside.

Combine sugar and soy sauce in medium saucepan and heat until sugar
dissolves. Add chicken chunks. Toss chicken in sesame seeds and onions. Serve
at once.

HINT:

Be careful not to overcook chicken pieces, this will make them tough.

BEST CHICKEN ARTICHOKE DINNER

SERVES 6-8

"When company is coming . . . "

6-8 whole chickens, boned
   and skinned
a dash of salt, pepper and paprika
1 · 14-ounce can artichokes, drained
   (reserve ½ the liquid), packed in water
6 tablespoons butter
¼ pound fresh mushrooms

¼ cup flour
1 cup half & half
1 · 10 ¾ ounce can chicken broth
¾ cup grated Parmesan cheese
2 tablespoons Sherry
¾ teaspoon rosemary
6 ounces egg noodles

DIRECTIONS:

OVEN TEMPERATURE: 350°

Boil noodles according to package directions, drain and set aside.

Butter or grease a 9 x 13 inch oven-proof baking dish. Layer noodles in bottom
of dish. Pour the reserved artichoke liquid over the noodles. Place the chicken
breasts over the noodles. Cut the artichoke hearts in half and layer over the
chicken.

In a sauce pan melt 2 tablespoons butter and sauté mushrooms until slightly
limp. Pour the mushrooms over the chicken mixture.

In same pan melt the remaining butter and add the flour. Cook until the flour is
absorbed and bubbly. Gradually add the half & half and chicken broth, stirring
constantly. Cook until thickened. Stir in half the Parmesan cheese, the rosemary
and Sherry. Cook until cheese is melted and then pour over the casserole.
Sprinkle the remaining cheese over the casserole. Bake at 350 degrees for 45
minutes.

CHICKEN BREASTS IN LEMON CREAM

SERVES 6

3 whole chicken breasts, split,
  boned and skinned
½ cup clarified butter
2 tablespoons Vermouth
2 teaspoons grated lemon peel
2 tablespoons lemon juice

½ teaspoon salt
¼ teaspoon pepper
1 cup cream
6 pats of butter
¼ cup Parmesan cheese, grated

DIRECTIONS:

OVEN TEMPERATURE: Broil

Wash chicken and pat dry. Sprinkle lightly with salt and pepper to taste.

In a large skillet heat clarified butter and sauté chicken breasts 8-10 minutes, turning once. Remove chicken to ovenproof serving platter.

To skillet add Vermouth, lemon peel and juice. Cook one minute, stirring constantly. Slowly add salt, pepper and cream; stir vigorously. Pour sauce over chicken. Place a pat of butter on each breast and sprinkle with grated cheese. Place under broiler until golden brown. Serve at once.

HINT:

Serve with fresh steamed asparagus.

CHICKEN COGNAC

SERVES: 2

"Easy, but elegant"

2 whole chicken breasts, halved
2 tablespoons milk
¼ cup biscuit mix
½ teaspoon salt
½ teaspoon paprika

Sauce:
1 tablespoon butter
¼ cup sliced green onions
1 egg yolk
½ cup whipping cream
½ cup Cognac

DIRECTIONS:

OVEN TEMPERATURE: 425°

Wash chicken and pat dry. Dip in milk and drain. Mix biscuit mix and seasonings in shallow pie plate. Coat chicken, and place in 9 x 9 x 2 inch baking dish skin side down. Bake chicken 15 minutes on each side in 425 degree oven. Keep warm.

In small fry pan melt butter and sauté onions until tender. Beat egg yolk into cream and pour gradually into onion mixture, stirring constantly over low heat. Cook until thickened.

Heat Cognac in small saucepan until hot. Pour Cognac over chicken and ignite. When flame dies out, pour sauce over chicken and serve immediately.

HINT:

Have on hand a damp dish towel to smother fire if necessary.

PINEAPPLE CHICKEN
SERVES 4-5

3 whole chicken breasts, skinned,
boned, and cubed
2 tablespoons vegetable oil
salt
pepper
18 canned pineapple chunks
1 green pepper, thinly sliced
1 cup diced celery

¼ cup white vinegar
1 cup apricot nectar
1 cup brown sugar
1 teaspoon Worcestershire sauce
½ cup tomato catsup
1 teaspoon cornstarch
2 tablespoons water

DIRECTIONS:

In large skillet heat oil and sauté chicken cubes. Lightly season with salt and pepper. Add pineapple chunks, green pepper and celery. Stirring constantly, cook until done. Set aside; keep warm.

Combine vinegar, nectar, brown sugar, Worcestershire sauce and catsup in a medium sized saucepan. Simmer 20 minutes. Dissolve cornstarch in water and add to sauce, cooking until thickened. Pour sauce over chicken; serve at once.

POLYNESIAN CHICKEN
SERVE 6

6 whole chicken breasts
1 teaspoon salt
½ teaspoon pepper
½ teaspoon paprika
6 tablespoons melted butter
1 · 6-ounce can frozen pineapple juice

¼ teaspoon garlic powder
1 teaspoon soy sauce
½ teaspoon ground ginger
¼ cup water
1 papaya, seeded, peeled and sliced

DIRECTIONS:
OVEN TEMPERATURE: 350°

Season chicken breasts with salt, pepper and paprika. In a large frying pan brown breasts in melted butter. Place breasts in baking dish and set aside.

Heat together in saucepan the pineapple juice, garlic powder, soy sauce, ginger and water. Reserve ¼ cup sauce and pour the remaining sauce over browned chicken breasts. Place in 350 degree oven and bake for 20 to 30 minutes, basting frequently. Add water to pan if necessary. Dip the sliced papaya in reserved sauce and bake with chicken the last 5 minutes of cooking time.

YAKITORI SKEWERED CHICKEN
SERVES 4

4 whole chicken breasts, skinned,
boned, and cut into bite sized pieces
2 tablespoons peanut oil
⅓ Shoyu (soy sauce)

5 tablespoons sugar
2 tablespoons Mirin Cooking Sake
2 bunches green onions, cleaned and
white end cut into 1 inch pieces

DIRECTIONS:
OVEN TEMPERATURE: Broil

In a large skillet heat oil and sauté chicken until partially cooked through. Mix together the shoyu, sugar, and Mirin. Pour this sauce over the chicken in the skillet and continue cooking until the chicken is done.

Thread the chicken chunks onto skewers with 1 or 2 onion pieces. Place under broiler or over grill and cook until lightly browned. Serve at once. Any remaining sauce may be served as a dip for the chicken.

CHICKEN CURRY

SERVES 12

"This is nice for a large group, and can easily be made ahead."

1 cup butter
1 cup minced onion
1 cup chopped celery
1 cup flour
4 teaspoons curry powder
2 teaspoons salt
2 teaspoons sugar
a dash of pepper

3 cups half & half
3 cups chicken broth
2 tablespoons Sherry
2 tablespoons lemon juice
5 pieces of candied ginger
2 · 4 ounce cans mushrooms, drained
grated peel of half an orange
6-8 cups chicken, cut in chunks

DIRECTIONS:

In a large skillet melt butter. Add onion and celery; sauté until transparent. Combine the flour, curry powder, salt, sugar, and pepper. Sprinkle this over onion and celery, cooking until absorbed by butter. While stirring, slowly add the half & half and chicken broth; cook until all lumps dissolve and sauce is smooth. Stir in the Sherry, lemon juice, ginger, mushrooms, and orange peel. Fold in the chicken chunks and cook until heated through.

CRAB STUFFED CHICKEN

SERVES 4

2 tablespoons butter
½ cup finely chopped green onions
1 cup cooked crab meat
1 · 3-ounce can chopped mushrooms, drained
½ cup coarsely crushed saltine crackers
2 tablespoons snipped parsley
2 tablespoons dry white wine
½ tablespoon salt
4 whole chicken breasts, skinned

and boned
vegetable oil

Shrimp Newburg Sauce:
2 tablespoons butter
2 tablespoons flour
¼ teaspoon salt
¼ teaspoon paprika
1½ cups half & half
1 cup cooked, shelled shrimp
2 tablespoons dry Sherry

DIRECTIONS:

OVEN TEMPERATURE: 375°

In a medium skillet melt butter and sauté green onion until tender. Stir in crab meat, mushrooms, cracker crumbs, parsley, wine and salt. Fill each breast with ⅓ cup stuffing mixture, roll and tie with string. Place stuffed breasts in baking dish and brush lightly with vegetable oil. Cover with foil and bake at 375 degrees for 30 minutes or until done. While chicken is cooking, prepare Newburg sauce.

In a medium saucepan melt butter and blend in flour, salt and paprika. Stirring constantly, add half & half and cook over medium heat until thickened. Add shrimp and Sherry. Remove from heat, but keep warm.

To serve, remove string from each breast and place on serving platter or individual plates. Spoon heated sauce over each breast.

SESAME CHICKEN BREASTS

SERVES 4-6

"Tender, tangy and delicious!"

3 whole chicken breasts, skinned,
  boned and halved
6 tablespoons soy sauce
¼ cup water
2 tablespoons sesame oil

1 · 3-inch piece of ginger, grated
  (amount varies according to taste)
2½ lemons, juiced
1½-ounce can sesame seeds, toasted
  in oven
lemon slices

DIRECTIONS:

OVEN TEMPERATURE: Broil

Combine soy sauce, water, sesame oil, ginger and lemon juice in a large enough
bowl to accommodate chicken breasts. Place chicken in marinade, cover and
refrigerate for 1 to 6 hours, turning occasionally.

Broil breasts for 8 to 10 minutes per side. Baste while broiling. Cooking time
may vary according to the thickness of each breast.

Roll cook breasts in sesame seeds, coating evenly on each side. Serve at once
with lemon slices.

TARRAGON CHICKEN

SERVES: 6

2 slices bacon
8 whole chicken breasts, halved,
  skinned, and boned
¼ cup butter
½ teaspoon leaf tarragon, crumbled
2 ounces Swiss cheese, grated

¼ pound fresh mushrooms, sliced
½ teaspoon salt
¼ teaspoon pepper
2 egg yolks
1½ cups cream

DIRECTIONS:

OVEN TEMPERATURE: Broil°

Cook bacon until crisp, drain and crumble. Set aside.

Pound the chicken breasts between 2 sheets of waxed paper until ¼ inch thick.

In large skillet heat butter and tarragon. Sauté chicken, part at a time, 3 to 4
minutes per side and remove to baking dish.

Add mushrooms, bacon, and remaining seasonings to skillet and sauté until
tender. Remove skillet from heat.

Beat egg yolks with cream in small bowl until blended; add to mushroom
mixture. Place over low heat and cook for 5 minutes, stirring constantly until
sauce thickens. Pour sauce over chicken and sprinkle with grated cheese. Place
under broiler until cheese bubbles. Serve immediately.

HINT:

This is nice with lemon buttered broccoli or fresh peas poached in wine.

BROCCOLI
CHICKEN CASSEROLE

SERVES: 4

"This is quite a popular recipe and everyone seems to love it."

2 whole chicken breasts, cooked, boned, skinned, and cut into bite sized pieces
1 fresh bunch broccoli cooked and cut into pieces, **or**
1 · 10-ounce package frozen broccoli cooked and cut into chunks

Sauce:

1 · 10¾ ounce can cream of
  chicken soup
½ cup mayonnaise

½ teaspoon lemon juice
¼ teaspoon curry powder
¾ cup buttered bread crumbs

DIRECTIONS:

OVEN TEMPERATURE: 350°

In an ovenproof baking dish layer broccoli pieces in the bottom. Add the cubed chicken pieces on top.

In a small bowl combine the soup, mayonnaise, lemon juice and curry; mix well. Pour the sauce over the chicken mixture. Top with buttered bread crumbs and bake at 350 degrees for 30 minutes or until bubbly.

CHICKEN BREAST
CASSEROLE SUPREME

SERVES 12-15

8 to 10 whole chicken breasts, cooked,
  skinned, boned, and cut into pieces
2 · 10¾ ounce cans cream of
  chicken soup
1½ cup mayonnaise
1 · 13-ounce can evaporated milk
2 tablespoons lemon juice
2 tablespoons minced onion
2 teaspoons Jane's Crazy Salt
  (found in gourmet spice section)

2½ cups diced celery
3 cups cooked white rice
1 · 2-ounce jar chopped pimento
2 · 4-ounce cans button mushrooms

Topping:

3 cups corn flakes
½ cup slivered almonds
½ cup melted butter

DIRECTIONS:

OVEN TEMPERATURE: 375°

In large mixing bowl combine the soup, mayonnaise, milk, lemon juice, onion, and salt. Mix well; set aside.

In another large bowl combine the chicken, celery, rice, pimento, and mushrooms. Fold in the soup mixture, and mix well.

Pour into a greased 9 x 13 inch ovenproof baking dish. In a small bowl mix all topping ingredients together and crumble over top of casserole.

Bake for 30 minutes at 375 degrees.

FILA CHICKEN CASSEROLE

SERVES: 12

"Don't be afraid of all the ingredients. This is a beautiful casserole for a buffet dinner. And what could be better — it can all be made ahead!"

Poached Chicken
1 · 3½ pound chicken
1 cup dry white wine
1½ teaspoons salt
1 bay leaf
1½ teaspoons thyme
¾ teaspoon rosemary
2 cups water

Casserole:
¾ cup butter
¼ cup flour
2 cups chicken broth
   (reserved poaching liquid)

½ cup whipping cream or half & half
½ teaspoon white pepper
2 cloves garlic, minced
1 large onion, chopped
½ pound fresh mushrooms, sliced
¾ cup long grain rice
1½ cups chicken broth,
   canned
¾ teaspoon summer savory
1 · 9-ounce package frozen artichoke
   hearts, thawed
12 to 14 sheets fila pastry
⅓ cup butter

DIRECTIONS:

OVEN TEMPERATURE: 350°

Prepare the chicken by combining all of the poaching ingredients in a 5 quart or larger stock pot. Bring to a boil, and reduce heat to a simmer. Cook 40 to 45 minutes until the meat is no longer pink. Remove the chicken, cool. Remove from bones and cut into bite sized pieces. Skim the fat from the broth, boil uncovered until it is reduced to 2 cups. Strain and set aside.

In a small saucepan melt ¼ cup of the butter over low heat. Stir in the flour and cook until it is bubbly. Slowly add the poaching liquid and the half & half. Cook, stirring until it boils and thickens. Stir in the pepper and set aside.

In a 2 to 3 quart pan melt 3 tablespoons butter and sauté the garlic, onion and mushrooms. Cook, stirring until the vegetables are limp. Stir in the rice, just enough to coat with the butter. Add the chicken broth (canned) and the summer savory, cover and cook 20 minutes or until rice is tender. Add the artichokes and cook another 5 minutes. Stir 1 cup of the cream sauce into the rice mixture and cool. Stir the remaining sauce into the chicken pieces and allow to cool.

Melt the ⅓ cup butter and brush the bottom of a 9 x 13 inch baking dish. Fit a sheet of fila in the bottom of dish and brush lightly with butter. Repeat this step to 6 or 7 more sheets. Spread half of the rice mixture over the fila, then add the chicken mixture. Layer the rest of the rice mixture over the chicken. Cover the casserole with the remaining fila, buttering each sheet as before. Cut lightly through the top 3 to 4 layers of the fila making 8 to 12 servings. Cover and chill if desired or bake immediately. Bake for 45 minutes if at room temperature, or 60 minutes if chilled. Bake at 350 degrees.

VARIATION:

Chopped asparagus may be substituted for the artichoke hearts, if desired.

HINT:

When working with this pastry, be sure to keep it covered with a damp dish towel to prevent excess drying.

CHEESY CHICKEN CASSEROLE

SERVES 6-8

1 · 3½ pound chicken, poached
2 · 10-ounce packages broccoli
2 cups milk
2 · 8-ounce packages cream cheese

1 teaspoon salt
1 teaspoon garlic salt
1½ cups grated Parmesan cheese

DIRECTIONS:

OVEN TEMPERATURE: 350°

Poach chicken. When chicken is cool, remove all meat from the bones and cut into bite sized pieces. Set aside.

Cook broccoli according to package directions and cut into bite sized pieces. Set aside.

In a medium sized saucepan or double boiler combine the milk, cream cheese, and seasonings. Add half the Parmesan cheese and cook until cheese is melted and sauce is heated through. Remove from heat and set aside.

Place the broccoli in the bottom of a 2 quart casserole dish. Pour 1 cup of the cheese sauce over the top. Add chicken pieces and pour remaining sauce over top. Sprinkle with the remaining Parmesan cheese and bake for 25 to 30 minutes at 350 degrees. Before serving, allow casserole to sit for 5 to 10 minutes.

ENCHILADAS De POLLO

SERVES 6

2 whole chicken breasts, cooked,
   boned, skinned, and cut into 12 pieces
1 cup chopped onion
1 clove garlic, minced
2 teaspoons butter
1 · 16-ounce can tomatoes, diced
1 · 8-ounce can tomato sauce
¼ cup chopped green chilies

1 teaspoon sugar
1 teaspoon ground cumin
½ teaspoon salt
½ teaspoon dried crushed oregano
12 corn tortillas
2½ cups grated Monterey Jack
   cheese
¾ cup sour cream

DIRECTIONS:

OVEN TEMPERATURE: 350°

In a medium sized saucepan sauté onion and garlic in butter until tender. Add tomatoes, tomato sauce, chilies, sugar and remaining seasonings. Bring to a quick boil and reduce the heat to simmer. Simmer covered for 20 minutes. Remove from heat and set aside.

Dip each tortilla into tomato mixture to soften. Place one strip of the chicken and 2 tablespoons of the grated cheese in each tortilla and roll up. Place each enchilada in a 9 x 13 inch ovenproof baking dish, seam side down. Pour the remaining sauce over the enchiladas and bake at 350 degree for 40 minutes. Spoon the sour cream over the enchiladas and serve.

HINT:

This dish will freeze very well without the sour cream. Simply add the sour cream at serving time.

CHICKEN WILDRICE CASSEROLE

SERVES 8-10

2 whole chickens (3 pounds each)
1 cup water
1 cup dry sherry
1½ teaspoons salt
½ teaspoon curry powder
1 medium onion, sliced
½ cup sliced celery

1 pound fresh mushrooms
¼ cup butter
2 · 6-ounce packages long grain
  and wild rice (combination)
1 cup sour cream
1 · 10¾ ounce can cream of
  mushroom soup

DIRECTIONS:

OVEN TEMPERATURE: 350°

Place chicken in large soup pot. Add water, sherry, salt, curry powder, onion, and celery. Bring to a boil and cover. Simmer for 1 hour. Refrigerate chicken when done and skim broth.

When chicken is cool, remove meat from bones and cut into bite sized pieces.

Wash mushrooms and pat dry. Sauté in butter until lightly browned. Reserve enough for garnishing the top of the casserole.

In a large pan combine the rice and chicken stock. Measure stock according to package directions for liquid measurements. If short on stock add enough water to compensate. Cook according to package directions.

Combine the chicken, rice, and mushrooms in a 4 quart casserole. Blend in the sour cream and mushroom soup. Arrange the reserved mushrooms on the top of the casserole. Bake for 1 hour at 350 degree oven.

WHITE GREEN CHILI ENCHILADAS

SERVES 12

10 fresh green chilies, blistered,
  peeled, and seeded
4 chicken breast halves, poached
  in 2 cups water
1 onion, chopped
2 tablespoons oil or chicken fat
1 clove garlic, crushed

1 teaspoon cumin seed
1 teaspoon oregano
2 tablespoons flour
1 dozen corn tortillas
oil
2 cups grated Jack cheese
3 cups hot cream

DIRECTIONS:

OVEN TEMPERATURE: 350°

Rinse the chilies and broil until blistered. Place into a plastic sack until cool, then peel and seed. Wear rubber gloves.

Remove the skin and the bones from the chicken after it is poached. Shred the chicken, and skim fat from the broth.

Melt the oil or chicken fat. Sauté the onion until transparent. Add the garlic and spices and flour. Cook for 2 minutes. Stir in the reserved chicken broth, the chilies, chopped coarsely, and the chicken. Cook until thickened.

Set out the chicken mixture, the shredded cheese, the tortillas, 1 inch of oil heated in a medium saucepan over medium heat, and the warm cream in a pie pan. Grease an oblong baking pan.

One at a time, dip the tortillas into the hot oil to soften, then into the cream, then place on a plate. Fill each tortilla with the chicken mixture, 2 tablespoons shredded cheese, and roll before placing seam side down in the baking dish.

When all tortillas are filled, pour remaining cream over all, sprinkle with remaining cheese, and set aside or refrigerate until ready to cook. Bake in a 350 degree oven for 30 minutes.

BARBECUED CHICKEN

SERVES 6-8

3 whole chicken split in half
3 tablespoons curry powder

½ cup French's mustard
½ cup honey

DIRECTIONS:

Wash and pat chicken dry. Rub 2 tablespoons of the curry powder over chicken.

Combine the remaining curry powder with the mustard and honey.

Place the chicken, skin side up, over the grill and brush with the sauce. Turn every 5 minutes and baste with remaining sauce. Cook approximately 45 minutes; this may vary depending on the intensity of the charcoal and the size of the chickens.

CHICKEN ADOBO

SERVES 4-6

"Even General McArthur would have returned to the Philippines for this dish."

3½ pounds chicken pieces, preferably
  dark meat
1 cup soy sauce
½ cup rice vinegar

½ cup water
1 teaspoon pepper
2 large cloves garlic, minced

DIRECTIONS:

In a large skillet combine all ingredients and bring to rapid boil for 2 minutes. Reduce heat to simmer and cover with lid. Cook 3 hours, turning chicken frequently. The last 15 to 20 minutes of cooking time, remove lid and allow some of the cooking liquid to evaporate.

Serve with rice and pass any extra cooking liquid as gravy.

FRIED CHICKEN

SERVES: 6-8

"Good & crispy"

2 whole chickens or equivalent
  parts
1 quart buttermilk

Breading:
2 cups self rising flour

  (no substitute)
1 tablespoon paprika
1½ teaspoons ground pepper
salt to taste
½ teaspoon nutmeg
Vegetable oil as required

DIRECTIONS:

Clean chicken and cut into pieces. Place chicken in a large bowl and pour buttermilk over pieces. Refrigerate overnight.

Remove chicken from refrigerator and immediately dredge pieces in seasoned flour. Coat evenly.

In a large frying pan pour at least 2 inches of oil and heat to 350 degrees. Fry chicken pieces for about 30 minutes or until done. Serve at once.

Be sure oil is to correct temperature before frying chicken.

HONEY GLAZED CHICKEN BAKE

SERVES 4-6

1 · 3-pound chicken, cut in pieces or equivalent parts
⅓ cup flour
½ teaspoon garlic powder
salt and pepper to taste

6 tablespoons butter
¼ cup honey
3 tablespoons lemon juice
2 tablespoons soy sauce
½ teaspoon ground ginger

DIRECTIONS:

OVEN TEMPERATURE: 350°

In a shallow dish combine the flour and seasonings. Dip each piece of chicken in flour mixture and coat evenly.

Melt 2 tablespoons butter in a shallow baking dish, large enough to accommodate chicken in a single layer. Arrange chicken, skin side down, in pan. Bake uncovered for 30 minutes, at 350 degrees.

Meanwhile, in a small saucepan, melt remaining butter and add honey, lemon juice, soy sauce and ginger.

After chicken has baked the 30 minutes, turn each piece over and pour sauce mixture evenly over chicken. Bake another 30 to 40 minutes, basting frequently.

PAN ROASTED CHICKEN

SERVES 4

1 · 2½-3 pound whole chicken
3 cloves garlic
2 tablespoons butter
2 tablespoons vegetable oil

1½ teaspoons rosemary
salt and pepper
½ cup white wine

DIRECTIONS:

OVEN TEMPERATURE: 375°

Wash chicken and pat dry. Place garlic in cavity of bird. Rub chicken with butter and oil. Sprinkle with salt, pepper and rosemary. Place bird on roasting pan. Bake 1 hour at 375 degrees and baste every 15 minutes.

To serve, remove bird to serving platter and spoon off all but 1 tablespoon of fat from pan. Place roasting pan over high heat on stove. Add wine and scrape the bottom of pan to deglaze. Pour juices over chicken and serve.

TIP:

Use a fresh chicken within three days of buying it and allow ¾ pound of chicken per serving.

SHOYU CHICKEN

SERVES 4

1 · 3½-pound chicken, split or quartered (skinned if desired)
¾ cup soy sauce
1 tablespoon honey
¼ cup brown sugar
1½ cups water
2 garlic cloves, minced
1 star anise

1 to 2 tablespoons grated fresh ginger or to taste
2 tablespoons Sherry
¼ cup chopped green onions
2 tablespoons cornstarch
2 tablespoons water
Optional:
½ pound pea pods

DIRECTIONS:

In a large dutch oven or pot, combine all of the ingredients *except* onions, cornstarch, water, chicken and peapods. Bring the sauce ingredients to a boil, stirring constantly for 2 minutes. Add chicken and simmer for 45 minutes or until tender.

Remove chicken to serving platter. Add the green onion, and pea pods to skillet. Combine the cornstarch with the water and stir into pan. Cook until thickened and pour over chicken.

SUSAN'S SPICED CHICKEN

SERVES 4-6

1 · 3-pound chicken, cut into pieces
¼ cup flour
¼ cup olive oil
1 cup diced onion
2 cloves garlic
½ pound fresh mushrooms, sliced
1½ cups white wine
½ cup pitted black olives

1 to 2 teaspoons capers — more if desired
1 · 1-pound can plum tomatoes, drained and chopped
1 teaspoon lemon juice
a dash of each — pepper, basil, oregano, and ground sage

DIRECTIONS:

Dredge chicken pieces in flour. In a large skillet heat oil and brown chicken evenly on both sides; remove from skillet and set aside.

In same skillet sauté onion and garlic until tender. Add mushrooms and cook 2 minutes. Pour in the wine and simmer for 10 minutes. Add the remaining ingredients including chicken pieces, cover and simmer for 30 minutes or until tender.

TIP:

Store fresh ginger in a plastic bag in the freezer. No need to thaw, just grate or slice when desired.

ELMEDA'S TURKEY ROLL-UPS

SERVES 16

1 · 8-ounce package cream cheese, softened
4 tablespoons melted butter
½ teaspoon pepper
2 cups cooked turkey or chicken, cubed
⅔ cup chopped mushrooms
2 · 8-ounce cans Crescent dinner rolls

6 tablespoons melted butter
1½ cups seasoned bread crumbs (or crushed stuffing croutons)
½ cup chopped nuts
1 envelope instant gravy mix, prepared according to directions (optional)
chopped chives (garnish)

DIRECTIONS:

OVEN TEMPERATURE: 375°

Cream together the cream cheese, butter and pepper. Stir in the turkey and mushrooms and set aside.

Separate the Crescent rolls into 16 individual pieces on a bread board. Spread each triangle generously with turkey mixture. Gently roll each triangle, starting with the longest point and tuck under to seal.

Combine bread crumbs and nuts in a shallow dish and mix together. Dip each roll up in the remaining melted butter and then gently roll in crumb mixture.

Place roll ups on an ungreased baking sheet and bake at 375 degrees for 15 to 20 minutes or until golden brown. Serve with gravy and chopped chives.

TURKEY ENCHILADAS

SERVES 6

"Quick and easy dinner from leftovers."

1½ cups sour cream
1 · 10¾ ounce can cream of mushroom soup
1 · 4-ounce can green chilies
½ cup chopped onions (scant)
1 teaspoon chili powder
1 teaspoon salt
1 teaspoon garlic powder
1 teaspoon black pepper

6 flour tortillas
1 · 1-pound piece cooked turkey breast, sliced
2 cups grated Cheddar cheese

Garnish:
Shredded lettuce
Sliced tomato
Sour cream

DIRECTIONS:

OVEN TEMPERATURE: 350°

In a large bowl combine the sour cream, soup, chilies, onions and seasonings. Mix well. Set aside.

Wrap turkey slices in flour tortillas and place in a 9 x 9 inch ovenproof baking dish, seam side down. Pour sauce over enchiladas and sprinkle with grated cheese. Bake at 350 degrees for 20 minutes or until heated through and cheese is bubbling. Garnish with lettuce, tomato, and sour cream. Serve at once.

HINT:

This is a great make ahead dish.

TURKEY ORIENTALE

SERVES 4-6

"Quick and easy dinner from leftovers."

1½ cups sliced fresh mushrooms
2 tablespoons vegetable oil
1 cup diagonally sliced celery
½ cup sliced onion
1 · 6-ounce package frozen snow peas
   or 1 small green pepper, cut into
   thin strips

2 tablespoons cornstarch
1 · 10½-ounce can chicken broth
1 tablespoon soy sauce
2 cups cooked chicken or turkey, diced
½ cup water chestnuts

Chinese noodles or steamed rice

DIRECTIONS:

In a large skillet brown mushrooms in oil. Add celery, onions, and peas, cook until tender. Stir in the cornstarch, chicken broth, and soy sauce. Cook until thickened. Add the turkey and water chestnuts.

Serve over a bed of rice or noodles. Pass additional soy sauce.

TURKEY STEAKS SUPREME

SERVES 4-6

"Kids love this one!"

1 · 2-pound package ground turkey steaks
1½ cups buttermilk baking mix
½ teaspoon salt
½ teaspoon pepper
¼ cup butter

1 · 10¾ ounce can cream of
   chicken soup
1 · 5-ounce can evaporated milk
1 · 4-ounce can button mushrooms,
   drained

DIRECTIONS:

In a shallow pie plate mix together the baking mix, salt and pepper. Evenly coat steaks on both sides.

In a large skillet, melt butter and fry steaks over medium heat until browned. Combine the soup and milk, pour over the steaks. Simmer over low heat for 45 minutes or until done. Add the mushrooms the last 20 minutes of cooking time. Serve at once.

TIP:

Turkey steaks, which are cross-cut from the turkey breast, can be easily done at home by partially freezing the breast and then slicing.

GRILLED BREAST
OF PHEASANT   SERVES 6

6 whole pheasant breasts,
  boned and skinned

Marinade:
1 cup olive oil
12 Juniper berries, toasted
  and crushed
1 teaspoon coriander seeds, toasted
  and crushed
2 hot red peppers, toasted and crushed
  (optional)

2 cloves garlic, minced
2 tablespoons chopped parsley
1 small onion, chopped
1 cup dry white wine or Vermouth

Sauce:
1 cup chicken stock
1 cup creme fraiche or
  1½ cup heavy whipping cream
salt and pepper to taste

DIRECTIONS:

Combine all the marinade ingredients together. Pour half the marinade in a shallow dish and arrange the pheasant breasts in the marinade. Pour the remaining half of the marinade on top. Cover and marinate for 2 to 3 days in the refrigerator.

Remove the breasts from the marinade, reserving marinade. Either broil or barbecue the pheasant breasts 3 to 5 minutes, turning once. Cooking time will vary according to the breast thickness. The meat should be fairly pink on the inside. When done remove from heat and keep warm.

The pheasant breasts may be served as is, or you may make a sauce by skimming the oil from the marinade, adding the stock, and boiling it down to ½ cup. Stir in the cream fraiche or cream. Simmer the sauce until it is creamy and starts to bubble. Add salt and pepper to taste.

Cut the pheasant breasts in diagonal slices and serve with sauce.

PHEASANT A LA
DUKE OF KENT   SERVES 2

2 pheasant breasts only
¼ cup flour
½ teaspoon salt
¼ teaspoon pepper
4 tablespoons clarified butter

½ onion, finely chopped
6 mushrooms, sliced
¼ cup Sherry or dry white wine
1 cup hot cream
4 slices bread, toasted

DIRECTIONS:

Season the deboned pheasant breasts with salt and pepper and dredge with flour.

In a sauté pan, heat enough clarified butter to cover the bottom of the pan. Add pheasant breasts and fry over moderate heat for 15 minutes, turning frequently. Add onion and mushrooms and sauté an additional 1 to 2 minutes.

Add the Sherry or wine and reduce slightly. Add the heated cream and heat until slightly thickened.

Serve over toast.

PHEASANT IN CHAMPAGNE

SERVES 6

6 thin slices of good french bread,
  toasted on both sides and buttered
6 single breasts of
  pheasant
4 tablespoons soft butter
1 carrot, chopped
1 onion, chopped
2 cups Champagne
1 cup chicken broth

Sauce:
4 tablespoons butter
½ cup chopped onion
1 cup fresh mushrooms, sliced
4 slices bacon, chopped
1 small basket white pearl onions,
  pealed (1 cup)
2 tablespoons flour
3 egg yolks
1½ cups heavy cream

DIRECTIONS:

OVEN TEMPERATURE: 425°

Rub pheasant with soft butter and roast in casserole dish for 10 minutes at 425 degrees. Add the carrot, onion, Champagne and broth. Cover, and roast for 30 minutes at 350 degrees. Remove pheasant from baking dish and strain cooking liquid. Reserve liquid. Keep pheasant warm.

Melt 4 tablespoons butter in large saucepan and sauté chopped onion, mushrooms and bacon. Add pearl onions. Blend in flour, reserved broth, and boil until 2 cups remain.

In a small bowl combine the egg yolks with cream and beat together. Add ¼ cup sauce to egg, cream mixture. Pour this mixture back into onion, mushroom sauce and heat through over very low heat. *Do not boil.*

To serve, place pheasant on serving platter and pour sauce on top. Top with toasted french bread slices. Delicious!

ROAST PHEASANT

SERVES 4-6

2 whole pheasants, cut in pieces
½ cup flour
½ teaspoon salt
½ teaspoon pepper
½ teaspoon paprika
¼ cup salad oil
½ cup brandy
1 clove garlic, minced

½ teaspoon thyme
½ teaspoon seasoned salt
1 · 10¾ ounce can cream of mushroom
  soup
1 · 4-ounce can mushrooms and liquid
½ cup milk
½ cup sherry
½ cup chopped parsley

DIRECTIONS:

OVEN TEMPERATURE: 350°

Wash birds and cut in pieces, leaving breasts intact. Pat dry. In a shallow pie dish combine flour, salt, pepper, and paprika. Dredge pheasant parts evenly in mixture.

Heat oil in large dutch oven and brown pheasant pieces on all sides. Remove from pan. Discard any fat and add brandy to pan to deglaze bottom. Cook for one minute and then add garlic, thyme, and seasoned salt. Stir in soup, mushrooms with liquid, milk, and sherry. Return pheasant to pan and simmer until tender for 1½ hours covered, in preheated 350 degree oven.

To serve, remove pheasant from oven and place on serving dish. Pour pan gravy over meat. This may also be used for game hens. Reduce cooking time by ½ hour.

STUFFED GAME HENS A LA GREQUE

SERVES 4

4 Rock Cornish Game Hens
butter
salt and pepper
½ cup white wine
½ cup water

Stuffing:
2 cups wild rice
4 cups chicken broth
¾ teaspoon salt

½ cup butter
giblets from hen (optional)
3 shallots, minced
1 celery stalk, minced
1 clove garlic, minced
2 tablespoons chopped parsley
½ teaspoon thyme
½ teaspoon sage
1 cup pine nuts, shelled
½ cup white wine

DIRECTIONS:

OVEN TEMPERATURE: 350°

In a large pan steam the rice in the chicken stock with salt and butter for 20 minutes. Remove from heat and set aside.

In 2 tablespoons butter, gently sauté the giblets, shallots, celery, garlic, and parsley. Add seasonings and simmer for 10 minutes over low heat. Add the rice, pine nuts, wine and mix well. Simmer covered for 5 minutes.

Wash and dry hens. Rub with butter. Stuff the birds and sprinkle with salt and pepper. Pour the wine over the birds and add ½ cup water. Roast for 45 minutes at 350 degrees, basting occasionally.

ROAST WILD GOOSE

SERVES 8

1 · 4-5 pound whole dressed goose
6 slices salt pork

Stuffing:
6 tablespoons butter
½ cup chopped onion
½ cup chopped celery
5 cups bread crumbs

2 teaspoons salt
2 cups apples, peeled and chopped
1 cup prunes, steeped in hot water
  or Madiera
1 teaspoon thyme
1 egg
pinch nutmeg

DIRECTIONS:

OVEN TEMPERATURE: 375°

Melt butter and sauté onion and celery in fry pan until limp. Add remaining stuffing ingredients and mix well.

Sprinkle the goose with salt and pepper. Stuff the goose loosely with the stuffing mixture. Lay the salt pork over the breast of the bird. Place goose in a shallow roasting pan and cover with foil. Bake one hour at 375 degrees. Remove foil from bird and bake one hour more. Baste the goose with pan juices during baking.

WILD DUCK A L'ORANGE

SERVES 2

2 wild ducks
¼ cup orange juice
¼ cup brandy
½ cup wild rice
4 cups boiling salted water
2 teaspoons instant chicken boullion
4 tablespoons butter
1½ tablespoons parsley, minced
1½ tablespoons green onion, minced

1½ tablespoons celery, minced
1½ tablespoons basil
½ teaspoon salt
½ teaspoon fresh pepper
1 cup orange juice
1 teaspoon grated orange rind
2 teaspoons lemon juice
1 cup red wine
4 slices bacon

DIRECTIONS:

OVEN TEMPERATURE: 450°

Rub the wild ducks inside and out with brandy and orange juice.

Wash the wild rice and cook in boiling salted water in which chicken boullion has been added. Simmer 30 to 45 minutes or until the rice is tender. Drain and set aside.

While the rice is cooking, combine butter with parsley, green onion, celery, basil, salt, and pepper. Mix this with the wild rice when it is done. Stuff loosely into the ducks. Place the ducks in an open roasting pan. Pour the orange juice, orange rind, lemon juice, and red wine in the bottom of the pan. Drape bacon over duck breasts. Roast in a pre-heated 450 degree oven for 25 to 35 minutes.

ROAST QUAIL WITH WILD RICE STUFFING

SERVES 8

8 · 6-ounce quail
2 teaspoons salt
½ teaspoon pepper
4 slices salt pork or bacon
6 tablespoons butter, melted

Wild Rice Stuffing:
2 tablespoons butter
½ cup chopped mushrooms
¼ cup finely chopped onion
2 cups chicken broth

½ cup wild rice
salt and pepper to taste

Sauce:
½ cup finely chopped onion or shallots
¼ cup sliced mushrooms
2 tablespoons flour
1 cup chicken stock
2 tablespoons brandy (optional)
⅛ teaspoon thyme
2 tablespoons heavy cream

DIRECTIONS:

OVEN TEMPERATURE: 475°

In a 3 quart pot, melt 2 tablespoons butter, add the mushrooms and onions, and cook until tender. Add chicken broth and bring to a boil. Add wild rice, salt and pepper and bring to a boil. Reduce heat and simmer 30 to 40 minutes. Cool.

Preheat oven to 475 degrees. Wash and dry the quail, sprinkle with salt and pepper, and stuff loosely with the cooked wild rice. Place the quail in a large, shallow roasting pan. Cut the bacon in half and drape over each breast. Roast for 20 minutes at 475 degrees, basting every 5 minutes. Remove from oven and keep warm.

Sauce: Pour off all but 2 tablespoons of the pan juices. Add the onions and mushrooms and cook 5 minutes. Add the flour and mix well. Add the chicken stock, brandy, and thyme. Cook, stirring constantly, until slightly thickened. Stir in the cream and serve with the quail.

BROILED BUTTERFISH

SERVES 2

2 large butterfish fillets,
  1 to 1½ pounds
2 tablespoons butter

2 teaspoons lemon juice
2 tablespoons dry bread crumbs
salt and pepper to taste

DIRECTIONS:

OVEN TEMPERATURE: Broil

Melt the butter. Place the butterfish in a shallow broiling or roasting pan lined with tin foil. Sprinkle the fish with lemon juice, salt and fresh pepper. Pour the melted butter over the top. Sprinkle with bread crumbs and broil for 5 minutes or until the fish flakes.

FILLET OF SOLE EN CROUTE

SERVES 8

8 large fillets of sole
1 box puff pastry

Scallop Mousse:
½ pound scallops, chilled
1 teaspoon salt
¼ teaspoon white pepper
1½ cups whipping cream,
  chilled
⅛ teaspoon paprika
⅛ teaspoon nutmeg
2 egg whites, chilled

Sauce Choron:
¼ cup white wine vinegar
¼ cup dry white wine
1 tablespoon shallots, minced
½ tablespoon tarragon
2 tablespoons parsley, minced
⅛ teaspoon pepper
½ teaspoons salt
3 egg yolks
2 tablespoons cold, ½ cup
  melted butter
2 to 4 tablespoons tomato paste

DIRECTIONS:

OVEN TEMPERATURE: 450°

Puff paste: Thaw and roll out each piece of puff pastry so that it can be cut into 4 · 5 inch squares. This can be done ahead of time and kept in the refrigerator until needed if lightly floured and covered.

Scallop mousse: Chill the blade of a food processor. Put the scallops, salt, pepper, paprika and nutmeg in the processor and puree until smooth. Add the egg whites and blend until smooth. Add the whipping cream, gradually, blending until smooth. Transfer to a small bowl, cover and refrigerate until needed.

Assembly: Preheat the oven to 450 degrees. Lightly salt and pepper the fillets. Put 2 to 3 tablespoons of the scallop mousse in the center of each fillet and roll up. Put each fillet in the center of a piece of puff pastry, roll up, pinch to seal and place seam side down on a greased baking sheet. Decorate with any left over puff pastry and brush with beaten egg. Punch a small hole in the center for the steam to escape and refrigerate 15 mintues.

Bake 10 minutes at 450 degrees and 10 minutes at 350 degrees.

Sauce choron: Boil vinegar, wine, shallots, herbs and seasonings over moderate heat until reduced to 2 tablespoons. Let it cool. Proceed with the rest as though making hollandaise. Beat the egg yolks until thick. Strain the vinegar mixture and add to the egg yolks. Place over low heat and add 1 tablespoon cold butter, then another, to thicken. Beat in the melted butter by drops. Add the parsley and tomato paste. Serve at once.

FILLET OF
SOLE MARYA
SERVES 8

8 fillets of sole
½ pound crab meat
½ pound tiny shrimp
1 teaspoon salt

White Sauce:
3 tablespoons butter
2 tablespoons flour
2 cups hot milk or half and half
½ teaspoon instant chicken
   boullion
salt and pepper to taste

1 to 2 tablespoons dry white wine
dash of nutmeg

Hollandaise Sauce:
½ cup butter, melted
3 egg yolks
½ teaspoon salt
2 tablespoons lemon juice
¼ teaspoon cayenne pepper

2 tablespoons grated Parmesan cheese
   to sprinkle over top

DIRECTIONS:
OVEN TEMPERATURE: 350°

Dry the fillets of sole and lightly salt them. Put 1 to 2 tablespoons of the crab meat on each fillet and roll it up. Do the same with each fillet and place them seam side down in a shallow baking dish.

White sauce: Melt the butter until it bubbles. Add the flour and cook 1 minute. Add the hot milk and stir with a whisk until it is thickened and smooth. Add the chicken boullion, salt, pepper, white wine and nutmeg. Stir in any remaining crab meat and shrimp.

Hollandaise sauce: Melt the butter until hot but not brown. Place the egg yolks, salt, lemon juice and cayenne in a food processor and process until blended. Slowly drizzle in the hot butter while the processor is on and process until thickened.

Add the hollandaise to the white sauce and pour over the fillets. Sprinkle with Parmesan cheese and bake in a preheated 350 degree oven for 30 minutes or unti heated and lightly brown.

HINT:
If you are in a hurry, use canned white sauce and Hollandaise sauce mix.

FISH
CASSEROLE
SERVES 4

1 pound fresh or frozen fish,
   any variety
2 tomatoes, sliced
2 green peppers, sliced
1 onion, sliced

½ cup olives, sliced
½ cup cooked peas or beans (optional)
1 teaspoon tarragon
½ tespon oregano
¼ cup melted butter

DIRECTIONS:
OVEN TEMPERATURE: 350°

In a shallow baking dish layer all the ingredients. Sprinkle the top with tarragon, oregano and melted butter.

Bake in a preheated 350 degree oven 30 to 40 minutes. Serve with rice.

POISSON AU SABAYON

SERVES 6

"A wonderful soufflé"

1 pound skinned white fish,
  cooked and flaked
1 carrot, sliced
1 onion, sliced
½ cup water
Bouquet garni: thyme, bay leaf and
  parsley

Bechamel sauce
2½ tablespoons butter
3 tablespoons flour
1 cup boiling milk
½ teaspoon salt
pepper

nutmeg
1 egg yolk
6 egg whites
pinch of salt
½ cup Swiss cheese, grated

Sauce Sabayon:
3 egg yolks
½ cup whipping cream
¼ cup reduced fish stock, strained
¾ cup unsalted butter
salt
pepper
juice of ½ lemon

DIRECTIONS:

OVEN TEMPERATURE: 425°

Place the fish in a buttered baking dish with the carrots and onion on the bottom. Add the wine, water and bouquet garni. Cover with buttered tin foil and poach in a 350 degree oven for 10 to 12 minutes.

Remove the fish from the liquid. Strain the liquid into another pan and reduce it to ¼ cup. Reserve for the sauce.

Bechamel sauce: Melt 2½ tablespoons of butter in a saucepan. Add the flour and cook for several minutes. Add the boiling milk, stirring until well mixed. Add the salt, pepper and nutmeg. Remove from the heat and add the egg yolk. Stir to keep the egg from scrambling. Set aside.

Whip the egg whites until stiff, add a pinch of salt and fold in all but 2 tablespoons of the grated cheese. Mix ¼ of the egg white mixture into the Bechamel sauce to lighten it. Then fold the Bechamel sauce into the egg whites, folding carefully.

Butter a shallow baking dish no more than 15 inches long, i.e. an oval dish. Spread a small amount of the egg whites on the bottom. Pile the flaked fish into 6 small mounds. Top with remaining egg whites and sprinkle with remaining cheese. Bake in a preheated 425 degree oven in a pan of hot water for 15 to 20 mintues. Serve with Sauce Sabayon.

Sauce Sabayon: Place the egg yolks, whipping cream and fish stock in a heavy pan and stir constantly over low heat until thickened. Slowly, piece by piece, stir the butter into the egg yolk mixture. When the butter has been incorporated, season with salt, pepper and the juice of ½ lemon. Serve immediately.

GRILLED HALIBUT STEAK

SERVES 4

4 · 6-ounce halibut steaks
½ cup oil
3 tablespoons soy sauce
¼ teaspoon pepper

2 tablespoons Sherry
1½ teaspoons grated fresh ginger
1 teaspoon grated orange rind
¼ cup butter, for basting

DIRECTIONS:

CHARCOAL GRILLED

Arrange the halibut steaks in a shallow baking dish. Mix together the oil, soy sauce, pepper, Sherry, ginger and orange rind. Pour over the halibut and marinate, coverd, 2 hours to overnight in the refrigerator.

Grill the fish on a barbecue 4 to 5 minutes on a side, basting frequently.

HINT:

This recipe is excellent with any fish, as long as the fish is cut into 1 inch thick steaks.

HALIBUT CASSEROLE

SERVES 8

2 pounds of halibut
1 bay leaf
1 onion, sliced
5 tablespoons butter
5 tablespoons flour

4 cups milk
½ pound Cheddar cheese, shredded
4 cups bread cubes, crust
   removed
½ cup buttered bread crumbs

DIRECTIONS:

OVEN TEMPERATURE: 350°

Steam the halibut with the bay leaf and onion slices for 10 minutes. Cool the halibut and break into bite sized pieces.

Melt the butter in a saucepan and add the flour. Cook for 1 minute, then add the milk and cook until slightly thickened. Add the cheese. The sauce will not be thick.

In a 3 quart casserole put a layer of fish pieces, a layer of bread cubes, and half the sauce. Repeat. Top with buttered bread crumbs. Bake uncovered in a preheated 350 degree oven for 30 minutes.

TIP:

Put lemon on fish just before or just after cooking. If the lemon is put on too early, the fish will get mushy.

SAUTÉED MAHI MAHI

SERVES 8

2 pounds Mahi Mahi, sole or grouper
2 eggs, beaten
½ cup flour
½ cup dry bread crumbs
½ teaspoon salt
¼ teaspoon pepper
½ teaspoon MSG (optional)

½ cup clarified butter
¼ cup dry white wine
1 cup coarsely chopped
   nuts: macadamia
   nuts or almonds
1 lemon for garnish

DIRECTIONS:

Cut the fish into 1½ inch chunks and dip in the beaten eggs. Combine the flour, breadcrumbs, salt, pepper and MSG. Dredge the fish pieces in the flour mixture.

In a large frying pan heat ¼ cup of clarified butter. Sauté the fish over medium high heat for about 10 mintues. Be sure to turn the fish to brown it on all sides. Remove the fish and keep warm.

Deglaze the pan with wine, and cook, stirring constantly, for 2 minutes. Add the remaining 4 tablespoons of butter and sauté the nuts for 2 minutes. Pour the butter/nut sauce over the fish and garnish with lemon slices.

POACHED SALMON WITH HOLLANDAISE

SERVES 8-10

3 pounds of salmon

Court Boullion
4 carrots, sliced
2 green onions, sliced
1 stalk of celery, sliced
1 bay leaf
1½ cups dry white wine
3 cups water

1 teaspoon salt
6 peppercorns

Hollandaise sauce:
½ cup butter
3 egg yolks
2 tablespoons lemon juice
¼ teaspoon salt
pinch of cayenne pepper

DIRECTIONS:

Mix all the court boullion ingredients together in a pot large enough to hold the salmon.Wrap the salmon in cheesecloth and put into the unheated court boullion. Bring to a boil, reduce heat and simmer 25 minutes. Remove the fish to a serving platter, take off the cheesecloth and serve with hollandaise sauce.

Hollandaise sauce: Heat ½ cup of butter to bubbling but not brown. In a food processor put the egg yolks, lemon juice, salt and pepper. Turn the motor on and add the hot butter gradually. Blend about 15 seconds or until thick. A blender may be used in place of a food processor if you wish.

HINT:

If your hollandaise sauce curdles, quickly beat in 1 teaspoon of boiling water.

BAKED PERCH

SERVES 2-3

1 pound perch fillets
water
¼ cup dry white wine
½ teaspoon salt
1 bay leaf
3 peppercorns

2 teaspoons lemon juice
2 to 3 tablespoons grated Parmesan
  cheese
¼ cup seasoned bread crumbs
1 tablespoon butter

DIRECTIONS:

OVEN TEMPERATURE: 400°

Pour ½ inch of water in the bottom of a rectangular baking dish. Add wine, salt, bay leaf, peppercorns and lemon juice. Put the fish fillets into the pan. Sprinkle with bread crumbs mixed with Parmesan cheese and dot with butter. Bake in a preheated 400 degree oven 30 minutes or until the fish flakes.

SWEET GRILLED SALMON

SERVES 4

4 · 1¼ inch thick Salmon steaks
½ cup dark brown sugar
2 tablespoons soy sauce

2 tablespoons dry Sherry
4 tablespoons melted butter

DIRECTIONS:

CHARCOAL GRILLED

Place the salmon steaks in a disposable aluminum foil baking pan. Combine all remaining ingrdients, pour over the salmon and let it sit for 15 minutes.

Place the foil pan over the coals or gas grill. Cook until the salmon begins to flake, brushing with the sauce as it cooks. Turn the steaks after 5 mintues.

HINT:

You may also use a whole salmon and cook it directly on the grill. Remove the skin when partly cooked and drizzle with the marinade. Oil the grill first and be careful not to overcook.

TUNA CASSEROLE

SERVES 6

6-ounces wide noodles, cooked
  and drained
1 · 10-ounce package peas, thawed
  and drained
1 · 6½-ounce can tuna
1 · 10¾ can cream of mushroom
  soup

½ cup chopped onion
1 cup Cheddar cheese, grated
1 · 4-ounce can mushrooms
¼ cup milk
2 teaspoons Worcestershire sauce
dash of pepper
½ cup slivered almonds

DIRECTIONS:

OVEN TEMPERATURE: 350°

In a large bowl combine all the ingredients except the almonds. Turn into a 2 quart cassrole, top with almonds and bake in a preheated 350 degree oven for 45 minutes.

BAKED STUFFED TROUT WITH HORSERADISH SAUCE

SERVES 4

4 trout, cleaned
5 tablespoons butter
6 fresh mushrooms, sliced
1 medium onion, chopped
¼ cup parsley, minced
1½ cups bread crumbs
½ teaspoon sage
¼ teaspoon onion salt
¼ teaspoon celery salt

¼ teaspoon garlic salt (optional)
freshly ground pepper to taste

Horseradish Sauce:
½ cup heavy cream
2 tablespoons prepared horseradish
salt to taste
parsley or dill sprigs for garnish
lemon slices for garnish

DIRECTIONS:

OVEN TEMPERATURE: 400°

Wash trout in cold water and pat dry. Set aside.

Melt 4 tablespoons of butter in a fry pan and sauté the mushrooms, onion and parsley until they are limp. Toss this mixture with the bread crumbs. Add sage, onion salt, celery salt, garlic salt and pepper. Stuff the trout cavities and place in a buttered baking dish. Brush with melted butter.

Bake the trout in a preheated 400 degree oven for 25 to 35 minutes. Garnish with parsley and lemon wedges. Serve with horseradish sauce.

Horseradish sauce: Whip the cream until stiff, fold in the horseradish and salt to taste.

TROUT ALMONDINE

SERVES 4

4 fresh, cleaned trout
¼ cups seasoned flour
¼ cup butter

¼ cup slivered almonds
¼ cup chopped parsley
1 lemon, sliced for garnish

DIRECTIONS:

Wash and dry the trout. Sprinkle with seasoned flour and fry in the butter which has been melted in a large fry pan. The trout will take 4 to 5 minutes per side to fry. When done, remove from the pan and garnish with any remaining melted butter, almonds, parsley and lemon.

HINT:

This is a simple, basic recipe, but one of the best for fresh trout.

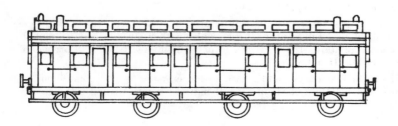

CRAB AND ARTICHOKE CASSEROLE

SERVES 4

1 pound crab meat
4 tablespoons butter
3 tablespoons flour
1 cup milk, heated
½ cup chicken broth
¾ cup grated Cheddar cheese
2 tablespoons Worcestershire sauce

¼ cup dry white wine or Sherry
2 · 9-ounce packages frozen artichoke
  hearts, cooked and drained
4 hard boiled eggs, peeled and sliced
(optional)
2 tablespoons Parmesan cheese
  grated

DIRECTIONS:

OVEN TEMPERATURE: 350°

Defrost the crab meat if frozen. Pick out any pieces of shell and set aside.

Melt 3 tablespoons of butter in a large saucepan. Add the flour and cook 1 minute. Blend in the milk and broth. Stir until smooth and thickened. Add the Cheddar cheese, Worcestershrie sauce and wine or Sherry. Cook over moderate heat until the cheese is blended and the sauce is smooth.

Spoon ⅓ of the sauce in the bottom of a 1½ quart casserole. Layer ½ of the artichoke hearts, saving 8 to garnish, ½ the eggs, ½ the crab meet with ⅓ the sauce on top. Repeat the layers. Top with the remaining ⅓ of the sauce. Sprinkle with Parmesan cheese.

Bake in a preheated 350 degree oven, uncovered, for 30 minutes. Just before serving melt 1 tablespoon butter in a skillet and cook the reserved artichoke hearts to 3 to 5 minutes and garnish the casserole.

CRAB LASAGNA

SERVES 8

1 pound crab meat
½ pound lasagna noodles
2 · 10¾-ounce cans cream of
  shrimp soup
1 · 8-ounce package cream cheese
2 cups cottage cheese, small curd
1 egg, slightly beaten

1 medium onion, chopped
2 teaspoons basil
½ teaspoon lemon juice
salt and pepper to taste
2 tomatoes, thinly sliced
1 cup shredded Cheddar cheese

DIRECTIONS:

OVEN TEMPERATURE: 350°

Cook noodles according ot package directions. Drain and rinse in cold water. Combine soup and crab meat.

In a small bowl mix together the cream cheese, cottage cheese, egg, onion, basil, lemon juice and salt and pepper to taste.

Butter a large shallow casserole. Place in it a layer of noodles, half of the cheese mixture and all of the crab mixture. Cover with another layer of noodles and the remaining cheese mixture. Top it with a layer of tomatoes. Bake in a preheated 350 degree oven for 15 minutes.

Add a layer of Cheddar cheese and return to the oven for 30 minutes or until golden brown and bubbly. Let stand several minutes before cutting into squares and serving.

CRAB WELLINGTONS

SERVES 8

¾ pound crab meat

Bechamel Sauce:
2 tablespoons butter
2 tablespoons flour
½ cup chicken broth
½ cup half and half
½ teaspoon salt
dash of nutmeg
2 tablespoons mayonnaise
3-ounces grated Swiss or Jack cheese
salt and pepper to taste

2 teaspoons butter
1 tablespoon minced shallot
2 large mushrooms, finely chopped
2 tablespoons finely chopped carrot
2 tablespoons finely chopped celery
1 · 17¼-ounce package puff pastry
1 egg, beaten
2 to 3 tablespoons dry wine or
  half and half
dash of nutmeg

DIRECTIONS:

OVEN TEMPERATURE: 375°

Bechamel sauce: Melt 2 tablespoons of butter in a 2 to 3 quart pan. Stir in the flour and cook 1 minute. Add the chicken broth, half and half, salt and nutmeg. Cook until it thickens and set aside.

In a bowl combine the bechamel sauce, crab, mayonnaise, cheese and salt and pepper to taste. Cover and chill.

In a fry pan melt the 2 teaspoons butter and cook the shallots, mushrooms, carrot and celery until limp. Cool.

To assemble: Roll out the puff pastry and cut each sheet into four 6 inch squares. Spoon an equal portion of the crab mixture into the center of each. Top with a portion of the mushroom mixture. Brush the edges with beaten egg to seal and bring the corners together to close.

Place the crab wellingtons, seam side down, on an ungreased pan and brush with the beaten egg. Bake in a preheated 375 degree oven for 20 to 25 minutes or until golden.

TIP:

How to clean a dungeness crab: Start from the bottom side of the crab and remove the cone shell, scrape out the waste in the center of the body cavity, wash well, crack and serve.

LOBSTER SAUCE

SERVES 3-4

1 · 2 pound lobster, cooked & cooled
3 tablespoons unsalted butter
1 celery stalk, sliced
1 carrot, sliced
½ cup chopped onion
1 tomato, peeled, seeded & chopped
½ teaspoon thyme
1 teaspoon salt

3 tablespoons brandy
1 cup white wine
3 cups chicken stock
1½ cups heavy cream
3 large egg yolks, beaten
⅛ teaspoon cayenne
pinch of nutmeg
1 pound of fettuccine noodles

DIRECTIONS:

Remove the meat from the cooked lobster and set aside. Cut the carcass into pieces.

In a 5 quart saucepan melt the butter. Add the celery, carrot, onion and tomato. Cook over medium heat, stirring until the ingredients are well coated, about 3 to 5 minutes. Add the thyme, salt and lobster carcass. Sauté slowly for 10 minutes.

In a small saucepan heat the brandy. Pour it over the vegetables and ignite. Cook 1 mintue. Add the wine and simmer 15 minutes. Heat the chicken stock and reduce to 2 cups. Add the stock to the vegetable mixture, simmer 30 minutes.

Strain the vegetable-lobster carcass mixture and place in a 2 to 3 quart saucepan. Heat the cream and reduce to ½ cup. Then add the cream to the strained stock. Whisk ¼ of this mixture into the egg yolks and return it all to the sauce. Cook stirring over low heat until thickened 2 to 3 minutes. Do not boil. Stir in the cayenne, nutmeg and lobster meat. Serve over cooked fettuccine.

HINT:

This is a time consuming recipe but worth it. The sauce, up to the final addition of the lobster, can be made ahead of time.

OYSTERS ROCKEFELLER

SERVES 4

12 oysters
1 · 10-ounce package frozen spinach
½ cup chopped scallions
¼ cup chopped celery
¼ cup chopped fresh parsley
1 clove garlic, mashed

4 tablespoons butter
2 teaspoons flour
¼ cup heavy cream
dash Tobasco
1 tablespoon Anisette liqueur
¼ cup grated Parmesan cheese

DIRECTIONS:

OVEN TEMPERATURE: 450°

Open oysters, drain and save liqueur; or place shucked oysters on shells or small heat proof dishes.

Defrost spinach and drain well. Blend with scallions, celery and parsley in blender or processor. Stir in garlic.

Heat butter in a skillet. Blend in flour. Add oyster liqueur and cream. Season with Tobasco. Add spinach mixture and Anisette. Let cool.

Spoon mixture on oysters, top with cheese and bake for 25 minutes at 450 degrees.

SEA SCALLOPS IN WINE SAUCE

SERVES 4-6

1½ to 2 pounds sea scallops
4 tablespoons butter
½ pound mushrooms, sliced
¼ cup onion, finely chopped
2 tablespoons flour
1 cup dry white wine

1 teaspoon salt
2 teaspoons lemon juice
freshly ground pepper to taste
2 tablespoons parsley, finely chopped
½ cup buttered bread crumbs
pinch of paprika

DIRECTIONS:

OVEN TEMPERATURE: 400°

Wash and dry scallops. Set aside.

Melt the butter in a sauté pan. Add the mushrooms and onion and sauté until tender. Stir in the flour and cook several minutes. Stir in the wine, salt, lemon juice, pepper and parsley. Bring to a boil and add the scallops. Remove from the heat.

Spoon the scallop mixture into a shallow casserole or individual baking dishes. Sprinkle the top with buttered bread crumbs and paprika. Bake in a preheated 400 degree oven 25 minutes for a large casserole or 15 minutes for individual ones.

SEAFOOD BROCHETTES

SERVES 4

8 large shrimp, shelled & deveined
8 sea scallops
½ pound halibut steak, cut in
  1 inch chunks
1 green pepper, cut in 1 inch chunks
1 onion, cut in 1 inch chunks

8 large mushrooms
½ teaspoon lemon pepper
1 teaspoon fresh dill
1 lemon
¼ cup clarified butter
8 · 8 inch wooden skewers

DIRECTIONS:

Charcoal Grilled

Steam the onion and pepper chunks for 5 minutes. Remove and drain.

Take eight 8 inch wooden skewers. Thread one mushroom, one piece of halibut, one piece of green pepper, one shrimp, one piece of onion and one scallop on each skewer. Sprinkle with lemon pepper, dill and the juice of 1 lemon. Grill the brochettes over charcoal 3 to 4 minutes per side basting with butter.

The brochettes can be fried if you prefer. Dredge them in seasoned flour and fry them in ½ inch of hot oil for 4 minutes, turning once.

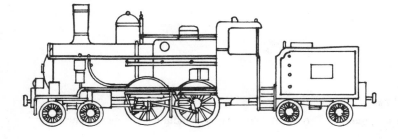

SEAFOOD SUPREME

SERVES 5-6

1 · 12-ounce package frozen scallops, thawed, drained and quartered
1 · 10-ounce package frozen cooked shrimp, thawed and drained
1 · 6-ounce can sliced mushrooms, drained or fresh are excellent
2 · 10¾-ounce cans cream of shrimp soup
1 tablespoon grated fresh lemon peel
1 tablespoon chopped chives
½ cup grated Parmesan cheese

DIRECTIONS:

OVEN TEMPERATURE: 400°

Preheat the oven to 400 degrees.

Mix all the ingredients except the cheese together and place 1 cup of the mixture in each of 5 or 6 baking shells or individual casseroles. Place the shells on a baking sheet and bake 15 minutes.

Remove from the oven, top with the cheese and bake 2 to 3 minutes longer.

VARIATION:

Before baking, make mashed potatoes, place in a pastry tube and pipe around the edge of each filled baking shell. Sprinkle with paprika and Parmesan cheese.

BARBECUED SHRIMP

SERVES 2-4

12 large shrimp
1 clove garlic, minced (optional)
1 inch piece of fresh ginger, minced
¼ cup soy sauce

¼ cup white wine
⅛ cup water
2 tablespoons olive oil
1 hot red pepper, broken

DIRECTIONS:

Charcoal Grilled

Remove the legs from the shrimp but keep the shells on. Slightly butterfly the shrimp to clean them.

Mix all the marinade ingredients together and marinate the shrimp for 1 hour. Barbecue the shrimp over hot coals for 2 minutes on each side. You may thread the shrimp on bamboo skewers if desired to keep them from curling up while cooking.

TIP:

One pound of shrimp should serve two adults as a main course.

HERBED SHRIMP DIABLE

SERVES 8

2 pounds raw shrimp, butterflied
½ cup butter
½ pound mushrooms, sliced
1 cup celery, sliced
1 cup green pepper, sliced
1 teaspoon parsley flakes
½ teaspoon tarragon

1 teaspoon dry mustard
2 teaspoons seasoned salt
2 teaspoons chives, chopped
½ teaspoon ground ginger
3 tablespoons lemon juice
12 cherry tomatoes, halved
¼ cup brandy, heated

DIRECTIONS:

Clean and butterfly the shrimp. Set aside.

Melt the butter in a large skillet or wok. Sauté the mushrooms, celery, and green pepper for 2 to 3 minutes. Push the vegetables to one side and add the shrimp. Sprinkle the shrimp with all the seasonings and sauté, stirring constantly, for 2 mintues. Add the lemon juice and tomatoes. Cover and cook for 3 minutes. Just before serving add the warmed brandy and flame.

Serve with rice.

PAELLA

SERVES 8-10

12 large raw shrimp
2½ pounds chicken breasts
½ cup seasoned flour
¼ cup olive oil
1½ pounds Italian sausage
¼ cup olive oil
½ cup onion, chopped
1 clove garlic, minced
1 green pepper, cut in strips

2 tomatoes, chopped
2 cups long grain rice, uncooked
1 teaspoon salt
¼ teaspoon pepper
¼ teaspoon saffron
4½ cups boiling chicken broth
1 · 10-ounce package frozen peas
2 to 3 lemons

DIRECTIONS:

OVEN TEMPERATURE: 375°

Clean the shrimp and set them aside

Skin, bone and cut the chicken breasts into bite sized pieces. Dredge in seasoned flour and fry in 2 cup olive oil until golden brown. Set aside.

Place sausage in a skillet, prick skins and add enough water to cover. Bring to a boil, reduce heat and simmer 5 minutes. Drain, peel and slice into 1 inch rounds.

In a very large skillet heat ¼ cup olive oil and cook the onion and garlic a few minutes. Add the green pepper and tomatoes and cook, stirring constantly, until barely tender. Stir in the rice, salt, pepper, saffron and boiling broth. Bring to a boil, stirring constantly. Immediately remove from the heat and place the mixture in a large casserole. Arrange the chicken, shrimp, sausage and peas on top. Set the casserole in the bottom of a 375 degree oven for 25 to 30 minutes or unti all the liquid is absorbed. Do not stir. Remove from the oven when done and cover with a towel. Let the mixture rest 5 to 10 minutes and serve garnished with lemons.

HINT:

Substitute any ingredients you like. Marinated artichoke hearts are a nice addition, as are lobster meat or squid.

SHUN LEE'S SZECHUAN SHRIMP

SERVES 4

1 pound deveined raw shrimp
½ cup minced scallions
¼ teaspoon minced fresh ginger
3 large cloves garlic, minced
¼ teaspoon hot pepper sauce
2 tablespoons sugar
½ cup catsup

3 tablespoons dry Sherry
1 tablespoon soy sauce
1½ teaspoons sesame oil, or 1
tablespoon toasted sesame seeds
1 tablespoon cornstarch
3 tablespoons water
1½ cups oil

DIRECTIONS:

Combine scallions ginger, garlic and pepper sauce in a small bowl.

Combine sugar, catsup, Sherry, soy sauce and sesame oil or seeds in another bowl. Set aside.

Combine cornstarch with 3 tablespoons water and mix thoroughly. Set aside.

Heat oil to 400 degrees. Have ready a strainer with a bowl for draining. Add shrimp to hot oil, stirring until done, about 2 minutes. Pour oil and shrimp into strainer to drain.

Heat 2 tablespoons of the strained oil in the same wok over high heat. Add scallion mixture and stir fry for 1 minute. Add drained shrimp and stir fry for 30 seconds more. Pour in catsup mixture. Stir until it comes to a boil. Add cornstarch mixture and cook until slightly thickened. Serve hot.

HINT:

You may add slivered almonds if desired. Cubed fish fillets or scallops may be used in place of shrimp.

TIP:

To remove the vein from raw or cooked shrimp, cut along the back of the shrimp with a sharp knife and remove the black vein.

BAKED LIMA BEANS

SERVES 12

4 cups dried lima beans	1 teaspoon freshly ground black pepper
1 pound thickly sliced bacon, diced	1 teaspoon ground ginger
6 tablespoons brown sugar	1¼ cups boiling water
1 tablespoon dry mustard	½ cup molasses
1 tablespoon salt	1 large onion, chopped

DIRECTIONS: OVEN TEMPERATURE: 250°

Cover beans with cold water and soak overnight. Drain well. Cover again with cold water, bring to a boil, reduce heat, and simmer until tender, about 40 to 45 minutes. Drain well.

Place beans in three quart bean pot or casserole. Add bacon. In a small bowl, combine sugar, mustard, salt, pepper and ginger with ¼ cup boiling water and blend well. Pour over beans, add onion, molasses, and remaining 1 cup boiling water. Mix well, cover, and bake 3 to 4 hours, adding more water if beans seem dry.

Stir through several times. Increase oven temperature to 300 degrees and bake uncovered until brown on top, about 45 minutes.

HINT:

Can be made up to two days ahead and reheated.

GREEN BEANS SUPREME

SERVES 6

"Excellent dish for Sunday dinner or with cold turkey!"

½ cup sliced onion	½ teaspoon grated lemon peel
1 tablespoon minced parsley	1 cup sour cream
2 tablespoons butter	5 cups canned green beans
2 tablespoons flour	1 cup grated Cheddar cheese
1 teaspoon salt	½ cup dry bread crumbs mixed with
¼ teaspoon pepper	2 tablespoons melted butter

DIRECTIONS: OVEN TEMPERATURE: 400°

Cook the onion and parsley in butter until tender but not brown. Add the flour, pepper, salt and lemon peel. Add the sour cream and mix well. Stir in the beans and pour into a buttered 2 quart casserole. Top with grated cheese and buttered bread crumbs. Bake in a preheated 400 degree oven for 20 minutes.

HINT:

You may substitute Swiss cheese for Cheddar cheese if you prefer.

MARINATED GREEN BEANS

SERVES 4

1 pound green beans
2 tablespoons olive oil
2 tablespoons salad oil
2 tablespoons cider vinegar

1 clove garlic, minced
½ teaspoon salt
½ teaspoon Dijon mustard

DIRECTIONS:

Trim the green beans and blanch in boiling water for 3 minutes.

Combine the other ingredients in a bowl, stir well, add the beans and refrigerate covered for 12 hours. Toss occasionally and serve at room temperature.

TERIYAKI GREEN BEANS

SERVES 4-6

"An unusual way to serve green beans!"

1 small onion, chopped
2 tablespoons butter
4 cups green beans

1 · 1-pound can bean sprouts, drained
1 · 3-ounce can mushrooms, chopped
3 tablespoons soy sauce

DIRECTIONS:

Sauté onion in butter until soft. In saucepan combine all ingredients. Simmer 15 minutes uncovered.

TIP:

After steaming, boiling, microwaving or otherwise cooking fresh vegetables, plunge them into ice water to preserve their color.

BROCCOLI AND BACON SOUFFLÉ FOR TWO

SERVES 2

1 tablespoon butter
1 tablespoon flour
½ cup milk
1 tablespoon lemon juice
2 egg yolks
4 slices bacon, diced and cooked

1 small onion, finely chopped
1¼ cup cooked and chopped broccoli
¼ teaspoon pepper
3 egg whites
⅛ teaspoon cream of tartar
½ teaspoon salt

DIRECTIONS:

OVEN TEMPERATURE: 375°

In a small heavy saucepan, melt the butter. Stir in the flour and gradually add the milk. Stir with a wire whisk until smooth and thick. Add the lemon juice. Remove from the heat and stir in the egg yolks. Set aside.

Fry the bacon and drain. Cook the onion in the bacon grease until limp. Drain and add the onion to the bacon.

Place the cooked broccoli in a blender and puree. Add the egg yolk mixture and process until smooth. Season with salt and pepper. Fold in the onions and bacon. (Make ahead to this point.)

Beat the egg whites, cream of tartar and salt, until stiff. Fold in the broccoli mixture and pour into two 2-cup prepared soufflé dishes. Place the soufflé dishes in a bain marie* and bake in a preheated 375 degree oven for 20 minutes.

HINT:

*A bain marie is a pan of hot water in which you cook soufflés in the oven. The water should come ¾ of the way up the side of the dishes.

BROCCOLI AND STUFFING

SERVES 8-10

3 · 10-ounce packages frozen chopped
   broccoli
¼ cup butter
¼ cup flour
2 cups milk
1 package Stove Top stuffing,
   poultry flavor

Topping:
6 tablespoons butter
1½ cups stuffing
⅔ cup water
⅔ cup slivered almonds or
   pinenuts

DIRECTIONS:

OVEN TEMPERATURE: 400°

Cook broccoli according to package directions, drain and set aside.

Combine the butter and flour in a saucepan and cook over medium heat until a roux is formed. Add milk and whisk until a smooth white sauce is formed. Add the stuffing seasonings to the white sauce and cook 1 minute, stirring constantly. Remove from the heat and set aside.

Topping: Melt the butter and add to the stuffing mix bread crumbs. Add water and nuts and set aside.

Place the broccoli in a 2 quart casserole. Pour the white sauce over the broccoli and then gently pat the stuffing mixture over the top. Bake 25 to 30 minutes in a preheated 400 degree oven or until bubbly.

HINT:

Two cups of cooked turkey can be substituted for one package of broccoli.

BROCCOLI WITH PINE NUTS AND GARLIC

SERVES 4-6

"Very fast and easy in the microwave!"

1 large bunch broccoli, cleaned and
  cut into spears
1 tablespoon olive oil
1 tablespoon butter
1 tablespoon thinly sliced fresh garlic

1 tablespoon pine nuts (others may
  be substituted)
¼ teaspoon pepper
salt (optional)

DIRECTIONS:

Place broccoli spears in large saucepan, add enough water to cover, and boil until just tender. (Broccoli may be cooked in a microwave oven.) Drain and arrange spears on serving platter.

In small saucepan, melt the oil and butter. Stir in the garlic and pine nuts. Pour over the hot broccoli. Add salt and pepper to taste.

MARINATED BRUSSEL SPROUTS

SERVES 6-8

"Nice substitute for salads!"

1½ pounds brussel sprouts
¼ cup olive or salad oil
2 teaspoons fresh parsley
¼ teaspoon minced garlic
½ teaspoon sugar
¼ teaspoon salt

¼ teaspoon tarragon
pepper
1 teaspoon lemon peel
3 tablespoons lemon juice
2 tablespoons white wine vinegar

DIRECTIONS:

Cut off the stems of the brussel sprouts and trim the outer leaves if necessary. Soak them in salted ice water for 30 minutes. Drain. Boil the brussel sprouts until tender, drain and place in a deep bowl.

Combine the oil, parsley, garlic, sugar, salt, tarragon, pepper and lemon peel and pour over the sprouts. Refrigerate overnight, stirring occasionally.

Before serving, sprinkle with lemon juice and wine vinegar.

HINT:

You might prefer these served at room temperature rather than cold.

BRUSSEL SPROUTS AND CHESTNUTS

SERVES 10

3 · 10-ounce packages frozen brussel
  sprouts
¼ cup butter
3 tablespoons flour
1 cup chicken broth
1 cup half & half

1 cup grated Swiss cheese
1 · 11-ounce can sliced water
  chestnuts, drained
salt and pepper to taste
4 slices cooked bacon, crumbled

DIRECTIONS:

OVEN TEMPERATURE: 325°

Cook the brussel sprouts in boiling salted water until they are barely tender and drain.

In a deep saucepan melt the butter, stir in the flour and cook 1 minute. Gradually add the broth and half & half. Cook, stirring constantly until thickened. Add the cheese and stir until the cheese is melted. Remove the sauce from the heat, fold in the brussel sprouts and water chestnuts. Season to taste and pour into a serving dish. Top with crumbled bacon.

HINT:

This can be prepared ahead of time, turned into a 2½ to 3 quart casserole and reheated in a 325 degree oven.

GERMAN RED CABBAGE

SERVES 6-8

1 medium red cabbage, chopped
2 large apples, pared and chopped
1 medium onion, chopped
1 teaspoon salt
1 cup vinegar
1 bay leaf
2 whole cloves

1 cup sugar
1½ cups water
2 whole allspice
6 peppercorns
2 tablespoons cornstarch (optional)
½ cup water (optional)

DIRECTIONS:

Combine all ingredients in a large pot and simmer 1½ hours. Remove the spices.

If you prefer a thicker sauce, mix 2 tablespoons cornstarch with ½ cup water, add to cabbage and cook several minutes before serving.

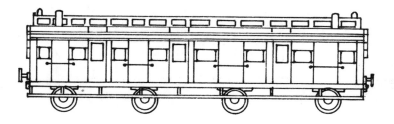

CARROT RING

SERVES 4-6

"An easy way to get children to eat carrots!"

½ cup oil
1 cup brown sugar
1 cup flour
1 teaspoon baking soda
½ teaspoon baking powder
pinch salt

2 cups grated carrots
grated rind of 1 lemon
3 tablespoons lemon juice
3 eggs
cinnamon (optional)
sugar (optional)

DIRECTIONS:

OVEN TEMPERATURE: 350°

In a mixing bowl, beat together the oil and sugar. Add the flour, baking soda and baking powder, salt, carrots, lemon rind, lemon juice and the eggs. Pour into a buttered 1 quart ring mold. Sprinkle with cinnamon and sugar, if desired.

Bake in a preheated 350 degree oven for 45 minutes or until set. When cool enough to handle, turn out onto a serving dish.

HINT:

This can be made in advance and reheated in the oven or microwave. It goes very well with any roasted, barbequed or broiled beef or chicken.

CARROT AND SPINACH CASSEROLE

SERVES 6

1 · 17-ounce can small whole carrots
   or 5 fresh carrots
1 package frozen spinach, cooked and
   drained
1 medium onion, chopped

3 tablespoons butter
3 tablespoons flour
1½ cup milk
1 cup grated Cheddar cheese
buttered bread crumbs

DIRECTIONS:

OVEN TEMPERATURE: 350°

Cut the carrots into thin slices or julienne strips. Cook and drain them. Sauté the onion in butter until limp. Add the flour and cook 1 minute. Add the milk and cook until thickened. Stir in the cheese.

Combine all the ingredients and place in a 1½ quart casserole. Top with buttered bread crumbs and bake in a preheated 350 degree oven for 20 to 30 minutes.

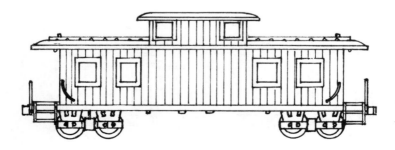

GLAZED CARROTS

SERVES 8

2 pounds carrots, peeled and sliced ⅛ thick
4 tablespoons butter
⅓ cup water

1 teaspoon salt
2 tablespoons chopped fresh parsley
1 teaspoon fresh dill or chervil

DIRECTIONS:

In a medium sized heavy saucepan bring the carrots, butter, water and salt to a boil over high heat. Cover, reduce the heat and simmer 10 minutes, or until the carrots are tender. Shake the pan 2 to 3 times during cooking. Uncover the pan, increase the heat and boil rapidly 2 to 3 minutes more, or until almost all the liquid has boiled away. Gently stir in the parsley and dill.

HINT:

If you are using dried herbs instead of fresh, add them to the pan when the water comes to a boil.

CELERY ROOT IN MUSTARD SAUCE

SERVES 6

"For a change of pace!"

3 cups celery root, cut in julienne slices
1½ teaspoons salt
1½ teaspoons lemon juice
3 tablespoons Dijon mustard

3 tablespoons boiling water
¼ - ⅓ cup oil
2 tablespoons wine vinegar
fresh parsley

DIRECTIONS:

In a bowl, toss the celery root with salt and lemon juice. Soak 30 minutes. Rinse with cold water and dry with paper towels.

Warm a mixing bowl in hot water. Dry the bowl. Add mustard and with a wire whisk, beat in the oil very slowly to make a thick creamy sauce. Slowly add the vinegar. Season with salt and pepper, if desired. Fold in the celery root. Let it marinate at least 2 hours.

Serve on lettuce leaves. Decorate it with parsley, cherry tomatoes or any colorful fresh vegetable.

HINT:

This can be made the day before. The dressing can be made quite easily in a food processor.

CORN CASSEROLE

SERVES 8

1 · 1-pound can cream style corn
1 · 3½-ounce can diced green chilies
½ cup yellow corn meal
¾ cup grated Longhorn cheese
1 egg, beaten

¾ cup milk
2 tablespoons sugar
2 tablespoons oil
salt and pepper to taste

DIRECTIONS: OVEN TEMPERATURE: 350°

Combine all of the ingredients. Place in a 1½ quart casserole dish and bake in a preheated 350 degree oven for 1 hour.

HINT:

This is very fast and easy. It can be made ahead and reheated.

EMILY MASSIE'S CORN PUDDING

SERVES 6

½ cup butter
4 tablespoons flour
2 cups cream style corn
1½ cups milk
½ cup grated sharp Cheddar cheese

4 tablespoons chopped green pepper
6 eggs
1 teaspoon salt
½ teaspoon pepper

DIRECTIONS: OVEN TEMPERATURE: 375°

In a saucepan melt the butter. Remove from the heat and mix in the flour. Set it aside. Mix all the other ingredients together and add the flour-butter mixture. Pour the corn pudding into a shallow casserole and bake in a preheated 375 degree oven for 1½ hours.

SAUTÉED CUCUMBERS

SERVES 4

1 cucumber   1 tablespoon butter

DIRECTIONS:

Peel the cucumber and cut it crosswise in 2-inch segments. Cut each segment in either matchstick or shoestring slices.

Sauté the slices quickly in hot butter. Do not overcook. They should remain crisp.

Serve immediately.

CAPANATA

YIELD: 3 quarts

"An excellent garden fresh hor d'oeuvre, meant to be eaten in the summertime with a red picnic wine and crusty french bread.""

½ cup olive oil
3 green peppers
1 medium eggplant
1 large onion
4 stalks celery
1 medium zucchini
1 · 6-ounce can pitted ripe olives
1 cup pimento stuffed green olives

½ cup finely chopped parsley
4 tablespoons oregano
5 cloves garlic
¼ cup capers
2 cups dry red wine
1 · 6-ounce can tomato paste
salt and pepper

DIRECTIONS:

Core the vegetables, but do not peel them. Cut them into reasonably uniform bite sized chunks. In a large skillet sauté each, one at a time, until cooked but still crisp. The eggplant cooks best if browned, and then covered for five minutes.

As each vegetable is cooked, remove with a slotted spoon to the bowl. Do not use an aluminum bowl for this.

Peel the garlic, chop it, and sprinkle it with salt. Let it stand for five minutes, then mash the garlic with the oregano into a paste. Sprinkle the layers of vegetables with garlic and oregano as they are put into the bowl. Grate fresh pepper over each layer.

When all vegetables are cooked, add the olives, parsley, and capers to the bowl. Pour the wine into the skillet, and mix well with the tomato paste. Pour this over the vegetables, and mix gently.

Allow to stand at room temperature for a few hours before serving. Can be refrigerated for at least a week.

FANCY FRIED EGGPLANT

SERVES 6

1 medium eggplant
½ cup flour
2 eggs, well beaten
¼ cup milk

1 cup saltine cracker crumbs
¼ - ½ cup oil
2 tomatoes, sliced ¼" thick
8 ounces Monterey Jack cheese, sliced

DIRECTIONS:

Clean and cut the unpeeled eggplant into ¼ inch slices. Coat the slices with flour. Dip them into the eggs beaten with milk and coat them with cracker crumbs. Fry the eggplant in oil until it is lightly browned and tender.

Leave the eggplant in the pan. Add a slice of tomato and a slice of cheese to each piece. Cover the pan and place on low heat until the cheese melts. Amounts may vary depending on the size of the eggplant or tomatoes.

CREAMED MUSHROOMS AND SPINACH

SERVES 4

2 tablespoons butter
⅓ cup chopped green onions
¼ cup flour
salt and pepper

1½ cups half & half
½ cup sauterne or white wine
2 cups cooked and chopped spinach
½ cup cooked mushrooms

DIRECTIONS:

Sauté onions in butter till tender. Stir in flour, salt and pepper. Slowly add the half & half. Cook and stir until thick. Add the wine and cook one minute more.

Drain the spinach well. Add the cooked mushrooms and spinach to the sauce and serve.

MUSHROOMS A LA GRECQUE

SERVES 4

2 pounds fresh whole mushrooms
2 cups water
1½ cups dry white wine
½ cup olive oil
juice of 2 lemons
2 large onions, sliced
2 bay leaves
1 teaspoon peppercorns

2 cloves garlic, crushed
4 sprigs Italian parsley
1 stalk celery, chopped
2 teaspoons salt
1 teaspoon oregano
1½ tablespoons chopped fresh parsley
1 tablespoon chopped fresh dill weed
1 teaspoon crushed black pepper

DIRECTIONS:

Wash and dry mushrooms and set aside.

Combine water, wine, olive oil, lemon juice, onions, bay leaves, peppercorns, garlic, parsley sprigs, celery, salt and oregano. Bring the mixture to a boil. Add the mushrooms, cover and simmer 8 to 10 minutes. Remove the mushrooms from the broth and put them in a deep bowl.

Boil the broth uncovered for 15 minutes. Strain it and discard the vegetables. Cool the broth and pour it over the mushrooms. Sprinkle them with chopped parsley, dill and pepper. Marinate the mushrooms in the refrigerator for several hours before serving.

HINT:

Cut the stems close to the mushroom caps, but do not remove the stem. This will ensure that the mushrooms will keep their shape.

MUSHROOMS MORNAY

SERVES 4-6

2 pounds fresh mushrooms, sliced
1 · 6-ounce can crabmeat or 1 pound
   fresh crab
2 teaspoons lemon juice
3 tablespoons flour

3 tablespoons butter
1½ cups milk
2 eggs, slightly beaten
1½ cups grated sharp American cheese
2 teaspoons Sherry

DIRECTIONS:

OVEN TEMPERATURE: 350°

Place the mushrooms in a shallow baking dish. Cover them with the crabmeat and sprinkle with lemon juice.

Mornay sauce: Brown the butter. Add the flour and cook 1 minute. Add the milk and cook until thick. Add the eggs and cook 1 more minute. Stir in 1¼ cups of the cheese and the Sherry.

Pour the sauce over the crab. Sprinkle the remaining cheese on top. Bake in a preheated 350 degree oven for 20 minutes or until bubbly. Serve over rice.

MUSHROOM SAUTÉ

SERVES 4-6

¼ cup butter
2-3 cloves garlic, minced
½ pound mushrooms, sliced

juice of ½ lemon
1 tablespoon Worcestershire sauce
salt and pepper to taste

DIRECTIONS:

Heat the butter in a large fry pan. Add the garlic and sauté a few minutes. Add the mushrooms, lemon juice, Worcestershire sauce and seasonings. Sauté until the mushrooms are brown and tender.

CRUMB BAKED ONIONS

SERVES 4-6

20 small white boiling onions, peeled
1 chicken boullion cube
¾ cup dry white wine or water
2 tablespoons melted butter
½ teaspoon sage
¼ teaspoon pepper

1½ teaspoons cornstarch mixed with 1
   tablespoon water
¼ cup crushed croutons
2 tablespoons grated Parmesan cheese
1 tablespoon chopped parsley

DIRECTIONS:

OVEN TEMPERATURE: 350°

Arrange the peeled onions in a single layer in an 8 or 9 inch baking dish.

In a small pan, crush the boullion cube, stir in the wine and heat until it dissolves. Stir in the melted butter, sage and pepper. Pour over the onions, cover and bake in a preheated 350 degree oven for 1 hour or until tender. Transfer the onions to a serving dish to keep warm and set aside.

Pour the cooking juices into a small saucepan. Stir in the cornstarch mixture and cook until it boils and thickens. Pour over the onions. Combine the croutons, Parmesan cheese and parsley. Sprinkle the mixture over the onions and serve.

FABULOUS FRIED ONION RINGS

SERVES 6

"They stay crispy."

1 cup all-purpose flour
1 cup beer
1 teaspoon salt

2 large onions, cut in rings
oil for frying

DIRECTIONS:

Mix together the flour, beer and salt. Let set, covered, at room temperature for 3 hours.

Place the onion rings in a large bowl of ice water in the refrigerator for 2 hours.

When ready to cook, drain and dry the onion rings. Dip them in batter and fry them in hot oil until golden brown.

HINT:

This beer batter is great for tempura vegetables.

DELUXE POTATO BALLS

SERVES 16-20

2 pounds potatoes (3-4 large)
3 ounces cream cheese
¼ cup milk
1½ tablespoons butter
1 tablespoon chopped green onion
¼ cup Parmesan cheese
2½ teaspoons instant onion soup mix

½ teaspoon pepper
½ teaspoon salt
½ teaspoon seasoned salt
dash Tabasco
1 egg, beaten
1½ cups corn flakes, crushed

DIRECTIONS:

OVEN TEMPERATURE: 400°

Peel the potatoes and cook in boiling water until tender. Drain and mash. Add the cream cheese, milk, butter, green onion, Parmesan cheese, onion soup mix, salt, pepper, seasoned salt and Tabasco to the potatoes and mix well.

Using an ice cream scoup dipped in water, form the potato mixture into balls. Dip each ball in beaten egg, roll in corn flakes and place on a greased baking sheet.

Bake in a preheated 400 degree oven 10 to 15 minutes or until the potato balls are hot and crisp.

HINT:

You can prepare potato balls in advance and keep in refrigerator. Bake them just before serving. If cold they will require longer baking time.

POTATO LATKE

SERVES 6

1 egg
1 small onion
2 tablespoons flour
½ teaspoon salt

3 medium potatoes, peeled and dried
oil for frying
sour cream, optional
apple sauce, optional

DIRECTIONS:

Place the egg, onion, flour, salt and potatoes in a food processor and process until blended together. Heat the oil and fry ⅓ cup of the potato mixture at a time over medium heat. Drain on paper towels and serve.

HINT:

Serve with sour cream or apple sauce.

MILLION DOLLAR POTATOES

SERVES 8

8 medium sized potatoes, peeled and
   sliced
2 pints of cream

2 teaspoons salt, or to taste
pepper to taste

DIRECTIONS: OVEN TEMPERATURE: 325°

Grease a 3-quart casserole. Layer some of the potatoes on the bottom and pour some of the cream over the top. Repeat until all the potatoes and cream are gone. Season each layer with salt and pepper. Be sure the potatoes are submerged in the cream and that no potatoes protrude through the top layer of cream. Bake uncovered 2½ to 3 hours in a 325 degree oven. If the potatoes begin to brown too quickly, cover.

HINT:

These potatoes are very good with pork, ham, or beef roast. They are also great reheated.

TIP:

Add 1 teaspoon lemon juice to the cooking water for potatoes, artichokes, mushrooms or cauliflower to preserve the vegetable's color.

HEAVENLY POTATO SOUFFLÉ

SERVES 8-10

6 medium (about 2 pounds) potatoes
¼ cup butter
2 egg yolks
1 cup hot milk or cream
3 drops Tabasco sauce
1 teaspoon salt

½ teaspoon dry mustard
¼ teaspoon MSG
⅛ teaspoon white pepper
½ cup (2 ounces) grated Cheddar
   cheese
2 egg whites

DIRECTIONS:

OVEN TEMPERATURE: 325°

Lightly grease a 1½-quart casserole. Wash, pare and cook potatoes until tender; drain. Whip or rice potatoes thoroughly. Whipping after each addition, add butter and egg yolks. Gradually stir in hot milk. Add Tabasco sauce and whip until potatoes are fluffy.

Mix together the salt, dry mustard, MSG and white pepper. Add this mixture to the potatoes and whip until light and fluffy. Add the grated cheese, all at one time, and beat until cheese is melted. Set aside.

Beat the egg whites until rounded peaks are formed. Spread egg whites over potato mixture and gently fold together. Turn mixture into casserole. Bake at 325 degrees about 50 minutes or until knife comes out clean when inserted halfway between center and edge of casserole. Serve immediately.

POTATOES MANHATTAN

SERVES 8

8 cups diced, peeled potatoes
2 small onions, finely diced
½ cup finely diced green pepper
1 · 3-ounce jar pimentos, finely
   chopped
4 tablespoons butter

1 · 10¾-ounce can cream of celery soup
½ cup milk
salt and pepper to taste
1 cup grated sharp Cheddar cheese
¼ cup fine bread crumbs

DIRECTIONS:

OVEN TEMPERATURE: 350°

Cook the potatoes in boiling salted water. Drain, place in a casserole and dot with butter. Add the onions, green pepper, pimentos and cheese. Mix thoroughly.

Dilute the cream of celery soup with milk, add salt and pepper and mix with the potatoes. Sprinkle with bread crumbs and bake in a preheated 350 degree oven for 30 minutes.

STUFFED POTATOES

SERVES 6-8

6-8 large baking potatoes
8 tablespoons butter
2 tablespoons chopped chives
1 teaspoon salt

½ teaspoon pepper
½ cup grated Parmesan cheese
½ cup heavy cream
½ teaspoon paprika

DIRECTIONS: OVEN TEMPERATURE: 375°

Wash the potatoes, prick the skins and bake for 1 hour at 375 degrees. When the potatoes are done, remove from the oven and cool 5 to 10 minutes. Cut the top off each potato, gently scoop the insides out and place in a large bowl. Be careful not to cut through the potato skin.

Mash the potatoes, adding butter, chives, salt, pepper, Parmesan cheese and cream. Stuff the mixture back into the potato skins, sprinkle with paprika and refrigerate until ready to serve.

When you are ready to serve the potatoes, place them in a shallow roasting pan and bake in a preheated 350 degree oven for 30 minutes or until heated.

HINT:

You may substitute any ingredients you might prefer, such as cooked bacon and Cheddar cheese for the chives and Parmesan cheese.

TABASCO CHEESE POTATOES

SERVES 4

5 medium potatoes, cut as for
   French fries
⅔ cup milk
1½ teaspoons salt

½ teaspoon Tabasco sauce
1 tablespoon melted butter
¼ cup grated American cheese
1 teaspoon paprika

DIRECTIONS: OVEN TEMPERATURE: 425°

Place the sliced potatoes in a greased, shallow casserole dish.

Combine the milk, salt, Tabasco, and butter and pour over the potatoes. Bake covered in a preheated 425 degree oven for 40 minutes. Uncover the potatoes and sprinkle with the cheese and paprika. Bake 5 minutes more or until the cheese melts.

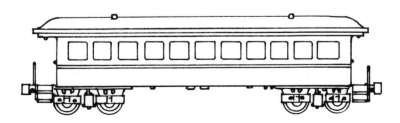

HARVEST SPINACH RING

SERVES 12

4 · 10-ounce packages frozen,
   chopped spinach
4 eggs, separated
2 cups grated sharp Cheddar cheese
3 tablespoons flour

3 tablespoons melted butter
2 tablespoons grated onion
1 tablespoon lemon juice
½ teaspoon salt
¼ teaspoon pepper

DIRECTIONS:

OVEN TEMPERATURE: 350°

Cook the spinach as directed on the package. Drain thoroughly and set aside.

Beat the egg yolks. Add the cheese, flour, butter, onion, lemon juice, salt and pepper. Add the spinach to this mixture.

In another bowl, beat the egg whites until stiff. Fold into the spinach mixture. Pour into a greased ring mold and bake in a preheated 350 degree oven for 30 minutes.

SPINACH SQUARES

SERVES 16-20

"A wonderful way to serve spinach to people who do not usually like it!"

3 packages frozen chopped spinach,
   thawed
2 cups plain bread crumbs
1½ cups Parmesan cheese
1 cup olive oil
1 cup chopped parsley
2 onions, finely chopped

2 cloves garlic, minced
1½ teaspoons Italian herbs (use any
   combination of oregano or basil)
2 teaspoons salt
½ teaspoon pepper
10 eggs

DIRECTIONS:

OVEN TEMPERATURE: 325°

Mix all the ingredients together by hand. Spread in a greased 9 x13 inch pan and bake in a preheated 325 degree oven for 40 minutes.

HINT:

This can be baked in small casseroles and frozen.

TIP:

When buying fresh spinach, look for crisp, undamaged leaves. Wash the spinach well to remove the sand and pull off the heavy stems.

CHEDDAR SQUASH BAKE

SERVES 8-10

2 pounds yellow crookneck squash
2 egg yolks, slightly beaten
1 cup sour cream
2 tablespoons flour
2 egg whites, stiffly beaten

1½ cups grated Cheddar cheese
4 slices bacon, cooked and crumbled
⅓ cup fine, dry bread crumbs
1 tablespoon melted butter
1 teaspoon salt

DIRECTIONS: OVEN TEMPERATURE: 350°

Scrub the squash, trim off the ends and cook in boiling salted water for 15 minutes or until tender. Drain, cut into thin slices and sprinkle with salt. Reserve a few slices for garnish.

Mix together the egg yolks, sour cream and flour. Fold in the egg whites. Layer half of the squash, half the egg mixture and half the cheese in a 12 x 7 x 2 inch baking dish. Sprinkle with bacon. Repeat the layers. Combine the bread crumbs and butter and sprinkle mixture around the edges. Arranged the reserved squash in the middle.

Bake in a preheated 350 degree oven 20 to 25 minutes.

HINT:

You may substitute zucchini for crookneck squash.

SPAGHETTI SQUASH PRIMAVERA

SERVES 8-10

1 · 3½-pound spaghetti squash
2 cups broccoli flowers
½ pound carrots, cut in 1" pieces
1 zucchini, cut into ¼" slices
½ cup chopped green onions
3 tablespoons olive oil
3 cups uncooked tomato sauce

Uncooked Tomato Sauce:
2 cups tomatoes, peeled, seeded, and chopped
½ cup olive oil
½ cup fresh basil
½ cup minced parsley
3 tablespoons grated Parmesan cheese
3 cloves garlic, minced
2 teaspoons salt

DIRECTIONS: OVEN TEMPERATURE: 350°

Bake the spaghetti squash in a preheated 350 degree oven for 1 hour. Let it stand for 15 minutes. Halve it lengthwise, remove the seeds and scrape the flesh into a bowl.

Heat the water to boiling in a sauce pan. Boil the broccoli for 1 minute and cool in ice water. Boil the carrots for 5 minutes and cool in ice water. Boil the zucchini for 1 minute and drain.

In a large skillet heat the oil and fry the green onions until soft. Add the rest of the vegetables and fry until just heated through. Mix in the tomato sauce and serve.

Tomato sauce: mix all the ingredients together and let stand, covered, for at least 1 hour.

THANKSGIVING SWEET POTATOES

SERVES 10

1 · 2½-pound can sweet potatoes, drained
⅓ cup sugar
1 egg
½ teaspoon cinnamon
¼ teaspoon nutmeg
4 tablespoons butter
1½ cups milk

¾ cup pecans

Topping:
¾ cup sugar
½ teaspoon cinnamon
½ cup flour
¾ cup pecans
4 tablespoons butter

DIRECTIONS:

OVEN TEMPERATURE: 350°

Combine the sweet potatoes, sugar, egg, cinnamon, nutmeg, butter, milk and pecans. Pour into a buttered casserole dish.

Combine the topping ingredients and spread over the top of the casserole. Dot with 4 tablespoons of butter and bake in a 350 degree oven for 40 minutes.

BROILED TOMATOES

SERVES 6

3 large beefsteak tomatoes
6 teaspoons creamy Italian salad dressing

2 teaspoons basil
2 teaspoons lemon pepper
½ cup grated Parmesan cheese

DIRECTIONS:

OVEN TEMPERATURE: Broil

Cut the tomatoes in half and place cut side up in a shallow pan. Put 1 teaspoon of salad dressing on the top of each half. Sprinkle each with basil, lemon pepper and Parmesan cheese. Broil tomatoes for 3 to 5 minutes.

TOMATOES STUFFED WITH MINCED MEAT

SERVES 5-10

10 large firm tomatoes
4 tablespoons butter
2 medium onions, chopped
1 pound lean hamburger
4 tablespoons wine
2 tablespoons chopped parsley

1 teaspoon chopped dill
salt and pepper to taste
¼ cup water
5 tablespoons grated cheese
5 tablespoons toasted bread crumbs

DIRECTIONS:

OVEN TEMPERATURE: 350°

Slice off the tops of the tomatoes and set aside. Scoop out the pulp and force through a sieve. Sprinkle the tomatoes with salt and turn upside down on paper towels to drain.

Heat 2 tablespoons of butter in a pan and fry the onions and meat until brown. Add the wine, tomato pulp, parsley, dill, and salt and pepper to taste. Pour in the water and simmer uncovered 30 to 40 minutes, or until the meat has absorbed all the liquid.

Remove the pan from the heat and mix in the cheese and bread crumbs. Fill each tomato with the mixture and cover with the cut-off slice. Arrange the tomatoes close together in a shallow baking dish. Melt the rest of the butter, pour over the tomatoes and bake in a 350 degree oven for 30 to 35 minutes.

LAYERED VEGETABLE PATÉ

SERVES 8-10

30 ounces frozen spinach, thawed
12 eggs
3 teaspoons salt
½ teaspoon pepper
½ teaspoon nutmeg

1 cup sour cream
1 small onion, chopped

¼ teaspoon basil
1 pound onions, chopped (about 2 large onions)
1 tablespoon butter
1 cup whipping cream
2 · 1-pound 12-ounce cans tomatoes, drained and chopped
2 teaspoons prepared horseradish

DIRECTIONS:

OVEN TEMPERATURE: 425°

Spinach layer: Squeeze the spinach to remove any moisture. Beat 4 of the eggs, 1 teaspoon salt, ½ teaspoon nutmeg, ¼ teaspoon pepper and mix with the spinach. Set aside.

Tomato layer: Cook the tomatoes and 1 small chopped onion over medium heat, stirring often, until the liquid evaporates. This will take about 30 minutes. Cool. When cool, beat the tomatoes in a bowl with 4 eggs, 1 teaspoon salt and the basil. Set aside.

Onion layer: Sauté 2 large onions in butter over medium heat until limp. Add the cream and cook, stirring often, over medium low heat until the cream evaporates and the mixture is thick. This will take about 20 minutes. Cool. In a bowl, beat together the remaining 4 eggs, 1 teaspoon salt, and ¼ teaspoon pepper. Add the onion mixture and set aside.

Line the bottom of a 5 x 9 inch loaf pan with tin foil and grease the foil. Layer half the spinach mixture, all the tomato, all the onion and the remaining spinach. Cover with greased foil, set in a 9 x 13 inch baking pan filled with 1½ inches of boiling water.

Bake in a preheated 425 degree oven for 1 hour 20 minutes or until a knife inserted comes out clean. Remove the foil and cool 10 minutes. Unmold on a platter and refrigerate until ready to serve. Let the paté come to room temperature for serving. Mix together the sour cream and horseradish for a sauce.

HINT:

This is so beautiful, it makes a lovely first course for an elegant dinner.

MIXED VEGETABLE CASSEROLE

SERVES 8-10

2 · 10-ounce packages of frozen mixed vegetables
1 · 10-ounce package frozen cauliflower

1 · 10¾-ounce can cream of mushroom soup
1 cup grated Cheddar cheese

DIRECTIONS:

OVEN TEMPERATURE: 350°

Cook the vegetables until barely tender. Mix in the cream of mushroom soup. Place in a 2-quart casserole, sprinkle with Cheddar cheese and bake in a preheated 350 degree oven for 45 minutes.

MARINATED VEGETABLES

SERVES 12

"Great for a picnic!"

1 pound mushrooms, sliced
⅓ cup lemon juice
1 head cauliflower, cut into
   flowerettes
1 bunch broccoli, cut into flowerettes
2 cups carrots, cut into matchstick
   slices

1 cup chopped onions
1 cup diced red pepper
1½ cups salad oil
1½ cups white wine vinegar
1½ tablespoons sugar
½ teaspoon freshly ground pepper

DIRECTIONS:

In a large bowl, toss together the mushrooms and lemon juice. Add the remaining vegetables and toss together.

In a medium bowl stir together the oil, vinegar, sugar and pepper until well blended. Pour this over the vegetables, cover and refrigerate overnight.

HINT:

These vegetables can be made well in advance and refrigerated up to a week.

ROASTED SUMMER VEGETABLES

SERVES 8

1½ pounds fresh ripe tomatoes,
   peeled, cored and thinly sliced
1 pound red onions, cut in wedges
1½ pounds new potatoes, pared
   and cut into wedges
1 pound zucchini, cut into 1½" chunks
2 ribs of celery, cut into 1½" chunks

⅓ cup minced parsley
1½ tablespoons fresh dill
1 teaspoon fresh mint or marjoram
2 teaspoons minced garlic
salt and pepper to taste
¼ cup olive oil

DIRECTIONS:

OVEN TEMPERATURE: 400°

Preheat the oven to 400 degrees. Place the oven rack in the upper third of the oven and grease a 9 x 13 inch baking dish.

Spread half the tomatoes over the bottom of the baking dish. Scatter onions, potatoes, zucchini and celery over the tomatoes. Arrange the remaining tomatoes over the top. Sprinkle with parsley, dill, mint, garlic, salt, pepper and oil.

Bake 30 minutes. Remove from the oven and stir. Bake an additional 30 minutes and serve hot or luke warm. The vegetables should be charred slightly to combine the flavors.

STEAMED VEGETABLES

SERVES 8

2 cups carrots, sliced
2 cups pearl onions, peeled
2 cups zucchini, thinly sliced
1 pound mushrooms, halved
6 tablespoons butter

2 tablespoons lemon juice
½ teaspoon salt
⅛ teaspoon pepper
½ teaspoon marjoram

DIRECTIONS:

Place the carrots, onions and zucchini in a steamer basket over boiling water and steam 8 to 10 minutes. Drain and set aside.

In a large fry pan melt the butter and sauté the mushrooms until tender, about 5 minutes. Add the lemon juice, salt, pepper and marjoram. Add the steamed vegetables and stir gently to mix. Turn into a serving bowl and spoon the juices over the top.

HINT:

This recipe may be cut in half or you may substitute any vegetable you might prefer. Fresh peas are good.

WINTER STEW

SERVES 8

7 slices bacon, cut in 1" pieces
½ pound hamburger (optional)
1 · 15-ounce can red kidney beans, drained
1 · 15-ounce can garbanzo beans, drained
1 · 30-ounce can pork and beans

1 small onion, chopped
¼ cup prepared barbecue sauce
⅓ cup catsup
2 tablespoons prepared mustard
1 clove garlic, minced
½ cup grated Cheddar cheese

DIRECTIONS:

Partially cook the bacon, drain and set aside. Add the hamburger to the drippings and brown. Add all the remaining ingredients, place in a crock pot and cook on low for 5 hours. Sprinkle with cheese before serving.

HINT:

This dish may also be made by cooking in a slow oven for 2 to 3 hours. You may substitute lima beans for garbanzo beans if your prefer.

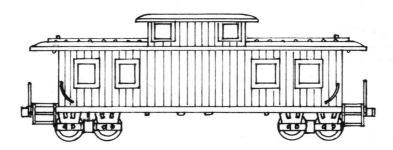

BAKED STUFFED ZUCCHINI

SERVES 6-8

4 · 6" zucchini
⅔ cup sour cream
½ cup Parmesan cheese
½ teaspoon minced onion

¼ cup finely chopped mushrooms
½ teaspoon oregano
¼ cup bread crumbs
2 tablespoons butter

DIRECTIONS:

OVEN TEMPERATURE: 350°

Cut the zucchini in half lengthwise and boil in salted, boiling water for 5 minutes. Scoop out the center place into a bowl and mix with the cheese, onion, mushrooms and oregano. Stuff the mixture back into the shells. Sprinkle with bread crumbs, dot with butter and bake for 20 minutes in a 350 degree oven.

ZUCCHINI OR EGGPLANT CASSEROLE

SERVES 8

5 small zucchini or 2 medium eggplant
2 cups chopped onions
2 green peppers, chopped
1 tablespoon oil
2 teaspoons salt or to taste

1½ cups sliced ripe olives
2 cups grated Cheddar cheese
1 · 4-ounce can tomato sauce
1½ tablespoons melted butter
1½ cups dry bread crumbs

DIRECTIONS:

OVEN TEMPERATURE: 350°

Slice the zucchini and blanch in boiling salted water until just tender. If eggplant is used, peel and slice. Dip slices in flour and brown in oil in fry pan. Layer the zucchini or eggplant in the bottom of a 9 x 13 inch baking dish.

Salt onions and peppers. Sauté in 1 tablespoon of oil until just tender. Pour on top of the zucchini. Sprinkle the olives and cheese over the top. Spread the tomato sauce over this and top with buttered bread crumbs. Bake in a preheated 350 degree oven for 30 minutes.

HINT:

This is a great meatless dinner, but you may add hamburger if desired.

ZUCCHINI ROUNDS

SERVES 12

⅓ cup Bisquick
¼ cup Parmesan cheese
⅛ teaspoon pepper

2 slightly beaten eggs
2 cups zucchini, grated
2 tablespoons butter

DIRECTIONS:

Stir together the Bisquick, cheese and pepper. Stir in the eggs until the mixture is just moistened. Stir in the zucchini.

In a fry pan heat the butter over medium heat. Drop the zucchini mixture into the pan, 2 tablespoons at a time. Cook until slightly brown and crisp. Drain on paper towels.

HINT:

Top each with a dollop of sour cream or yogurt if you like.

AUNT RITA'S SOURCREAM COFFEE CAKE

YIELD: 1 Coffee Cake

½ cup butter
1 cup sugar
2 eggs
2 cups flour
1 teaspoon baking soda
1 teaspoon baking
   powder
pinch of salt

1 cup sour cream
1 teaspoon vanilla

Streusel
½ cup chopped walnuts
1 teaspoon cocoa
1 teaspoon cinnamon
½ cup brown sugar

DIRECTIONS:

OVEN TEMPERATURE: 350°

Cream the butter and sugar. Add the eggs one at a time. Combine the flour, soda, baking powder, and salt alternately with the sour cream, mixing well. Add the vanilla. Beat for 10 minutes.

Mix together the nuts, cocoa, cinnamon, and brown sugar in a separate bowl.

Pour half of batter in a greased and floured tube cake pan. Spoon half of streusel on batter and swirl. Repeat with the remaining batter and streusel. Bake the coffee cake at 350 degrees for 45 minutes or until done.

HINT:

This can be halved or doubled and baked in any shaped pan, except a bundt pan. It freezes beautifully.

BOTERKOEK

YIELD: 2 Coffee Cakes

"Dutch Coffee Cake"

3 cups flour
2 cups sugar
2 eggs
1 cup butter

2 teaspoons almond extract
2 teaspoons baking powder
1 cup slivered almonds

DIRECTIONS:

OVEN TEMPERATURE: 375°

Mix all the ingredients together, except the almonds, until the mixture forms a smooth ball. Divide it into two equal parts. Spread each in an ungreased 8-inch cakepan. Spread the dough evenly with your fingers. Make an edge with a fork. Press ½ cup of almonds on top of each cake. Bake for 30 minutes at 375 degrees.

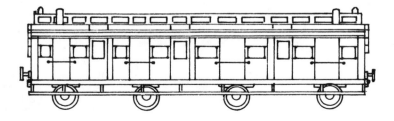

COCONUT BRUNCH BREAD

YIELD: 1 · 10-inch bundt pan

4 eggs
2 cups sugar
1 cup vegetable oil
2 teaspoons coconut
  flavoring
3 cups flour
½ teaspoon baking soda
½ teaspoon baking powder
½ teaspoon salt

1 cup buttermilk
1 cup flaked coconut
1 cup chopped walnuts

Topping:
1 cup sugar
½ cup water
2 tablespoons butter
1 teaspoon coconut flavoring

DIRECTIONS:

OVEN TEMPERATURE: 325°

Beat the eggs in a large mixing bowl. Add the sugar, oil and coconut flavoring and blend well. Sift together the flour, soda, baking powder, and salt. Add this to the egg mixture, alternating with the buttermilk. Fold in the flaked coconut and walnuts.

Pour into a greased and floured 10 inch bundt pan. Bake at 325 degrees for 1¼ hours.

Combine the sugar, water and butter. Bring it to a boil and simmer for 5 minutes. Remove the topping from the heat and add 1 teaspoon coconut flavoring. Pour immediately over the warm bread. Let it stand 4 hours before removing the bread from pan.

PECAN-CINNAMON RING

YIELD: 1 Bundt Ring

"Perfect for Christmas Morning"

½ to 1 cup chopped pecans
18 frozen dinner rolls
1 · 3-ounce package butterscotch
  pudding (not instant)

½ cup margarine
¾ cup brown sugar
¾ teaspoon cinnamon

DIRECTIONS:

OVEN TEMPERATURE: 350°

Grease the bottom and sides of a bundt pan. Sprinkle nuts evenly on the bottom of the pan. Place the frozen rolls on the nuts and sprinkle the dry pudding on top. Melt the margarine and combine it with the brown sugar and cinnamon. Pour this mixture over the top of the rolls.

Set it out uncovered overnight or for 6 to 8 hours. Bake at 350 degrees for 25 to 30 minutes. Tip out on large platter immediately.

BAKED APPLE "DOUGHNUTS"

YIELD: 12 Muffins

1½ cups flour
1 cup sugar, divided
1¾ teaspoons baking powder
½ teaspoon salt
½ teaspoon nutmeg
½ cup shortening

1 egg, beaten
½ cup milk
1 cup grated Golden Delicious Apple
¼ cup butter, melted
1 teaspoon cinnamon

DIRECTIONS:

OVEN TEMPERATURE: 350°

Sift together the flour, ½ cup sugar, baking powder, salt, and nutmeg. Cut in the shortening until crumbly. Stir in the egg and milk. Fold in the grated apples.

Fill greased muffin cups one-half full. Bake at 350 degrees for 20 to 25 minutes. Cool slightly. Dip the tops in melted butter, then in the remaining sugar combined with cinnamon.

BUTTERMILK BRAN MUFFINS

YIELD: 58 to 60 Muffins

3 cups All Bran or Bran Buds Cereal
2 cups boiling water
4 eggs
1 cup brown sugar
1 cup oil

1 quart buttermilk
5 cups flour
5 teaspoons baking soda
½ teaspoon salt

DIRECTIONS:

OVEN TEMPERATURE: 400°

Soak the bran in the boiling water for twenty minutes. In a separate bowl beat the eggs, then add all the other ingredients, mixing after each addition, adding the bran mixture last.

Pour the muffins into paper baking cups ¾ full. Bake at 400 degrees for 15 to 20 minutes.

VARIATION:

Use 1 cup of orange juice and 1 cup of water in place of 2 cups of boiling water.

CARROT-SPICE MUFFINS

YIELD: 10 Muffins

1½ cups all-purpose flour
½ cup unprocessed bran
1 teaspoon salt
1 teaspoon cinnamon
¾ teaspoon baking soda
¼ teaspoon baking powder
¼ teaspoon allspice

1 cup shredded carrots
⅔ cup orange juice
⅓ cup raisins
¼ cup vegetable oil
¼ cup brown sugar
1 egg

DIRECTIONS:

OVEN TEMPERATURE: 425°

In a large bowl combine the flour, bran, salt, cinnamon, baking soda, baking powder, and allspice. Mix well. Combine all the remaining ingredients and add to the bran mixture, mixing just until the dry ingredients are moistened.

Fill the muffin cups ⅔ full. Let stand 5 minutes. Bake 20 to 25 minutes at 425 degrees.

"GOBLIN" MUFFINS

YIELD: 18-20 Muffins

½ cup butter, melted
1 teaspoon vanilla
1 egg
1¼ cups canned
   pumpkin
1 cup sugar
3 cups flour

4 teaspoons baking powder
1 teaspoon salt
1 teaspoon cinnamon
½ teaspoon ground cloves
½ teaspoon nutmeg
1 cup milk
Dates or raisins are optional

DIRECTIONS:

OVEN TEMPERATURE: 400°

With a beater, blend together the butter, vanilla, egg, pumpkin, and sugar.

Add all the dry ingredients. While beating add the milk. Blend well. Stir in dates or raisins if desired. Fill muffin cups ¾ full. Bake at 400 degrees for 18 to 20 minutes.

HEALTHY MUFFIN MIX

YIELD: 4 Dozen Muffins

2 cups oats (not instant)
2 cups Bran Buds
2 cups Shredded Wheat (5 large squares)
2 cups water
3 cups sugar
1 cup oil

4 eggs
2 teaspoons salt
5 teaspoons baking soda
5 cups flour (may use half wheat)
1 quart buttermilk
raisins or dates are optional

DIRECTIONS:

OVEN TEMPERATURE: 350°

Mix the cereals and water together and set aside. Blend the sugar, oil, eggs, salt and baking soda together; mix well. Alternate the buttermilk and flour, mixing well after each addition. Stir in the cereal mixture and mix well.

Store in the refrigerator for up to 6 weeks in an air tight container. Bake at 350 degrees for 25 to 30 minutes filling muffin cups ⅔ full.

POPPY SEED MUFFINS

YIELD: 16 Muffins

¾ cup sugar
¼ cup butter
½ teaspoon grated orange peel
2 eggs
2 cups flour
2½ teaspoons baking powder

½ teaspoon salt
¼ teaspoon nutmeg
1 cup milk
½ cup raisins, preferrably white
½ cup chopped pecans
1 can poppy seeds (1 · ⅝-ounces)

DIRECTIONS:

OVEN TEMPERATURE: 400°

Cream the sugar and butter together. Add the orange peel and eggs. Mix all the dry ingredients together and add to the creamed mixture alternately with the milk. Fold in raisins, pecans, and poppy seeds.

Fill paper-lined muffin tins ¾ full and bake at 400 degrees for 20 minutes.

STRAWBERRY MUFFINS

YIELD: 20 Muffins

1½ cups flour
½ cup chilled butter
¾ cup sugar
1 teaspoon baking soda
¼ teaspoon salt

2 eggs
¼ cup milk
2 teaspoons Sherry
½ cup walnuts
1 cup fresh strawberries

DIRECTIONS:

OVEN TEMPERATURE: 350°

In a food processor using the knife blade mix the flour, butter (cut into six pieces), sugar, baking soda, and salt. Process 10 seconds.

Add the eggs and milk; process 10 to 15 seconds. Add the Sherry; turn processor on and off fast. Add the nuts; then strawberries. Process 10 seconds.

Bake in muffin cups filling ½ full for 18 to 20 minutes at 350 degrees.

YELLOW SQUASH MUFFINS

YIELD: 18 to 24 Muffins

2 pounds yellow squash
2 eggs
1 cup butter, melted
1 cup sugar

3 cups flour
1 tablespoon plus 1 teaspoon
  baking powder
1 teaspoon salt

DIRECTIONS:

OVEN TEMPERATURE: 375°

Wash the squash thoroughly, trim off the ends, cut into 1 inch pieces and cook in a small amount of water for 15 to 20 minutes or until soft. Drain well and mash (it's okay if it's lumpy). Measure 2 cups of squash.

Combine the squash, eggs and butter. Stir well and set aside.

Combine the remaining ingredients in a large bowl. Make a well in the center of mixture; add the squash mixture. Stir just until moistened. Spoon into greased muffin pans and bake at 375 degrees for 20 minutes.

NOTE:

Can substitute 2 cups cooked frozen squash.

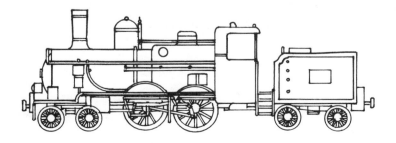

APPLE PANCAKES WITH CINNAMON SYRUP

YIELD: 12 Pancakes
3¼ Cups Syrup

1½ cups sifted flour
1½ teaspoons baking
   powder
1 tablespoon sugar
¾ teaspoon salt
1 egg, beaten
1 cup evaporated milk
1 tablespoon butter,
   melted

2 medium apples, peeled
   and chopped

Syrup
1 cup light corn syrup
2 cups sugar
½ cup water
2 teaspoons cinnamon
1 cup evaporated milk

DIRECTIONS:

Sift together the flour, baking powder, sugar and salt. Combine the beaten egg, milk, and melted butter. Add the liquid mixture gradually to dry ingredients, stirring only until the batter is smooth. Fold in the chopped apples. The batter will be very thick. Drop the batter by generous tablespoons onto a hot, greased griddle, spreading to make the pancakes round. Allow plenty of cooking time as the pancakes are very thick.

Syrup: Mix together the corn syrup, sugar, water and cinnamon in a medium size sauce pan. Bring the syrup to a full boil over medium heat, stirring constantly. Continue stirring and boiling for 2 minutes longer. Cool five minutes. Stir in the evaporated milk. Serve warm or cold.

This is also good on ice cream or pancakes. If the syrup is made and refrigerated, warm very slowly to avoid curdling the milk.

HOOTENANY PANCAKE

SERVES 8

"Great Puffed Pancake"

6 eggs
1 cup milk
½ teaspoon salt
1 cup flour

½ cup butter or margarine
fruit such as fresh peaches
   or frozen strawberries,
   thawed

DIRECTIONS:

OVEN TEMPERATURE: 425°

Combine the eggs, milk, and salt in a blender. Blend the batter until fluffy. Tap in the flour a little at a time, beating the ingredients until well blended. Melt the butter in a 9 x 13 inch baking dish in a 425 degree oven. When the butter is bubbly, pour on the batter. Immediately return the mixture to the oven. Bake it at 425 degrees for 25 minutes.

Cut it into squares and serve immediately with fruit topping.

YEAST PANCAKES

YIELD: 12 Pancakes

1 cup milk
2 tablespoons sugar
¼ cup butter or margarine
¼ cup warm water

1 package active dry yeast
1 egg, beaten
1 teaspoon salt
1 cup unsifted flour

DIRECTIONS:

Scald the milk; stir in the sugar and butter. Cool it to lukewarm. Measure the warm water into a bowl. Sprinkle or crumble in the yeast and stir until it is dissolved. Add the lukewarm milk mixture. Add the egg, salt and flour, beating with an egg beater. Beat the mixture until smooth; about 1 minute.

Cover the batter and allow to rise in a warm place free from draft until double in bulk; 30 minutes to an hour. When double in bulk, stir mixture a few times. Using ¼ cup batter, cook pancakes on a lightly greased griddle.

YOGURT PANCAKES

YIELD: 16 · 3 Inch Pancakes

1 cup flour
1 tablspoon sugar
1 teaspoon baking powder
½ teaspoon baking soda

½ teaspoon salt
1 egg, slightly beaten
1 cup milk
½ cup plain yogurt

DIRECTIONS:

Combine the flour, sugar, baking powder, baking soda, and salt. Beat the eggs and milk together and stir into the dry ingredients. Using ¼ cup batter for each pancake, pour it on a buttered grill and cook until golden brown, turning once.

BANANA NUT BREAD

YIELD: 2 Loaves

"The Best You've Ever Tasted"

¾ cup butter
1½ cups sugar
4 bananas, mashed
2 eggs, well beaten
1 teaspoon vanilla

2 cups sifted flour
1 teaspoon baking soda
¾ teaspoon salt
½ cup buttermilk
¾ cup chopped walnuts

DIRECTIONS: OVEN TEMPERATURE: 325°

Cream the butter and sugar thoroughly. Add the bananas, eggs and vanilla. Beat well. Sift the baking soda, salt and flour together. Stir it into the banana mixture, alternating with the buttermilk. Add the nuts and mix well.

Pour the batter into greased and floured loaf pans. Bake it at 325 degrees for one hour and fifteen minutes. Let the bread cool in the pan ten minutes before turning it out onto a cooling rack to cool completely.

BUTTERMILK CORN BREAD

SERVES 6

½ cup butter or margarine, melted
⅔ cup sugar
2 eggs
½ teaspoon baking soda

1 cup buttermilk
1 cup corn meal
1 cup unsifted flour
½ teaspoon salt

DIRECTIONS:

OVEN TEMPERATURE: 375°

In a mixing bowl combine the melted butter and sugar. Add the eggs and beat the batter until it is well blended. Combine the baking soda and buttermilk. Stir it into the egg mixture. Add all the remaining ingredients and stir until well blended.

Pour the corn bread into a greased 8 x 8 inch baking pan. Bake at 375 degrees for 30 minutes or until it starts to pull away from sides of pan.

CARROT BREAD

YIELD: 2 Loaves

4 eggs
2 cups sugar
1½ cups vegetable oil
3 cups flour
2 teaspoons baking powder

1½ teaspoons baking soda
¼ teaspoon salt
2 teaspoons cinnamon
2 cups finely shredded raw carrots
raisins or chopped nuts are optional

DIRECTIONS:

OVEN TEMPERATURE: 350°

In a mixing bowl beat the eggs. Add the sugar and beat until thick. Add the oil gradually, beating until well blended. Stir in the flour, baking powder, baking soda, salt and cinnamon. Mix until smooth. Stir in the carrots. Add raisins or nuts if desired. Pour the batter into two well greased bread tins. Bake at 350 degrees for one hour.

ENVY OF THE NEIGHBORHOOD ZUCCHINI BREAD

YIELD: 2 Loaves

3 eggs
¾ cup cooking oil
2 cups sugar
2 cups grated zucchini
3 teaspoons vanilla
3 cups sifted flour
1 teaspoon salt

1 teaspoon baking soda
1 teaspoon baking powder
½ teaspoon cloves
3 tablespoons cinnamon
½ teaspoon nutmeg
1 cup chopped walnuts

DIRECTIONS:

OVEN TEMPERATURE: 350°

Beat the eggs until foamy. Add the oil, sugar, zucchini, and vanilla and mix lightly, but well. In a separate bowl, combine flour, salt, soda, baking powder, cloves, cinnamon and nutmeg. Blend the two mixtures together and add chopped walnuts.

Pour the batter into greased and floured bread tins. Do not use glass. Bake at 350 degrees for one hour or until done.

LEMON NUT BREAD

YIELD: 1 Large Loaf

¼ cup margarine
1 cup sugar
2 eggs
1½ cups flour
½ teaspoon salt
1 teaspoon baking powder
½ cup milk

1 cup chopped walnuts
grated rind of 1 lemon

Glaze
juice of 1 lemon
½ cup sugar

DIRECTIONS:

OVEN TEMPERATURE: 325°

In a mixing bowl cream together the margarine and sugar; add the eggs and beat well. Sift together the dry ingredients and add to the sugar mixture alternating with the milk. Fold in the chopped nuts and lemon rind.

Pour the batter into a greased bread tin. Bake at 325 degrees for 50 to 60 minutes. Remove the bread from pan and let stand for 5 minutes. To glaze, combine the lemon juice with the sugar. Mix well and drizzle over the warm loaf.

ORANGE-RAISIN NUT BREAD

YIELD: 2 Loaves

¾ cup orange juice
1 cup sugar
½ cup raisins
½ cup coarsely chopped walnuts
   or pecans
1 egg, slightly beaten
2 tablespoons grated orange
   rind
2 tablespoons butter or
   margarine

1¾ cups flour
1 teaspoon baking powder
½ teaspoon baking soda
½ teaspoon salt

Glaze
1 cup sifted powdered sugar
1½ tablespoons water
optional: orange twist, maraschino
   cherries, whipped cream

DIRECTIONS:

OVEN TEMPERATURE: 350°

Combine the orange juice, sugar, raisins, nuts, egg, orange rind, and butter, mixing well. Stir together, in a separate bowl, the flour, baking powder, baking soda and salt. Combine the two mixtures and mix well.

Pour the batter evenly into two greased and floured loaf pans. Bake at 350 degrees for 30 to 35 minutes. Cool the bread in pans for five minutes. Turn out onto wire racks. Combine the powdered sugar and water, stirring well. Drizzle the glaze over loaves.

The bread can be garnished with orange twists and cherries on a platter. It also can be served as a dessert with a spoonful of whipped cream on top.

PUMPKIN RAISIN BREAD

YIELD: 2 Loaves

"Nice and moist"

⅔ cup butter
2⅔ cups sugar
4 eggs
⅔ cup water
1 · 1-pound can pumpkin
2½ cups white flour
1 cup whole wheat flour

2 teaspoons baking soda
½ teaspoon baking powder
1½ teaspoons salt
1 teaspoon cloves
1 teaspoon cinnamon
½ teaspoon cardamon
1½ cups raisins

DIRECTIONS:

OVEN TEMPERATURE: 350°

Cream together the butter and sugar. Add the eggs and blend in the water and pumpkin, beating well. Add the remaining dry ingredients, stirring just until blended. Stir in the raisins.

Pour the mixture into two greased bread tins. Bake at 350 degrees for 1¼ hours or until browned. Cool in tins for ten minutes. Turn out onto racks.

HINT:

If you cannot find cardamon, omit and increase other spices, or add a bit of coriander.

SIMPLE-DIMPLE BEER BREAD

YIELD: 1 Loaf

3 cups *self-rising* flour
3 tablespoons sugar

12-ounces beer
(do not use light beer)

DIRECTIONS:

OVEN TEMPERATURE: 350°

Mix all the ingredients together very well. Pour the mixture into a greased and floured bread tin. Bake the bread in a 350 degree oven for 30 minutes or until the top is brown. The cooked bread will sometimes appear bumpy on top.

TIP:

To test for doneness: Notice if the loaf has fallen from the sides of the pan, or test by tapping the top of the loaf and listening for a hollow sound with yeast breads.

RHUBARB BREAD

YIELD: 2 Loaves

"Delicious for brunch or as dessert with ice cream"

1½ cups brown sugar
⅔ cup vegetable oil
1 egg
1 cup sour milk*
1 teaspoon vanilla
2½ cups flour
1 teaspoon baking soda
1 teaspoon salt

½ teaspoon cinnamon
½ teaspoon nutmeg
1½ cups finely chopped rhubarb

Topping
1 cup brown sugar
1 teaspoon cinnamon
2 tablespoons butter, melted

DIRECTIONS:

OVEN TEMPERATURE: 350°

In a mixing bowl combine the sugar and oil. Beat in the egg, milk and vanilla. Blend in the dry ingredients. Stir in the rhubarb.

Pour the batter into two greased bread tins. Sprinkle with a topping made of brown sugar, cinnamon, and butter. Bake the bread at 350 degrees for 50 to 60 minutes or until a toothpick inserted comes out clean. Leave in pans 10 minutes. Turn out onto racks.

*Sour milk: Add 1 tablespoon vinegar to 1 cup milk; let stand for 5 minutes.

RASPBERRY BREAD

YIELD: 2 Loaves

"Good and different for a fruit bread"

3 cups flour
1 teaspoon baking soda
1 teaspoon cinnamon
2 cups sugar
1 teaspoon salt
1¼ cups vegetable oil
4 eggs

2 · 10-ounce packages frozen raspberries, thawed reserve ½ cup juice and a few berries for filling
1 · 8-ounce package cream cheese, softened

DIRECTIONS:

OVEN TEMPERATURE: 350°

Combine the flour, soda, cinnamon, sugar and salt. Add the oil, eggs and raspberries; mix well. Pour the batter into greased and floured loaf pans.

Bake the bread at 350 degrees for 60 to 70 minutes. Allow to cool ten minutes before removing the loaves from the pans.

Beat the cream cheese with the reserved berries and juice to a spreading consistency. Cut the bread into thin slices. To make sandwiches spread one slice with cream cheese filling. Top with a second slice; cut in half to serve.

HINT:

This bread slices best when frozen.

BUTTERMILK CRESCENTS

YIELD: 3 Dozen Rolls

"Great recipe to make ahead"

2 packages active dry yeast
⅓ cup water
pinch of sugar
2 eggs, room temperature
½ cup sugar
1 teaspoon salt

1 teaspoon baking soda
1 cup buttermilk, warmed
½ cup margarine
4½ to 5 cups flour
¼ cup butter, melted

DIRECTIONS:

OVEN TEMPERATURE: 400°

In a very large mixing bowl dissolve the yeast in warm water. Add a pinch of sugar and let it sit 15 to 20 minutes.

Beat the eggs with the sugar. Add the salt and soda. Mix well and add this mixture to the yeast. Blend in the warm buttermilk and margarine. Beat well. Blend in 3 cups of flour with a mixer. Stir in the remaining flour. Do not make the dough too stiff.

Knead the dough for two to three minutes. Grease the dough with vegetable oil. Let it rise until it is double in bulk. Roll it out into 3 circles. Cut each into twelve pie shaped wedges. Roll each up crescent style. Brush with melted butter.* Let them rise until double in bulk.

Bake at 400 degrees for 12 to 15 minutes.

To make ahead, follow the directions to the *asterick. Cover and freeze. Before serving remove from the freezer. Allow to rise (approximately 4 hours). Bake as directed.

CHALLAH BREAD

YIELD: 2 Braided Loaves

"Very easy, looks beautiful"

2 packages active, dry yeast
1¾ cups lukewarm water
1 tablespoon salt
½ cup sugar
¼ cup butter, melted

4 large eggs, beaten
7 cups flour
1 egg yolk
1 tablespoon water
sesame or poppy seeds

DIRECTIONS:

OVEN TEMPERATURE: 350°

Dissolve the yeast in water. Add the salt, sugar, butter, eggs and flour. Knead by hand until it is mixed well. Place the dough in a greased bowl. Cover with a damp cloth and let it rise until it is doubled in bulk. Punch it down.

Divide the dough into six equal parts and form each into a rope. Using three ropes at a time, weave them into two braids. Place the braids on a baking sheet, cover, and let them rise until double in size.

Mix 1 egg yolk with 1 tablespoon water. Brush it on top of the bread. Sprinkle with seeds. Bake at 350 degrees for 45 minutes or until the bread sounds hollow when tapped. Remove from the baking sheet and cool.

CARMEL PECAN STICKY BUNS

YIELD: 15 Rolls

"Best Served Warm"

½ cup milk
4 tablespoons butter
2 tablespoons water
2¾ to 3 cups flour
¼ cup sugar
½ teaspoon salt
1 package active dry yeast
1 egg

Filling
3 tablespoons butter, melted

1 cup chopped pecans
½ cup packed brown sugar
1¼ teaspoons cinnamon

Topping
¾ cup packed brown
sugar
4 tablespoons butter,
melted
2 tablespoons light corn
syrup

DIRECTIONS: OVEN TEMPERATURE: 375°

Grease a large bowl and set it aside. In a medium sauce pan, mix together the milk, butter and water. Heat it only until it is warm (130 degrees). In a large bowl mix together 1 cup flour, sugar, salt and yeast. Add the warm milk mixture. Beat with an electric mixer on medium speed for 2 minutes. Add one egg and ½ cup flour. Beat with a mixer on high for 2 minutes. By hand stir in enough of the remaining flour to make a moderately stiff dough. Knead three to five minutes. Place in a greased bowl, turning once to grease the top. Cover and let it rise in a warm place for 1 hour or until double in bulk. Punch down and let stand for 10 minutes.

Grease a 9 x 13 inch baking dish and set it aside. Roll out the dough into a 12 x 15 inch rectangle. Brush it with 3 tablespoons of butter. In a small bowl, mix together 1 cup pecans, ½ cup brown sugar and the cinnamon. Sprinkle this mixture evenly over the dough. Roll the dough tightly from the long side, jelly-roll fashion. Seal the edges. Cut the roll into fifteen 1-inch slices.

In a small bowl mix together the brown sugar, 4 tablespoons butter, and corn syrup. Spread this mixture over the bottom of a greased baking dish. Place the rolls cup side up on top of the brown sugar mixture in the baking dish. Cover and let rise in warm place about 30 minutes. Bake at 375 degrees for 25 to 35 minutes or until done. Cool in pan for ten minutes. Invert on a platter. Serve warm.

TIP:

Yeast: To proof yeast, add 1 tablespoon to yeast warm-water mixture in your recipe. If the mixture bubbles up within 5 minutes, yeast is good. If nothing happens, yeast is dead.

One package of yeast will raise as much as eight cups of flour. To get faster action, use 1 package to every 4 cups flour.

CINNAMON BUBBLE BREAD

YIELD: 2 Loaves

1 cup scalded milk
½ cup shortening
½ cup sugar
1 teaspoon salt
2 packages active dry yeast
½ cup warm water

2 eggs beaten
4½ cups flour
½ cup butter, melted
1 cup sugar
1 tablespoon cinnamon

DIRECTIONS:

OVEN TEMPERATURE: 350°

Combine the milk, shortening, sugar and salt in a large bowl and cool to lukewarm. In a small bowl dissolve the yeast in ½ cup of warm water. Add the yeast and eggs to the milk mixture. Mix well. Add the flour. Add enough additional flour to knead to a soft dough. Cover and let rise until double in bulk. Punch down and let rise 10 more minutes.

In another small bowl mix the sugar and cinnamon together. Break off walnut sized pieces of dough. Roll them in melted butter and then the sugar mixture. Make two layers with eight dough balls per layer in two greased loaf pans.

Cover and let rise until double in bulk. Bake at 350 degrees for 30 to 35 minutes.

HINT:

Can be made in a bundt pan or angel food cake pan.

ENGLISH MUFFIN BREAD

YIELD: 2 Loaves

4½ cups flour
¼ teaspoon baking soda
1 tablespoon sugar
2 teaspoons salt

2 packages active, dry yeast
2 cups milk
½ cup water

DIRECTIONS:

OVEN TEMPERATURE: 375°

Mix 4 cups of flour, baking soda, sugar, salt and yeast in a mixing bowl. Heat the milk and water to 110 to 120 degrees using a thermometer. Pour the milk mixture over the dry ingredients stirring constantly. Add the remaining flour, stirring the mixture until it is sticky.

Spoon the mixture into two well-greased loaf pans. Let it rise 45 minutes. Bake at 375 degrees for 35 minutes. Remove from pans immediately.

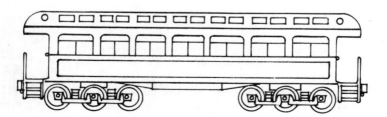

CUBAN BREAD

YIELD: 2 Loaves

"Makes marvelous grilled cheese sandwiches"

1-2 packages active dry yeast
1 tablespoon salt
2 tablespoons sugar

2 cups lukewarm water
5 to 6 cups flour
Cornmeal

DIRECTIONS:

OVEN TEMPERATURE: 400°

Dissolve the yeast, salt, and sugar in a cup with some of the water. With a wooden spoon, beat enough of the flour into the rest of the water until you have a batter. Stir in the yeast mixture and continue adding flour until you have a manageable dough. Turn it out onto the counter and knead well. Add flour until you have a fairly stiff dough. Then knead again for approximately 10 minutes.

Place the dough in a greased bowl, cover with a damp towel, and let rise until doubled in bulk. Turn out onto counter and cut in two equal parts. Shape it (squeezing out yeast gases) into two plump, high, round loaves. (You can make loaves smaller and get three loaves.)

Sprinkle cornmeal on a greased baking sheet in an area large enough for both loaves. Place the loaves on the sheet and let rise for five minutes.

Slash in a criss-cross pattern on the top of each loaf with a sharp knife. Place them in a cold oven. Set the oven for 400 degrees placing a large pan of boiling water on the lower shelf of the oven. Bake 45 to 50 minutes.

This is a delicious, crusty bread. Since it has neither milk nor shortening it is complemented by garlic or herb butter.

VARIATIONS:

Use either unbleached flour, or whole wheat and unbleached or white flour – half and half.

DILLY CASSEROLE BREAD

YIELD: 1 Loaf

1 package active dry yeast
¼ cup warm water
1 cup creamed cottage cheese
2 tablespoons sugar
1 tablespoon instant minced onion
1 tablespoon butter

2 teaspoons dill seed or weed
1 teaspoon salt
¼ teaspoon baking soda
1 egg
2¼ to 2½ cups flour

DIRECTIONS:

OVEN TEMPERATURE: 350°

Dissolve the yeast in water. Heat the cottage cheese to lukewarm. Combine the sugar, onion, butter, dill seed, salt, baking soda, and egg in a bowl with the cheese and yeast mixture. Add the flour to form a stiff dough.

Cover the bread and let it rise until doubled in bulk. Stir down the dough. Turn it into a well greased 1½ quart casserole or 8-inch round pan. Let it rise 30 to 40 minutes more. Bake the bread at 350 degrees for 40 to 50 minutes. Brush it with butter and sprinkle with salt.

DELICIOUS ONE-BOWL CINNAMON ROLLS

YIELD: 5 Dozen Rolls

6 packages active dry yeast
1 cup warm water
¼ cup sugar
12 cups flour
4 cups hot water
6 eggs
1 cup vegetable oil
2 cups powdered milk
6 teaspoons salt
¼ cup sugar

½ cup butter, melted
1 cup brown sugar
2 tablespoons cinnamon
1 cup raisins, optional
1 cup walnuts, optional

Frosting, optional:
½ cup milk
2 cups powdered sugar
1 teaspoon vanilla

DIRECTIONS:

OVEN TEMPERATURE: 350°

In a small mixing bowl dissolve the yeast in 1 cup of warm water and add ¼ cup sugar. Set aside.

Place the flour in a large mixing bowl. Make a hole in the center and add the water, eggs, oil, powdered milk, salt and sugar. Mix these well with a wire whip without stirring in the flour. Add the yeast mixture and mix well, again without mixing in the flour. Let rise covered in a warm place until bubbly and high. Blend in the flour. Let rise again for 1 hour. The dough will seem thin.

Roll it out on a floured surface ¼ at a time into an 18-inch rectangle one inch thick (if the dough is hard to handle sprinkle with additional flour to make it manageable). Spread with butter and the sugar-cinnamon mixture. Also spread with raisins or nuts if desired. Roll up lengthwise and seal edges. Cut 1 inch thick. Place the rolls in greased muffin tins. Let them rise for 45 minutes. Bake at 350 degrees for 10 minutes. Frost with powdered sugar frosting if desired.

VARIATION:

Orange rolls; ½ cup butter, melted, 1 cup sugar, 2 tablespoons grated orange rind in place of cinnamon mixture.

LIGHT ROLLS

YIELD: 5 Dozen Rolls

"Light as a cloud rolls"

1 cup shortening
¾ cup sugar
2 teaspoons salt
1 cup boiling water
2 packages active dry yeast

½ cup warm water
1 tablespoon sugar
4 eggs
1 cup cold water
7½ cups flour

DIRECTIONS:

OVEN TEMPERATURE: 400°

In a large bowl cream the shortening, sugar and salt. Add the boiling water and mix until smooth. Dissolve the yeast using ½ cup warm water and a tablespoon of sugar. Add this to the creamed mixture. Beat in the eggs. Add the cold water and flour. Beat until the dough is well combined and smooth.

Let the dough rise until double in bulk, approximately two to three hours. Punch it down and form into rolls. Allow it to rise for ½ hour. Bake at 400 degrees for twelve minutes.

ELIZABETH'S CINNAMON ROLLS

YIELD: 3½ to 4 Dozen Rolls

1 cup milk, scalded
1 package active dry yeast
¼ cup lukewarm water
⅔ cup shortening
1 cup cooked and mashed potatoes
2 eggs, beaten
1 cup sugar
1 teaspoon salt

4 cups flour
½ cup butter, melted and cooled
1 cup sugar
1 cup raisins
2 tablespoons cinnamon
½ cup milk
2 cups powdered sugar
1 teaspoon vanilla

DIRECTIONS:

OVEN TEMPERATURE: 350°

Scald the milk and allow it to cool to lukewarm. In a large bowl dissolve the yeast in ¼ cup lukewarm water. Add the scalded milk to the yeast mixture. Add the shortening, mashed potatoes, eggs, sugar and salt. Beat by hand until all the ingredients are dissolved. Add the flour one cup at a time, mixing well. When enough flour is added to make a sticky dough, cover with plastic wrap and let rise in warm place unti double in bulk.

Roll the dough out onto a floured surface to a 12 x 15 inch rectangle. Spread with butter; sprinkle with sugar, raisins and cinnamon. Roll it lengthwise sealing the edges. Cut it into 1-inch thick rolls. Place the rolls in greased pans. Let them rise until double in bulk (about ½ hour). Bake at 350 degrees for 25 minutes or unti golden brown.

Mix together the milk, powdered sugar, and vanilla. Ice the rolls while they are still hot.

FLAT FRENCH BREAD

YIELD: 1 Large Loaf

2 cups warm water
1 tablespoon sugar
1 package active dry yeast
4 cups flour

2 teaspoons salt
¼ cup butter, melted
Parmesan cheese or sesame seeds

DIRECTIONS:

OVEN TEMPERATURE: 350°

In a large bowl mix together the water, sugar and yeast. Let it stand for several minutes. Then add the flour and salt, beating well with a spoon. Put it aside and let it rise until double in bulk.

Grease a large jelly roll pan. With greased hands spread the dough in the pan. Pour melted butter over the dough. Sprinkle with Parmesan cheese or sesame seeds as preferred. Let it rise again until the bread is several inches high.

Bake at 350 degrees for 30 minutes. Spread the butter more evenly on the bread as it bakes. Remove from oven and slice bread in diagonal slices and serve warm.

FRENCH BREAD

YIELD: 1 Large Loaf

"Great with homemade soup"

1½ cups hot tap water	1 package active dry yeast
1 teaspoon shortening	4 cups flour
1 tablespoon sugar	1 tablespoon milk
1½ teaspoons salt	sesame seeds, optional

DIRECTIONS:

OVEN TEMPERATURE: 375°

Combine all the dry ingredients. Add the liquid (shortening and water together). Knead the dough until smooth. Let it rise. Punch it down every 10 minutes. Do this 5 times or for 50 minutes. Roll the dough out into a rectangle. Roll it up on the diagonal. Slash it with a sharp knife about ¼ inch deep every inch or inch and a half. Brush with milk, sprinkle with seeds if desired. Let the bread rise for 1 hour. Bake it at 375 degrees for 25 to 30 minutes.

VARIATION:

For flour use 1 cup whole wheat and 3 cups white.

GRETA'S HOT DINNER ROLLS

YIELD: 2 Dozen Rolls

"Excellent dough for cinnamon rolls or doughnuts"

½ cup butter, melted	⅔ cup warm water
½ cup sugar	1 teaspoon sugar
2 eggs	1 cup milk
1 teaspoon salt	4 cups flour
1 package active dry yeast	

DIRECTIONS:

OVEN TEMPERATURE: 375°

Mix together the butter, sugar, eggs and salt. Dissolve the yeast in warm water with 1 teaspoon sugar. Add the milk and yeast mixture to the first mixture. Add the flour and beat well. This should be a sticky dough.

Cover the dough and let it rise until double in bulk. Roll it out and cut the dough into rolls. Place them on a greased baking sheet. Let them rise again until double in bulk.

Bake the rolls at 375 degrees about 25 minutes or until lightly brown. Brush with butter.

TIP:

Kneading: To knead, press dough flat with heels of hands, folding to the center. Repeat process of pressing and folding dough in rhythmic motion. You should knead dough at least 15 minutes, unless using a mixer with a dough hook. Kneading is important because it evenly distributes the gas bubbles formed by the yeast. Flat bread is usually caused by insufficient kneading, too much liquid, stale yeast or the humidity.

HERB BREAD

YIELD: 2 Loaves

2 cups milk
4 tablespoons sugar
1 tablespoon salt
1 package active dry yeast
2 eggs, beaten

1 teaspoon nutmeg
1 teaspoon sage
8 cups flour
4 tablespoons shortening, melted

DIRECTIONS:

OVEN TEMPERATURE: 425°

Scald the milk. Add the sugar and salt. Allow it to cool to lukewarm. Sprinkle the yeast into the milk, and stir to dissolve it. Add the eggs, nutmeg, sage and ½ cup flour; beat until smooth. Add the melted shortening and remaining flour, or enough to handle easily.

Knead the dough until it is smooth and elastic. Let it rise until double approximately 2 hours. Divide the dough into two equal parts and shape into round loaves. Let it rise about one hour.

Bake in a 425 degree oven for fifteen minutes. Reduce the heat to 375 degrees and bake for 35 minutes. Allow it to cool.

MONKEY BREAD

YIELD: 2 Large Bundt Rings

2 cups lukewarm water
½ cup sugar
1 teaspoon salt
1 package active, dry yeast

2 eggs
7 cups flour
4 tablespoons vegetable oil
1 cup butter

DIRECTIONS:

OVEN TEMPERATURE: 350°

Combine the water, sugar, salt and yeast, let rest 5 to 10 minutes or until yeast is bubbly. Beat 2 eggs and add them to the yeast mixture. Sift in 3 cups of flour. Mix well. Add the oil and then the additional 4 cups of flour. Mix well.

Cover the dough with a damp cloth and let it rise until double in bulk. Punch it down and let it rise again.

Melt the butter. Pour ½ cup in each bundt pan. Roll the dough out to ½ inch thick. Cut it with a circular cookie cutter. Fold the circles in half, and stand them on end in the pan. Let rise until doubled in bulk.

Bake 20 minutes at 350 degrees. Cover with foil for the last 5 mintues to prevent over browning.

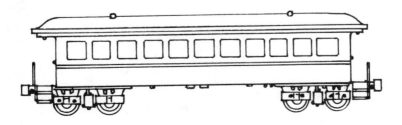

OATMEAL BREAD

YIELD: 2 Loaves

2 packages active, dry yeast
½ cup warm water
1½ cups boiling water
1 cup rolled oats
½ cup molasses

⅓ cup shortening
1 tablespoon salt
5½ cups flour
2 eggs

DIRECTIONS:

OVEN TEMPERATURE: 375°

Dissolve the yeast in warm water and set aside. Combine the boiling water, oats, molasses, shortening, and salt. Cool to lukewarm. Stir in 2 cups of flour. Add 2 eggs. Stir in the yeast mixture. Beat well. Add additional flour until the dough is no longer sticky. Knead well. Cover and refrigrate 2 hours or overnight.

Shape the dough into 2 loaves. Place it in greased bread pans. Cover and let rise until double in bulk, approximately 2 hours. Bake at 375 degrees for 40 to 50 minutes.

POTTED DILL BREAD

YIELD: 2 · 4-Inch Loaves

2 clay flower pots 4 inches across
shortening
1 package active dry yeast
½ cup warm water
3 tablespoons sugar

1 tablespoon dry dillweed
1 cup evaporated milk
2 tablespoons butter, melted
1 teaspoon salt
3½ cups flour

DIRECTIONS:

OVEN TEMPERATURE: 350°

Wash the pots and grease them well. Bake them on a cookie sheet at 350 degrees for ten minutes. Grease the pots again and repeat the procedure three more times. Cool slightly between bakings.

Dissolve the yeast in the water in a large bowl. Stir in 1 tablespoon of the sugar and all the dillweed. Let it stand fifteen minutes. Stir in the remaining sugar, milk, butter and salt. Stir in the flour to make a stiff sticky dough. Line the bottom of the pots with foil

Fill the pots ⅔ full. Cover with wax paper and let them rise in a warm place 30 minutes. Bake the pots on a cookie sheet at 350 degrees for 35 minutes until browned. Let the bread cool in the pots for 10 minutes. Run a knife around the edge to loosen. Cool on wire rack.

HINT:

To give as a gift, return the bread to a pot and wrap in plastic.

TIP:

Rising: To facilitate rising of bread or rolls, place, covered with a towel, in cold oven. On a lower shelf place a pan of hot water and close the oven door. Dough has risen enough when a slight pressure from the fingers leaves an imprint.

ORANGE ROLLS
YIELD: 24 Rolls

½ cup warm water
2 packages active dry yeast
1½ cups lukewarm milk
½ cup sugar
2 teaspoons salt
2 eggs
½ cup shortening
7 to 7½ cups flour

Filling
2 tablespoons melted butter
½ cup sugar
2 tablespoons grated orange peel

Topping:
1 cup powdered sugar
2 tablespoons orange juice

DIRECTIONS:
OVEN TEMPERATURE: 400°

Dissolve the yeast in warm water. Scald the milk and cool it to lukewarm. Mix together the yeast, milk, sugar, salt, eggs and shortening. Add half of the flour. Mix well and add the rest of the flour. Knead for 5 minutes.

Place the dough in a greased bowl and allow it to rise until double (about 1½ hours). Punch it down and allow it to rise for 30 minutes. Roll the dough out into 10 x 20-inch rectangle. Mix the filling ingredients and spread them over the dough. Cut the dough into 20 1-inch strips. Stack 5 strips together. Cut into 6 equal pieces.

Place the pieces in greased muffin tins. Let them rise until double. Bake at 400 degrees for 15 to 20 minutes. Brush with topping mixture.

PERFECT ORANGE ROLLS
YIELD: 3 Dozen

2 packages active dry yeast
¼ cup warm water
1¼ cup milk, scalded
½ teaspoon salt
½ cup sugar
½ cup margarine or butter
3 eggs, well beaten

5 to 5½ cups flour

Orange-Sugar Mixture
1 cup sugar
½ cup butter
grated rind from two
    oranges

DIRECTIONS:
OVEN TEMPERATURE: 375°

Dissolve the yeast in warm water and set it aside. Scald the milk; add the sugar, butter, and salt and stir to dissolve the sugar. Cool the mixture to lukewarm. Add this to the yeast. Beat the eggs until light and fluffy. Beat them into the yeast mixture. Add two cups of flour, beat with a mixer. Add the rest of the flour, blending it in by hand. Knead it for a good five minutes. Cover the dough and allow to rise until double in bulk.

Divide the dough in half. Roll it out into a rectangle 18 inches long and ¼ inch thick. Cream together the sugar, butter, and orange rind and spread it over the dough. Roll it up jelly roll style. Cut the dough into one-inch slices. Place in greased muffin pans. Let it rise until double in bulk. Bake 12 to 15 minutes at 375 degrees.

Dough can be refrigerated one day in advance. Allow to reach room temperature approximately three hours before making rolls.

REFRIGERATOR ROLLS

YIELD: 3 Dozen Rolls

½ cup warm water
2 packages active dry yeast
½ cup sugar
½ cup shortening
1 cup warm water

3 eggs, slightly beaten,
   room temperature
4½ cups flour
2 teaspoons salt
½ cup butter, melted

DIRECTIONS:

OVEN TEMPERATURE: 400°

In a large bowl dissolve the yeast in warm water. Add the sugar and shortening. The water should not be hot enough to dissolve shortening. Add 1 cup of warm water. Stir in the eggs one at a time. Sift the flour and salt together. Add this to yeast mixture. Stir well. Cover and refrigerate overnight.

Six hours before serving, remove the dough from the refrigerator to allow it to reach room temperature. Three and one-half to four hours before serving, roll the dough out into a rectangle. Spread with melted butter. Roll the dough up lengthwise and cut it into one-inch slices. Place the slices cut side down in greased muffin tins. Allow the rolls to rise about the three and one-half hours. Bake 10 to 12 minutes at 400 degrees.

WHEAT BREAD

YIELD: 6 Large or 8 Small Loaves

½ cup warm water
2 packages active dry yeast
5 cups hot water
11 cups wheat flour
2 cups white flour

2 tablespoons molasses
⅔ cup honey
⅔ cup oil
2 tablespoons salt
2 eggs, unbeaten

DIRECTIONS:

OVEN TEMPERATURE: 350°

Dissolve the yeast in ½ cup of warm water. Place 5 cups of hot water in a mixer and add 7 cups of whole wheat flour to it. Mix it until it is quite smooth. While the mixer is running, add molasses, honey, oil, salt and eggs. Then add the yeast mixture. When mixed, add 4 cups of wheat flour and 2 cups of white flour. Beat 10 minutes.

Place the dough on a greased surface and let it rest 10 minutes. Grease the bread tins. Cut the dough into 6 equal pieces place them in the bread tins. Let them rise until level with the top of the tins.

Bake the loaves at 400 degrees for 10 minutes. Lower the heat to 350 degrees and bake 30 minutes for small loaves and 35 minutes for large loaves.

TIP:

To make rolls extra light — have eggs at room temperature and beat until very thick.

BUTTERMILK SCONES

YIELD: 100 to 150 Scones

2 packages active dry yeast
¼ cup warm water
1 quart buttermilk, warmed
2 tablespoons sugar
2 eggs

2 tablespoons vegetable oil
2 teaspoons salt
3 teaspoons baking powder
½ teaspoon baking soda
8 cups flour
oil for frying

DIRECTIONS:

Soften the yeast in warm water. Pour warm buttermilk into a large warm bowl. Add the sugar, eggs, oil, salt, baking powder, and baking soda. Mix well. Add the softened yeast and mix; then add 4 cups of flour and beat until smooth. Add the remaining 4 cups of flour to make dough soft.

Cover; let the dough rise in a warm place about 1 hour or until double in bulk. Punch the dough down to its original size. Cover and refrigerate overnight. Remove the desired amount of dough; roll it out on a lightly floured surface. Cut it into squares; fry in hot oil (375 degrees) until golden brown, (3 to 5 minutes). Do not allow the dough to rise prior to frying. Serve the scones with honey butter or jam. The dough will keep 4 to 6 weeks in the refrigerator in an air tight container.

PARMESAN BISCUITS

YIELD: 10 Biscuits

1 can buttermilk biscuits
¼ cup butter, melted

½ cup poppy seeds
½ cup grated Parmesan cheese

DIRECTIONS:

OVEN TEMPERATURE: 375°

Dip each biscuit in butter, poppy seeds and cheese. Place them in a shallow baking dish, overlapping each biscuit. Bake at 375 degrees for 15 to 20 minutes or until golden brown.

VARIATION:

Sliced white bread or quartered pita bread may be substituted for the biscuits.

POPOVERS

YIELD: 6 Popovers

3 eggs
1 cup milk
3 tablespoons butter, melted

1 cup flour
½ teaspoon salt

DIRECTIONS:

OVEN TEMPERATURE: 400°

Beat the eggs until frothy in a mixer or blender. Next beat in the milk and butter. Slowly beat in the flour and salt. The mixture should be light but not foamy. If it is bumpy, strain it.

Generously oil custard cups (6-4 ounce pyrex cups) and fill to one-half inch from the top. Place the cups on a cookie sheet with a small amount of water in the pan. Bake them fifteen minutes at 425 degrees or 30 minutes at 400 degrees.

When done, cut two slits on top of each popover to release the steam and bake them another five minutes. Remove the popovers at once. Do not cover tops.

Serve immediately.

CROISSANTS

YIELD: 2 Dozen

1½ cups unsalted softened butter
¼ cup unsifted flour
¾ cup milk
2 tablespoons sugar
1 teaspoon salt

½ cup very warm water (105 to 115)°
2 packages active dry yeast
3 cups unsifted flour
1 egg yolk
1 tablespoon milk
waxed paper

DIRECTIONS: OVEN TEMPERATURE: 425°

With a spoon, beat the butter and ¼ cup flour until smooth. Spread on waxed paper (on wet cookie sheet) in a rectangle, 12 x 6 inches. Refrigerate. Heat the milk; stir in the sugar and salt to dissolve. Cool to lukewarm.

With a thermometer, check the temperature of the water (105 to 115 degrees). Sprinkle the yeast on the water and stir to dissolve.

With a spoon, beat the milk mixture and 3 cups flour into the yeast. Stir until smooth. Turn onto lightly floured pastry cloth. Knead until smooth. Let rise, covered, in a warm place (85 degrees), free from draft until double in bulk (1 hour). Refrigerate ½ hour.

On a lightly floured pastry cloth, with stockinette-covered rolling pin, roll the dough into a 14 x 14 inch square. Place the butter mixture on half of the dough: remove the paper. Fold the other half over the butter: pinch the edges to seal. With the fold at right, roll from the center to 20 x 8 inches.

From the short side, fold the dough into thirds, making three layers; seal the edges. Chill one hour wrapped in foil. With the fold at left, roll to 20 x 8 inches: fold as before and chill one-half hour. Repeat and chill overnight.

Next day, roll to 20 x 8 inches; fold twice and chill ½ hour. Repeat and chill one hour longer.

To shape, cut the dough into 4 parts. On a lightly floured pastry cloth, roll each into a 12 inch circle. Cut each circle into six wedges. Roll them up beginning at the wide end. Form each into crescent. Place point side down, two inches apart on brown paper on a cookie sheet.

Cover; let rise in warm place (85 degrees), free from draft until double (1 hour). Heat the oven to 425 degrees. Brush with yolk beaten with milk. Bake five minutes. Reduce oven to 375 degrees. Bake 10 minutes and until croissants are puffed and brown. Cool on rack ten minutes.

HOT CHEESE CROUTONS

YIELD: 20 to 25 Pieces

1 loaf uncut sandwich bread
½ cup butter, melted

½ cup mayonnaise
½ cup Parmesan cheese

DIRECTIONS: OVEN TEMPERATURE: 350°

Cut the crusts off a loaf of bread. Slice the bread into 2 inch thick slices. Cut each slice into thirds, making three lady-finger shaped croutons from each bread slice.

Combine the butter, mayonnaise and cheese. Spread it on all sides of the croutons, except the bottoms. Bake them at 350 degrees for 10 to 15 minutes. Serve hot as an appetizer or with meal.

The croutons can be prepared early and frozen or refrigerated. Bake them just before serving.

BARLEY PILAF

SERVES 10-12

"A nice alternative to rice or potatoes"

1 ½ cups pearl barley
½ cup butter
2 medium onions, chopped

½ pound fresh mushrooms, sliced
4 cups chicken broth or
    boullion

DIRECTIONS:

OVEN TEMPERATURE: 350°

In a heavy skillet, lightly brown the barley in half of the butter. Remove to a 2 quart buttered casserole.

Sauté the onions and mushrooms in the remaining butter until tender. Add to the barley. Pour the chicken broth over all and combine well.

Bake covered in a preheated 350 degree oven for 1 hour. Remove the cover and bake another 1 to 1 ½ hours, stirring occasionally. Add additional broth or water if barley gets too dry.

HINT:

This can be made ahead and then frozen in batches. Reheat them in the oven or microwave. Add more liquid if reheating in the oven.

ARMENIAN WEDDING RICE

SERVES 8

6 ounces coiled fideo pasta
¼ cup butter
1 cup long grain rice, uncooked
2 cups hot chicken broth
salt and pepper to taste

2 tablespoons butter
2 ½ ounces slivered almonds
6 ounces pitted dates, sliced
½ cup raisins

DIRECTIONS:

Heat the butter in a large casserole or large sauce pan and brown the fideo. Add the rice, 2 cups hot chicken broth and salt and pepper to taste. Bring to a boil, cover and simmer for 20 minutes.

While the rice is cooking, heat 1 tablespoon butter in a fry pan and sauté the slivered almonds until golden brown. Remove and set aside. Add another tablespoon of butter and sauté the dates and raisins briefly. When the rice is done, stir in the almonds, dates, and raisins and serve.

TIP:

One cup of uncooked rice will yield about three cups of cooked rice.

GREEN RICE

SERVES 12

2 cups uncooked rice
4 cups water
2 cups grated sharp cheddar cheese
⅓ cup chopped green onion
½ cup chopped green pepper

2 tablespoons chopped parsley
2 eggs, slightly beaten
1 cup milk
¼ cup oil
salt and pepper to taste

DIRECTIONS:

OVEN TEMPERATURE: 350°

Cook the rice in 4 cups of water until it is light and fluffy.

Combine the rice, cheese, onion, green pepper and parsley. In a bowl beat together the eggs, milk, oil and salt and pepper. Add this to the rice mixture. Pour into a casserole and bake in a preheated 350 degree oven for 45 minutes.

MEXICAN RICE

SERVES 6

"A nice way to use leftover rice!"

4 cups cooked rice
2 cups sour cream
1 · 4-ounce can diced green chilies

2 cups grated Monterey Jack cheese
   (¾ pound)
dash of paprika

DIRECTIONS:

OVEN TEMPERATURE: 350°

Mix together all the ingredients but the paprika saving some of the cheese to sprinkle on top of the casserole.

Put the rice mixture in a shallow casserole dish. Top with remaining cheese and a dash of paprika.

Bake in a preheated 350 degree oven for 30 minutes.

HINT:

This is very good when served with Mexican food. It can be made ahead, refrigerated and reheated in the microwave.

RICE CASSEROLE

SERVES 12

1 cup rice
2 cups water
2 tablespoons chopped green pepper
½ cup butter
1 onion, chopped

1 cup canned consomme
¾ cup water
1 cup sliced fresh mushrooms
1 teaspoon salt

DIRECTIONS:

OVEN TEMPERATURE: 350°

Cook the rice in 2 cups of water until light and fluffy.

Add the remaining ingredients and mix. Place mixture in an 8 x 10 inch baking dish. Cover with aluminum foil and bake in a preheated 350 degree oven for 2 hours.

HINT:

This can be made in advance and reheated in the oven or microwave.

FRIED RICE

SERVES 8-10

4 cups cold cooked rice
3 tablespoons oil
1 cup shredded ham or shrimp
2 eggs, slightly beaten

6 green onions, chopped
2 tablespoons soy sauce
½ teaspoon sugar (optional)

DIRECTIONS:

Heat the oil in a large fry pan and cook the rice for 10 minutes, stirring frequently. Add ham or shrimp. Pour eggs over the mixture. Cook slowly for 5 minutes. Add onions, soy sauce and sugar. Heat through and serve.

HINT:

You may substitute any left over meat in place of the ham or shrimp. Some optional additions or substitutions to the rice might be chopped water chestnuts or raisins.

WILD RICE CASSEROLE

SERVES 6-8

½ cup butter
2 stalks celery (with leaves), chopped
1 small onion, finely chopped
4 ounces wild rice, cooked (you may substitute wild and white rice)

1 small can mushrooms with liquid
½ pound Velveeta cheese, cut in small chunks
salt and pepper to taste

DIRECTIONS:

OVEN TEMPERATURE: 350°

Sauté butter, celery and onion till soft.

Mix all ingredients together in a casserole dish. Bake in a preheated 350 degree oven for 30 minutes or in a microwave till hot.

HINT:

This may be prepared in advance. It freezes and reheats well.

RICE MUSHROOM RING

SERVES 10

1 cup butter or ¾ cup margarine
⅓ cup chopped onion
¾ pound fresh mushrooms, sliced
3 cups cooked rice
1 teaspoon seasoning salt
⅛ teaspoon sage

⅛ teaspoon marjoram
⅛ teaspoon pepper
⅛ teaspoon thyme
⅓ cup chopped nuts, pecans, almonds or walnuts

DIRECTIONS:

OVEN TEMPERATURE: 350°

Sauté the onions and mushrooms in butter or margarine until the onions are translucent. Add the rice, seasonings and nuts. Mix well. Pack into a ring mold and let age 6 hours to overnight in the refrigerator. Reheat in a pan of water for 1 hour in a 350 degree oven, covered.

CRAB CHAFING DISH

SERVES 6

"A chance to use your chafing dish"

1 pound spaghetti, cooked
2 · 7½-ounce cans crab meat
2 tablespoons oil
2 tablespoons minced onion
1 clove garlic, minced
1 cup milk
¾ cup grated sharp Cheddar cheese

1 · 10-ounce package frozen
   artichokes, thawed
½ teaspoon seasoned salt
½ teaspoon pepper
¼ cup Sherry
¼ cup parsley, minced

DIRECTIONS:

Before guests arrive, cook and drain spaghetti, drain crabmeat and thaw artichokes.

At the table in an electric skillet or chafing dish, heat the oil. Sauté the onion and garlic until golden. Add the milk, cheese, artichokes and seasonings. Cook until the cheese melts and the artichokes are tender. Add the Sherry, spaghetti and parsley and toss until well mixed.

PASTA NESTS WITH VEGETABLES

SERVES 6

2 cups frozen, loose-pack cauliflower,
   broccoli and carrots
6 ounces fettuccine noodles
3 tablespoons butter
2 tablespoons flour
1 teaspoon grated lemon peel

½ teaspoon salt
¼ teaspoon pepper
¾ cup milk
1 cup sour cream
1 beaten egg
¼ cup grated Parmesan cheese

DIRECTIONS: OVEN TEMPERATURE: 350°

In separate pots cook the vegetables and pasta until tender. Drain and set aside.

In another saucepan melt the butter, stir in the flour, lemon peel, ½ teaspoon salt and a dash of pepper. Stir in the milk. Cook and stir until thickened and bubbly. Stir in the sour cream and vegetables. Heat almost to boiling. Spoon half the vegetable sauce mixture into a shallow baking dish.

Toss together the cooked pasta, egg and Parmesan cheese. Using a long-tined fork, twirl a few strands of the fettuccine around the tines. Remove the pasta from the fork, standing the pasta upright in the baking dish to form a nest. Continue forming the nests and arranging in the baking dish until you have 6 nests. Spoon the remaining vegetable sauce over the pasta. Cover and bake in a preheated 350 degree oven 20 minutes or until heated through.

FETTUCCINE CON PESTO

SERVES 8

Pesto:
2 cups fresh basil leaves
½ cup olive oil

2 tablespoons pine nuts
2 cloves garlic, minced
1 teaspoon salt

1 pound fettuccine noodles, plain and spinach
½ cup freshly grated Parmesan or Romano cheese
2 tablespoons sweet butter, room temperature

DIRECTIONS:

Pesto: Put the basil, olive oil, pine nuts, garlic and salt in a food processor and mix at high speed. Stop from time to time to scrape the ingredients down toward the bottom of the bowl. When the ingredients are evenly blended, remove and reserve.

Cook the fettuccine noodles in boiling salted water until al dente. Drain the noodles and toss with butter. Arrange the noodles on a platter, sprinkle with the grated cheese and spoon the pesto over this. Freeze any left over pesto.

HINT:

al dente, firm to the bite

STRAW AND HAY

SERVES 4

½ pound each green and white pasta
3 tablespoons butter
7 tablespoons unsalted butter
2 shallots, finely chopped

6 ounces prosciutto
¾ cup heavy cream
salt and pepper to taste
½ cup Parmesan cheese

DIRECTIONS:

In a large kettle heat salted water to boiling. Add the pasta and cook al dente. The white pasta will take a little longer to cook than the green pasta. Drain the pasta and toss with 3 tablespoons of butter.

While the pasta is cooking, heat ¼ cup of the unsalted butter in a skillet. Add the shallots and cook a few minutes. Slice the prosciutto and add to the shallots. Add the heavy cream and heat until slightly thickened.

Pour the sauce over the pasta and season with salt and pepper. Sprinkle with Parmesan cheese and serve.

HINT:

To vary the dish, add garlic, mushrooms or even cooked asparagus to the pasta.

LASAGNE AL FORNO

SERVES 8-10

Meat Sauce:
1 cup chopped onion
1 clove garlic, minced
½ cup chopped celery
2 tablespoons butter
1 pound mild Italian sausage
1 pound hamburger
2 tablespoons olive oil
½ cup dry white wine
2 cups chopped, seeded tomatoes
3 tablespoons tomato paste
1 cup beef stock
1 bay leaf
½ teaspoon sugar
½ teaspoon dried oregano

⅛ teaspoon allspice
salt and pepper to taste

Bechamel Sauce:
3 tablespoons butter
6 tablespoons flour
2 cups milk
1 cup heavy cream
1 teaspoon salt
dash of nutmeg

1 pound lasagna noodles, preferably green
1 pound grated mozzarella cheese
½ cup grated fresh Parmesan cheese

DIRECTIONS:

OVEN TEMPERATURE: 350°

Meat Sauce: Combine the onion, garlic and celery and sauté over low heat in 2 tablespoons butter until golden brown, about 8 minutes. Stir often. Remove to a heavy 3-4 quart saucepan. In the fry pan sauté the sausage and hamburger in olive oil until browned. Break up the lumps and drain excess grease. Add the wine to the meat and cook until it has almost evaporated. Add meat to the saucepan with the onions. Add the remaining sauce ingredients and simmer 1 hour.

Bechamel Sauce: Melt butter over low heat, stir in the flour and cook 2-3 minutes. Stir constantly. Add the milk to the cream and add to the flour mixture. Stir until smooth and thick. Add the salt and nutmeg and set aside.

In a large pot with boiling salted water cook the lasagna noodles and drain. Butter a 9"x13" baking dish. To assemble: layer ¼" of meat sauce on the bottom, ⅓ of the noodles, ⅓ of the bechamel sauce and ⅓ of the mozzarella cheese. Repeat 2 more times, ending with the mozzarella. Sprinkle the top with Parmesan cheese.

Bake in a preheated 350° oven for about 30 minutes or until bubbly.

TIP:
Add 1 to 2 tablespoons of olive oil to the water in which you boil the pasta to keep the water from boiling over and the pasta from sticking together.

SPAGHETTI PRIMAVERA

SERVES 6-8

1 pound spaghetti or spaghettini
2 tablespoons butter or oil
1½ cups coarsely chopped broccoli
1 cup chopped zucchini
1 cup peapods
6 asparagus stalks, sliced
½ cup tiny peas, fresh or frozen
1 tablespoon olive oil
2 tomatoes, chopped
1 teaspoon minced garlic

¼ cup chopped parsley
salt and pepper to taste
¼ cup olive oil
¼ cup pine nuts
1 cup sliced mushrooms
½ cup cream, more if needed
½ cup Parmesan cheese
⅓ cup butter
1 teaspoon dried basil

DIRECTIONS:

Cook the spaghetti with oil in boiling, salted water until barely tender.

Blanch the broccoli, zucchini, peapods, asparagus and peas in boiling water 3 to 4 minutes. Rinse in cold water.

In a medium pan, heat 1 tablespoon olive oil. Add tomatoes, garlic, parsley and salt and pepper to taste. Sauté 2 to 3 minutes and set aside.

Heat ¼ cup olive oil in a skillet and brown pine nuts. Add the mushrooms and blanched vegetables. Simmer a few minutes. Add the spaghetti, cream, Parmesan cheese, butter and basil. Mix with a fork. Top with the sautéed tomatoes and serve immediately.

SPAGHETTI SAUCE WITH ITALIAN SAUSAGE

SERVES 6-8

2 tablespoons butter
¼ cup chopped onion
1 stalk celery, chopped
1 pound hamburger
1 pound Italian sausage
1 · 1-pound can stewed tomatoes
1 · 6-ounce can tomato paste

1 bay leaf
½ teaspoon Italian herbs
2 tablespoons Parmesan cheese
¼ cup water
½ teaspoon garlic salt
salt and pepper to taste

DIRECTIONS:

Sauté onion and celery in butter until transparent. Remove to a crock pot or other large pot.

Brown the hamburger and sausage with the skins on. Cut the sausage into pieces and add to the pot.

Add remaining ingredients and simmer in a crock pot all day or 2 to 3 hours over low heat on the stove.

SALMON STUFFED PASTA SHELLS

SERVES 6-8

1 · 8-ounce package shell shaped
   pasta (25-30)
2 eggs, beaten
2 cups Ricotta cheese
½ cup finely chopped green pepper
¼ cup finely chopped onion
¼ cup minced fresh parsley
¼ cup milk or light cream

½ teaspoon lemon peel grated
½ teaspoon salt
¼ teaspoon ground mace
1 · 15-ounce can salmon, drained
   and flaked
⅓ cup fine dry bread crumbs
⅓ cup grated Parmesan cheese
2 tablespoons melted butter

DIRECTIONS: OVEN TEMPERATURE: 350°

Cook pasta in boiling salted water until just tender. Drain, rinse in cold water, drain again and set aside.

In a medium bowl combine the eggs, ricotta cheese, green pepper, onion, parsley, milk or cream, lemon peel, salt and mace. Stir in the salmon. Spoon the mixture into the cooked pasta shells.

Place the shells, filled side up, in a 13 x 9 x 2 inch baking dish. Add 2 tablespoons of water to the dish, cover and bake at 350 degrees for 30 minutes.

Combine the bread crumbs, Parmesan cheese and butter. Sprinkle over the shells. Bake the shells 5 minutes more, uncovered. Serve hot and garnish with lemon wedges and parsley if desired.

SMOKED SALMON WITH PASTA

SERVES 4

6 tablespoons butter
2 tablespoons shallots, finely chopped
1 clove garlic, minced
¾ pound mushrooms, cleaned and diced
1 teaspoon salt
freshly ground pepper to taste

6-8 ounces smoked salmon
¾ cup heavy cream
½ pound fresh fettuccine
½ pound fresh spinach pasta
½ cup freshly grated Parmesan cheese

DIRECTIONS:

Melt 3 tablespoons of butter in a large skillet. Add the shallots and garlic and sauté over medium heat for a few minutes. Add the mushrooms, salt and pepper. Turn the heat to medium high and cook 3 to 5 minutes, stirring often. Reduce heat to medium, add the salmon and cook 1 minute. Add half the cream and cook until thickened. Set aside.

Bring 4 quarts of salted water to a boil and cook the pasta. Fresh pasta will take only about 1 minute to cook and the spinach pasta will not take that long. Drain the pasta when done.

Melt 3 tablespoons of butter and the rest of the cream in a large skillet. Turn to low, add the pasta, half of the salmon mixture and toss 1 minute. Serve by placing a portion of pasta on a plate. Spoon some extra sauce over the top and sprinkle with grated cheese.

ARTICHOKE FRITTATA

SERVES 6

"A wonderful meatless main dish."

2 · 6-ounce jars marinated artichoke hearts
1 bunch green onions, chopped
1 clove garlic, minced
2 tablespoons minced parsley
10 soda crackers

2 cups grated Cheddar or Swiss cheese
4 eggs, slightly beaten
¼ teaspoon salt
⅛ teaspoon pepper
⅛ teaspoon Tabasco
¼ teaspoon oregano

DIRECTIONS:

OVEN TEMPERATURE: 325°

Drain the artichoke hearts and chop. Reserve the oil from the jars. Heat the oil in a large fry pan and sauté the artichokes, onions, garlic and parsley.

Crumble the soda crackers and mix with the cheese, eggs and spices. Combine with the other ingredients until well blended. Pour into an ungreased 9 x 13 inch pan. Bake in a preheated 325 degree oven for 35 to 40 minutes or until firm to the touch. Cool and cut into 1 inch squares.

HINT:

The frittata may be frozen and reheated in a 325 degree oven for 10 to 12 minutes.

BREAKFAST SOUFFLÉ

SERVES 10-12

"Make ahead and refrigerate overnight!"

10-12 slices day-old bread
1 pound sausage or bacon
½ cup sliced mushrooms (optional)
½ pound Cheddar cheese, grated

12 eggs
1¼ cups milk
salt and pepper to taste

DIRECTIONS:

OVEN TEMPERATURE: 250°

Place the day-old bread (crusts removed) in a buttered 9 x 11 inch baking pan. Bakery bread, not soft "Wonder" bread, is best.

Cook the sausage or bacon and drain. Break the meat into bits and sprinkle over the bread. Sauté the mushrooms and add to the meat. Sprinkle the cheese over this.

Beat the eggs in a blender with the milk, salt and pepper. Pour over the other ingredients and refrigerate over night. (The cheese may float.)

Remove the casserole from the refrigerator 2 hours before cooking to allow it to get to room temperature. Bake for 1 hour in a preheated 250 degree oven. Cut in squares to serve.

HINT:

You may add or change ingredients as you like. Substitute ham for the sausage or bacon, or you may add chopped onion, zucchini, tomatoes or potatoes, if you prefer. This recipe may also be cut in half using a smaller sized dish.

BROCCOLI-CHEESE PIE

YIELD: 8 or 9 Inch Pie

"Not for every night, but wonderful for a dinner party!"

1 medium onion, finely chopped
(about ½ cup)
4 tablespoons butter
2 pounds fresh broccoli, chopped and
parboiled 5 minutes or
3 · 10-ounce packages frozen broccoli,
thawed and drained
3 eggs

½ pound feta cheese, crumbled
¼ cup chopped fresh parsley
2 tablespoons chopped fresh dill
or 1 tablespoon dried dill weed
salt and pepper to taste
½ cup butter, melted
8 filo pastry leaves, room
temperature

DIRECTIONS:

OVEN TEMPERATURE: 350°

Sauté onions in 4 tablespoons butter until golden. Add broccoli and cook 1 minute. Remove from heat.

In large bowl, beat eggs slightly. Add feta cheese, parsley, dill, salt and pepper. Add broccoli mixture and mix well.

Place 9" springform pan on baking sheet to catch drippings. Line it with 6 filo leaves, overlapping the edges. Brush each leaf with melted butter. Pour filling over filo. Bring filo edges up to cover filling. Top with the remaining 2 filo leaves which have been cut into four 9-inch circles, and pour any remaining melted butter over everything.

Bake in a 350 degree preheated oven for 40-45 minutes or until crust is puffy and golden-brown. Cool on rack 10 minutes before serving.

CHEESE ENCHILADAS

SERVES 6

2 tablespoons butter
2 medium onions, chopped
1 · 4-ounce can green chilies
1 · 4½-ounce can sliced olives
½ cup sour cream
6 flour tortillas, softened

¾ pound Monterey Jack cheese
1 · 10-ounce can medium-hot enchilada
sauce
4 ounces grated Cheddar cheese
¼ cup chopped green onions
¼ cup chopped cilantro

DIRECTIONS:

OVEN TEMPERATURE: 350°

Melt the butter in a medium saucepan. Add the chopped onions and cook 2 to 3 minutes. Add half of the chilies, half of the olives and all the sour cream. Heat through and set aside

Soften the tortillas by wrapping them in foil and heating them in a 350 degree oven for 10 minutes. Fill each with 2 tablespoons of the onion mixture. Cut the Monterey Jack cheese into ¼" to ½" wedges and put two in each tortilla. Roll up the tortillas. Place seam side down in a buttered 9 x 13 inch baking dish and pour the enchilada sauce over the top of each tortilla. Sprinkle with cheddar cheese, green onions, cilantro and remaining olives and green chilies.

Bake the enchiladas in a preheated 350 degree oven for 30-40 minutes or until the cheese melts.

CHEESY VEGETABLE BURRITOS

SERVES 8-10

¼ cup butter
1 large onion, thinly sliced
2 cloves garlic, minced
½ pound mushrooms, sliced
1 large green pepper, cut in strips
2 carrots, peeled and thinly sliced
4 medium zucchini,
   sliced in ½" pieces
2 large tomatoes, peeled and

cut in ½" wedges
1 · 4-ounce can diced green chilies
1 can black olives, sliced
1 teaspoon salt
1 teaspoon chili powder
½ teaspoon oregano
½-1 pound Jack cheese, grated
½-1 pound Cheddar cheese, grated
12 flour tortillas

DIRECTIONS:

OVEN TEMPERATURE: 250°

Have all the above ingredients sliced or grated before you start the recipe.

Melt the butter in a large skillet and sauté the onion and garlic for a few minutes. Add the mushrooms, green pepper, carrots, zucchini and tomatoes. Bring the mixture to a boil and simmer, covered, for 10 minutes.

Add the chilies, olives, salt, chili powder and oregano. Boil until the liquid evaporates, about 20 minutes. Sprinkle ½ of the cheeses on top and stir gently until melted. Add more cheese according to taste.

Serve immediately in warmed flour tortillas or place the burritos, rolled up, in a 9 x 13 inch pan in a 250 degree oven. Sprinkle any remaining cheese over the top. You may keep the burritos warm until ready to serve.

CHILI RELLENOS CASSEROLE

SERVES 6-8

1 · 1-pound 10-ounce can whole green
   chilies
1 pound Monterey Jack cheese
1 pound Cheddar cheese, grated
5 eggs
¼ cup flour

1¼ cups milk
½ teaspoon salt
pepper and Tabasco to taste
8 ounces tomato sauce or taco sauce
   (optional)

DIRECTIONS:

OVEN TEMPERATURE: 350°

Open each chili and remove the seeds. Cut the Monterey Jack cheese into strips 1 x 3 inches long and ¼ inch thick. Stuff the cheese strips into the chilies, one into each chili. Arrange half the stuffed chilies in a greased 3 quart casserole. Sprinkle with half of the cheddar cheese. Repeat the layers.

Beat the eggs. Gradually add the flour and milk. Add the salt, pepper and Tabasco. Pour over the chilies. Top with tomato sauce, if desired.

Bake, uncovered, in a preheated 350 degree oven for 45 minutes or until golden brown. Let stand 5 to 10 minutes before serving.

HINT:

This is excellent as a main dish with a tossed salad or as an accompaniment to other Mexican favorites.

GRATIN OF LEEKS AND HAM

SERVES 6-8

12 small leeks
½ teaspoon salt
2 tablespoons unsalted butter
12 thin slices of smoked ham
2 ounces Gruyere cheese, grated

2 ounces Parmesan cheese, grated
3 large eggs
2 large egg yolks
2 cups heavy cream
white pepper to taste

DIRECTIONS:

OVEN TEMPERATURE: 375°

Butter the bottom and sides of a 10 inch quiche pan and set aside.

Wash the leeks and trim a 3 inch section from the white part of each leek. Discard the green tops or save for another use. Arrange the leeks in a layer in a large skillet. Season with salt and add enough water to cover the leeks by ½ inch. Add the butter and bring to a boil, reduce to a simmer and cook covered for 15 minutes or until tender. Drain and dry the leeks thoroughly.

Place a leek on the short end of each ham slice and roll up the ham to enclose the leek. Place the ham rolls, seam side down, spoke fashion in a single layer in the prepared baking dish. Set aside.

Combine ½ of the Parmesan cheese, all of the Gruyere cheese, the eggs, egg yolks, cream and pepper to taste. Beat thoroughly or process in a food processor. Pour over the ham and sprinkle with the remaining Parmesan cheese. Bake in the center of a preheated 375 degree oven for 45 minutes or until the custard is set and the top is lightly browned. Cover loosely with foil and bake another 10 minutes. Cool 10 minutes and serve.

HAM SOUFFLÉ CASSEROLE

SERVES 10-12

2 cups fresh bread crumbs
2 pounds ground ham
1 pound sharp Cheddar cheese, grated
8 eggs

1 tablespoon dry mustard
2 cups milk
1 tablespoon minced parsley

DIRECTIONS:

OVEN TEMPERATURE: 325°

Butter a 9 x 13 inch baking dish and cover with 1 cup of fresh bread crumbs or more if needed to cover the bottom. Over the crumbs spread the ham and cheese. Top this with more fresh bread crumbs, enough to cover it well.

Beat together the eggs, mustard, milk and parsley. Pour this over the ham mixture and refrigerate overnight. Bake in a preheated 325 degree oven for 1 hour or until set.

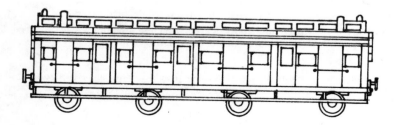

MACARONI AND CHEESE

SERVES 8

¼ cup butter
¼ cup flour
2 cups warm milk
½ teaspoon pepper
½ teaspoon Tabasco sauce

½ cup heavy cream
3 cups sharp, grated Cheddar cheese
8 ounces elbow macaroni, cooked and
   drained

DIRECTIONS: OVEN TEMPERATURE: 350°

Melt the butter in a heavy saucepan over low heat. Add the flour and stir 2 minutes. Gradually add the warm milk, stirring constantly, and heat to boiling. Turn the heat down and simmer a few minutes. Add the pepper, Tabasco sauce, heavy cream and simmer briefly. Stir ¾ of the cheese into the sauce and stir until melted.

Combine the sauce with the cooked macaroni and pour into a greased 2 quart casserole. Sprinkle the remaining cheese over the top. Bake in a preheated 350 degree oven for 30 minutes.

MEATLESS LASAGNE

SERVES 12

6 tablespoons butter
½ cup chopped onion
1 clove garlic, minced
2 · 2-pound 3-ounce cans Italian
   tomatoes
½ pound fresh mushrooms, sliced
½ cup wheat germ
¼ cup milk
3 eggs
1 cup grated Parmesan cheese
½ cup chopped fresh parsley

1 teaspoon salt
½ teaspoon pepper
2 · 6-ounce cans tomato paste
3 cups water
1 tablespoon honey (optional)
1½ teaspoons basil
1½ teaspoons oregano
1 pound lasagna noodles
1 pound ricotta cheese
1 pound mozzarella cheese, grated

DIRECTIONS: OVEN TEMPERATURE: 350°

In a saucepan melt the butter and sauté the onion, garlic and tomatoes for 10 minutes.

In a large fry pan combine the mushrooms, wheat germ, milk, eggs, ½ cup Parmesan cheese, parsley, salt and pepper. Cook until the mushrooms are soft. Add this mixture to the tomatoes. Simmer a few minutes. Add the tomato paste, water, honey, basil and oregano and simmer 45 minutes.

Cook the lasagna noodles and drain.

In a 13 x 9 x 2 inch pan pour in 1 cup of sauce. Cover with ⅓ of the noodles, ⅓ of the mozzarella, ⅓ of the ricotta, 2 tablespoons of Parmesan cheese. Repeat two more times, ending with sauce on top. Sprinkle with remaining Parmesan cheese. Bake in a preheated 350 degree oven for 30 minutes.

QUICHE ELEGANT

SERVES 8

1 · 9"-10" pastry lined pie plate
1½ cups finely chopped ham
½ cup finely chopped onion
1 tablespoon butter
1 · 10-ounce package frozen chopped
   spinach, cooked and drained
1½ cups grated Swiss cheese
½ cup grated Monterey Jack cheese

1 tablespoon flour
4 eggs, beaten
1 cup cream
½ cup milk
¼ teaspoon Tabasco
⅛ teaspoon nutmeg
⅛ teaspoon pepper
½ teaspoon salt

DIRECTIONS:

OVEN TEMPERATURE: 450°

Bake the pastry at 450 degrees to set. Remove from the oven, cool and sprinkle the ham on the bottom of the shell.

Melt the butter in a frying pan and sauté the onion until limp. Sprinkle the onion over the ham. Spread the spinach over this. Mix together the cheese and flour and spread over the spinach. Combine the remaining ingredients, pour into pastry shell and bake in a preheated 450 degree oven for 15 minutes. Reduce the oven to 350 degrees and bake an additional 15 to 20 minutes or until set.

FREEZE AHEAD QUICHE LORRAINE

SERVES 6

1 · 9" pie shell, uncooked, frozen
4 eggs, beaten
1¾ cups half & half
1 teaspoon salt
¼ teaspoon pepper

½ cup mushrooms, sautéed in butter
½ pound bacon, cooked, drained and
   broken into pieces
1 cup grated cheese (Swiss and
   Cheddar are good)

DIRECTIONS:

OVEN TEMPERATURE: 400°

Place the bacon on the bottom of the pie shell. Sprinkle grated cheese over the top. Next add the mushrooms. Mix the beaten eggs, half & half, salt and pepper by hand. Pour over the crust and freeze until ready to use.

Bake the quiche, frozen, in a preheated 400 degree oven for 15 minutes. Reduce the heat to 350 degrees and bake 45 minutes more or until a knife inserted into the quiche comes out clean. Bake in 350 degree oven for 1 hour if not frozen.

HINT:

This is an excellent basic quiche recipe which can be changed by using different fillings such as crab, shrimp, ham, broccoli, or chicken.

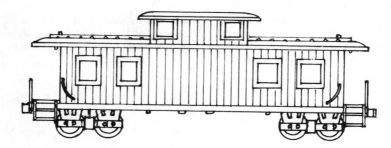

SPINACH QUICHE

SERVES 6

1 · 9" pastry shell
1 · 10-ounce package frozen chopped spinach
6 eggs
1 · 3-ounce package cream cheese
¼ cup grated Cheddar cheese
3 green onions, finely chopped

½ cup slivered almonds
3 tablespoons minced parsley
½ teaspoon salt
¼ teaspoon pepper
3 tablespoons Parmesan cheese
1 large tomato, cut in wedges

DIRECTIONS: OVEN TEMPERATURE: 425°

Cook the spinach and drain thoroughly; set aside.

Combine the eggs, cream cheese and Cheddar cheese. Stir in the green onions, spinach, almonds, parsley, salt and pepper. Pour into a pastry shell, sprinkle with 1 tablespoon Parmesan cheese and bake in a preheated 425 degree oven for 15 minutes.

Top with tomato wedges and 1 tablespoon Parmesan cheese and bake 4 minutes more. Let stand 10 minutes before serving.

STUFFED EGGS MORNAY

SERVES 4-6

Mornay Sauce:
¼ cup butter
3 tablespoons flour
¾ cup chicken broth
¾ cup cream
2 egg yolks, slightly beaten
⅓ cup grated Parmesan cheese

Stuffed Eggs:
6 hard boiled eggs
1 teaspooon lemon juice
½ teaspoon finely chopped onion
¼ teaspoon salt
⅛ teaspoon pepper
1 cup crab or shrimp meat
1 tablespoon Mornay sauce

DIRECTIONS:

Mornay sauce: Melt 3 tablespoons butter in a 2 to 3 quart pan. Add the flour and cook 1 to 2 minutes. Add the broth and cream, stirring until it boils, and cook another 2 minutes. Stir 3 tablespoons of the sauce into the egg yolks and then stir the yolks into the sauce. Cook 3 to 4 minutes. Cool. Add the cheese and remaining butter and stir. Pour the sauce into a chafing dish to keep it hot while preparing the eggs.

Stuffed eggs: Halve the hard boiled eggs, remove the yolks and mash them in a bowl. Mix in the lemon juice, onion, salt and pepper. Add the crab or shrimp and 1 tablespoon of Mornay sauce. Spoon this mixture back into the egg whites, put into the chafing dish and spoon the sauce over the top.

Sprinkle with parsley and serve with English muffins.

HINT:

This can be made ahead and reheated in a chafing dish.

BANANA CAKE

SERVES 12

1 cup sugar
½ cup melted butter
2 eggs
1 teaspoon vanilla
2 cups flour
1 teaspoon baking soda

1 teaspoon baking powder
½ teaspoon salt
3 bananas, mashed
½ cup sour milk (add ½ teaspoon
   white vinegar to fresh milk)

DIRECTIONS:

OVEN TEMPERATURE: 350°

Cream butter; add sugar, eggs and vanilla. Sift together flour, baking soda, baking powder, and salt. Alternately add bananas, milk, and dry ingredients to the butter and egg mixture. Mix well. Pour into greased 9 x 13 inch pan. Bake in preheated 350 degree oven for 30 minutes. Cool and frost with Butter Frosting. (See index.)

BLACK BOTTOM CUPCAKES

YIELD: 2 Dozen Cupcakes

Easy Method:
1 package Devils food cake mix.
Make batter according to package directions.

Scratch Method:
½ cup cocoa
3 cups sifted flour
2 cups sugar
1 teaspoon salt
2 teaspoon soda

¾ cup oil
2 tablespoons vinegar
2 teaspoons vanilla
1 egg
2 cups cold water

DIRECTIONS:

OVEN TEMPERATURE: 350°

Mix cocoa, flour, sugar, salt and soda in large bowl. Make four depressions in batter. Mix oil, vinegar, vanilla, egg in small bowl and pour about one fourth in each depression, using all the mix. Add water and blend until lumps disappear. Fill 24 to 30 muffin cups two thirds full. Add 2 teaspoons filling to each. Bake at 350 degrees for 25 minutes. Cool before frosting.

Filling:
1 · 8-ounce package cream cheese,
   softened
1 egg
1 teaspoon vanilla

⅓ cup sugar
6-ounce package semi-sweet
   chocolate chips

Combine all ingredients.

Black Bottom Frosting:
¾ cup butter
3 tablespoons sour cream
2 tablespoons peanut butter

5 tablespoons cocoa
1 · 16-ounce box powdered sugar
4 tablespoons evaporated milk

THIS MAKES ENOUGH FROSTING FOR TWO BATCHES CUPCAKES. Mix all ingredients, cream to spreading consistency.

BROWNIE CAKE

YIELD: 1 Cake

⅔ cup cooking oil
5 tablespoons cocoa
½ cup evaporated milk
4 tablespoons water
2 cups sugar
2 tablespoons light corn syrup

2 teaspoons vanilla
1½ cups flour
1 teaspoon salt
1 teaspoon baking powder
4 eggs

DIRECTIONS:

OVEN TEMPERATURE: 350°

In bowl, blend cooking oil and cocoa. Stir in, gradually, evaporated milk, water; add sugar, light corn syrup and vanilla. Set aside.

Mix flour, salt, and baking powder together. Mix with cocoa mixture.

Beat in eggs. Pour in 9 x 13 inch pan; bake at 350 degrees, for 40 to 45 minutes.

CHOCOLATE 'ICEBOX' CAKE

YIELD: One 9 x 13 inch cake

2 cups graham cracker crumbs
  (24 single crackers)
¾ cup margarine, melted
¾ cup brown sugar
½ cup chopped walnuts

½ teaspoon cinnamon
1 · 18.25-ounce chocolate cake mix
½ pint whipping cream
2 to 3 tablespoons baking cocoa
⅓ cup powdered sugar

DIRECTIONS:

OVEN TEMPERATURE: 350°

Grease 9 x 13 inch baking pan.

Roll graham crackers very fine and combine them with the melted margarine, sugar, nuts and cinnamon in a bowl.

Mix the chocolate cake mix as directed on package.

Spoon half of the graham cracker mix (1¾ cups) into bottom of pan. Pour half of the chocolate cake batter over cracker mixture (approximately 2¾ cups). Spoon rest of cracker mixture over batter. Pour remaining batter on top.

Bake at 350 degrees for 35 to 40 minutes or until cake springs away from sides of pan. Cool.

Whip cream, adding sifted cocoa and powdered sugar gradually.

Spread cream over cake. Refrigerate overnight.

COCOA APPLE CAKE

YIELD: 1 Cake

"Moist and flavorful"

3 eggs
2 cups sugar
1 cup margarine
½ cup water
2 tablespoons cocoa
2½ cups flour
1 teaspoon baking soda

1 teaspoon cinnamon
1 teaspoon allspice
1 cup chopped nuts
1 cup chocolate chips
2 apples, peeled and chopped,
    or grated
1 tablespoon vanilla

DIRECTIONS:
OVEN TEMPERATURE: 325°

In a large bowl, beat eggs, sugar, margarine and water. Add dry ingredients, beat. Fold in apples, nuts and chips, and vanilla. Pour cake into a greased and floured 10-inch tube or bundt pan. Sprinkle with powdered sugar or drizzle with chocolate glaze. Bake at 325 degrees for 60 to 70 minutes.

COINTREAU GLAZED POUNDCAKE

YIELD: 1 Cake

1 cup unsalted butter
2½ cups sugar
5 large eggs
4 cups flour, sifted
2½ teaspoons baking powder
½ teaspoon salt
1⅓ cups whole milk

grated rind of two bright skinned
    oranges

Glaze
¾ cup sugar
½ cup orange juice
2 tablespoons orange liqueur

DIRECTIONS:
OVEN TEMPERATURE: 350°

Beat butter and sugar; add eggs one at a time, beating after each.

Sift flour, baking powder and salt together, add dry ingredients alternating with milk to butter sugar mixture.

Pour into greased and floured bundt pan. Bake 1 hour at 350 degrees or until toothpick comes out clean. Cool in pan 15 minutes. Invert on baking rack. Brush with glaze allowing as much glaze to soak in as possible.

Glaze: Cook in small saucepan until bubbly and sugar is dissolved.

HINT:
Cake is best served second day.

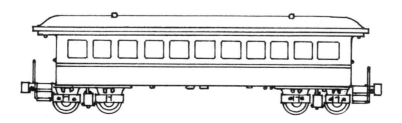

DATE CHOCOLATE CHIP CAKE

YIELD: 24 Small Servings

"A delightful combination"

1 cup chopped dates
1 teaspoon baking soda
1½ cups boiling water
¾ cup shortening
1 cup sugar
2 eggs
2¼ cups flour
1¼ teaspoon baking powder

1 teaspoon cinnamon
½ teaspoon salt
1 teaspoon vanilla

Topping
½ cup brown sugar, packed
½ cup finely chopped nuts
½ cup chocolate chips

DIRECTIONS:

OVEN TEMPERATURE: 350°

Sprinkle baking soda over dates; cover with boiling water, let cool. Cream shortening, sugar, eggs, add to dates. Sift dry ingredients, add vanilla and mix well. Combine topping ingredients and sprinkle on top.

Bake in 9 x 13 inch pan at 350 degrees for 30 minutes.

FRESH PEACH CAKE

YIELD: One 9 x 11 inch cake

1½ cups sugar
2 eggs
¾ cup oil
1⅓ cups mashed peaches
  (about 4 medium peaches)
2 cups flour
1 teaspoon baking soda
1 teaspoon cinnamon
¼ teaspoon salt

Frosting:
1 cup sugar
1 teaspoon flour
½ cup margarine
2 egg yolks
⅔ cup evaporated milk
  (or ½ cup regular milk)
1 teaspoon vanilla
½ cup chopped pecans (optional)

DIRECTIONS:

OVEN TEMPERATURE: 350°

Mix sugar, eggs and oil with a beater. Stir in mashed peaches. Sift together the flour, baking soda, cinnamon and salt. Add to the batter and stir until well mixed.

Grease and flour one 9 x 13 inch cake pan or three 8 or 9 round pans. Pour batter into the pans and bake at 350 degrees for 40 minutes. Cool and frost.

Frosting: In a small sauce pan, combine sugar, flour, margarine, egg yolks and milk. Boil on medium heat for 10 minutes, stirring constantly. Add vanilla and nuts. Pour over the 9 x 13 inch cake or between the layers of the layer cake.

VARIATION:

For a fresh peach taste, peel and slice 4 to 5 fresh peaches and lay on top of cooled cake. Pour frosting over the peaches.

GOOD AND EASY CARROT CAKE

SERVES 8

1½ cups salad oil
3 eggs
1 · 7-ounce can crushed pineapple, drained
2 teaspoons vanilla
2 cups flour
2 teaspoons baking soda
1 teaspoon salt
2 cups white sugar

2 teaspoons cinnamon
1 · 7-ounce bag shredded coconut
2 cups shredded carrots
1 cup chopped walnuts

Frosting:
2 · 3-ounce packages cream cheese
⅓ cup butter, softened
1 · 1-pound box powdered sugar

DIRECTIONS:

OVEN TEMPERATURE: 350°

Cake: In a large bowl combine the oil and the eggs. Fold in the pineapple and the vanilla. Stir in the flour, and the remaining ingredients. Pour into a greased 9 x 13 inch cake pan. Bake at 350 degrees for 35 to 45 minutes. Cool and frost.

Frosting: Cream the cream cheese and butter. Add the sugar and beat until smooth.

HUMMINGBIRD CAKE

SERVES 10-12

3 cups flour
2 cups sugar
1 teaspoon salt
1 teaspoon soda
3 eggs, beaten
1½ cup oil
1½ teaspoon vanilla
1 · 8-ounce can pineapple

1 cup nuts, chopped
1 cup chopped bananas

Frosting:
½ cup butter margarine
1 · 8-ounce package cream cheese
1 pound powdered sugar
2 teaspoons vanilla

DIRECTIONS:

OVEN TEMPERATURE: 350°

Combine dry ingredients in a large bowl. Add eggs and salad oil stirring by hand until dry ingredients are moistened. Do not beat with mixer. Stir in vanilla, pineapple, nuts, and bananas. Spoon batter into three well greased and floured 9-inch cake pans or one large 9 x 13 inch pan. Bake at 350 degrees for 25 to 30 minutes for layers or 40 to 50 minutes for large pan, or until inserted toothpick comes out clean.

Cool in pans for 10 minutes then remove from pans and cool completely. If baked in rectangular pan leave in pan and frost when completely cool. Frost layers and refrigerate.

For frosting cream all ingredients together until fluffy.

LEMON CAKE

SERVES 12-16

1 · 18½-ounce package yellow cake mix
4 eggs
½ cup oil
1 cup water
1 · 3-ounce package lemon-flavored
  gelatin

Icing:
2 cups sifted powdered
  sugar
grated rind of 2 lemons
juice of 2 lemons

DIRECTIONS:

OVEN TEMPERATURE: 350°

Combine all cake ingredients and mix with electric beater for 4 minutes. Pour into a buttered and floured 9 x 13 inch pan. Bake 40 minutes, in preheated 350 degreee oven. Punch full of holes with heavy meat fork and pour on icing.

Icing: Combine all ingredients until sugar is thoroughly mixed. If desired, top with whipped cream before serving.

NOTE:

Use high altitude directions on cake mix.

SURPRISE POUND CAKE

YIELD: 1 Cake

Cake
1 · 6-ounce package (1 cup)
  chocolate chips
1⅓ cups milk, divided
3 cups unsifted flour
2 teaspoons baking powder
½ teaspoon salt
1 cup butter, softened
2 cups sugar
3 eggs
2½ teaspoons vanilla

Filling
1 cup heavy cream
2 tablespoons powdered sugar
1 teaspoon vanilla

Glaze
1 · 6-ounce package (1 cup)
  chocolate chips
2 tablespoons white corn syrup
2 tablespoons water

DIRECTIONS:

OVEN TEMPERATURE: 350°

In double boiler over hot (not boiling) water, combine chocolate chips and ⅓ cup milk, stir until chocolate chips melt and mixture is smooth. Remove from heat and set aside.

In small bowl, combine flour, baking powder and salt; set aside.

In large bowl, combine butter and sugar, beat until creamy, about five minutes. Add eggs, one at a time, beating well after each addition. Alternately blend in flour mixture with remaining 1 cup milk. Blend in melted chocolate mixture and vanilla extract. Pour into greased and floured 10 inch tube pan. Bake at 350 degrees for 1 hour or until inserted toothpick comes out clean.

Cool 15 minutes, remove from pan, cool completely. Cut off top layer of cake about ½ inch from top edge. Hollow out a half inch deep tunnel in bottom part of cake leaving a half inch border all around the inside and outside edges. Cut hollowed out cake pieces into half inch cubes. Fold into filling. Spoon filling into tunnel. Replace top of cake.

Drizzle top with glaze. Serve remaining glaze over cake slices.

Filling: In small bowl, combine heavy cream, powdered sugar and vanilla extract, beat until soft peaks form.

Glaze: Combine over hot water, chocolate chips, corn syrup, and water. Heat until chocolate melts and mixture is smooth.

PUMPKIN LOAF CAKE

1¾ cups flour
1 teaspoon baking soda
½ teaspoon salt
1 teaspoon cinnamon
½ teaspoon nutmeg
¼ teaspoon ginger
¼ teaspoon ground cloves
1 cup butter, soft
1 cup sugar
2 eggs

¾ cup pumpkin
¾ cup semi-sweet chocolate chips
¾ cup walnuts (chopped)

Glaze
½ cup powdered sugar (sifted)
⅛ teaspoon nutmeg
½ teaspoon cinnamon
1 to 2 tablespoons cream

DIRECTIONS: OVEN TEMPERATURE: 350°

Grease bottom and sides of loaf size pan. Combine flour, soda, salt and spices. Set aside in larger bowl. Cream butter, gradually adding sugar. Blend eggs, beating well.

At low speed, add dry ingredients to butter mixture, alternating with pumpkin. Start and end with flour. Stir in chocolate chips and walnuts. Pour into pan and bake 60 minutes at 350 degrees.

For glaze: Combine powdered sugar, nutmeg, cinnamon. Blend in enough cream until glaze consistency.

SNOW BALL CAKE

YIELD: 1 Cake

"An old favorite"

1½ cups milk, scalded
5 egg yolks
1 cup sugar
¼ teaspoon salt
1½ teaspoons vanilla
1 tablespoon gelatin (dissolved in
   ¼ cup water)

1 cup chopped pecans
½ cup maraschino cherries
   (cut in 8ths)
1 pint whipping cream, whipped
1 large angel food cake

DIRECTIONS:

In a double boiler combine scalded milk, egg yolks, sugar, salt and vanilla. Cook over medium heat stirring constantly for 15 minutes or until thickened. (Be careful this will burn easily.) Remove from heat and add dissolved gelatin. Cool. Fold in nuts, cherries and whipped cream.

Split cake in half or thirds. Frost each layer with a generous layer of custard and stack together. Frost top and sides with remaining custard. Cover and refrigerate 24 hours before serving.

SUGGESTION:

Leftover egg whites might be used for Chocolate Divinity or Winnie's Cookies. (See index.)

SOUR CREAM POUND CAKE

YIELD: 1 Cake

"Perhaps a touch of lemon or an orange rind to top a perfect cake."

1 cup butter
3 cups sugar
6 eggs, separated
1 teaspoon vanilla extract
1 teaspoon lemon juice

1 teaspoon grated lemon rind
¼ teaspoon baking soda
1 cup sour cream
2½ cups flour

DIRECTIONS:

OVEN TEMPERATURE: 325°

Grease and flour bundt cake pan or angel food pan. Beat butter with 2½ cups sugar. Add egg yolks one at a time, beat after each. Add vanilla, lemon juice and soda. In separate bowl, beat egg whites with remaining ½ cup sugar, adding 1 tablespoon at a time. Beat until stiff and glossy. Set aside. Add sour cream and flour alternately to butter and egg mixture. Fold in egg whites. Pour into prepared pan. Bake in slow oven, 325 degrees for 1 hour and 30 minutes, or until pick comes out clean. Cool on rack 10 minutes. Remove from pan.

TEMPTATION CAKE

SERVES 16

3 cups unsifted flour
1½ teaspoons baking soda
1½ teaspoons cinnamon
1 teaspoon nutmeg
¼ teaspoon ground cloves
1¾ cups sugar

¾ cup butter, room temperature
3 eggs
1½ cups applesauce
1¼ cups chopped walnuts
2 cups semi-sweet chocolate pieces
2 tablespoons powdered sugar

DIRECTIONS:

OVEN TEMPERATURE: 350°

Generously grease and flour 10-inch tube pan or a 12 cup bundt pan. Set aside.

In large bowl, combine flour, soda, cinnamon, nutmeg and cloves. Set aside.

In large mixer bowl at medium speed, cream sugar and butter until light and fluffy, scraping sides of bowl occasionally. Add eggs, one at a time, beating well after each. Reduce speed to low. Add flour mixture alternating with applesauce. Beat until smooth.

Fold in 1 cup chocolate pieces and ¾ cup of the chopped nuts. Pour batter into pan. Sprinkle remaining chocolate pieces and nuts on top of batter. Bake 1 hour at 350 degrees or until inserted toothpick comes out clean. Place on wire rack and cool completely before removing from pan.

Cake can be baked and frozen for one month. Thaw, wrapped at room temperature for three hours. To serve, sprinkle with powdered sugar.

ALMOND ROCA

YIELD: 2 Pounds Candy

2 cups sugar
2 cups butter (1 pound)
⅓ cup water

*2 cups sliced almonds
2 · 8-ounce Hershey bars –
    broken into pieces

DIRECTIONS:

Mix sugar, butter, and water in a large heavy saucepan. Cook on high, stirring until sugar is dissolved. Reduce to medium high and cook until tan – 276 degrees (285 sea level).

While cooking, spread almonds in an 11 x 15 inch buttered jelly roll pan. Pour hot candy on almonds. Cool slightly. Sprinkle with broken chocolate. Let melt. Smooth evenly with knife. Break into pieces when completley cool.

*If preferred, almonds can be toasted.

TIP:

Pour out candy when cooked, DO NOT scrape pan or the texture may be grainy. Scape left over candy in cup with cool water for children to taste.

CHOCONUT CARAMEL BARS

YIELD: 32 Bars

1 · 11-ounce package milk chocolate
   morsels
2 tablespoons shortening
1 · 14-ounce package caramels

5 tablespoons margarine
2 tablespoons water
1 cup coarsely chopped peanuts

DIRECTIONS:

Melt chocolate and shortening over hot (not boiling) water. Stir until mixture is smooth. Remove from heat.

Pour ½ of melted chocolate into an 8-inch foil lined square pan; spread evenly. Refrigerate until firm (about 15 minutes).

Return remaining chocolate mixture to *low* heat.

In a separate saucepan, combine over boiling water, caramels, margarine and water. Stir until caramels melt and mixture is smooth. Stir in nuts.

Pour into the chocolate-lined pan and spread evenly. Refrigerate until tacky, about 15 minutes. Top with remaining melted chocolate and spread evenly to cover caramel filling. Return to refrigerator and chill until firm (about 1 hour). Cut into 1 by 2 inch rectangles and refrigerate until ready to serve.

TIP:

Never double a recipe. If a larger amount of candy is desired, make another batch or two.

CRAZY CRUNCH

YIELD: 2 Pounds

2 quarts popped pop corn
1⅓ cups pecans
⅔ cup almonds
1⅓ cups sugar

1 cup butter
½ cup light corn syrup
1 teaspoon vanilla

DIRECTIONS:

Mix popcorn and nuts in large container.

Combine sugar, butter and syrup in 1½ quart sauce pan. Bring to a boil over medium heat, stirring constantly. Boil, stirring occasionally, 10 to 15 minutes or until mixture turns a light caramel color. Remove from heat. Stir in vanilla.

Pour over popped corn and nuts, mix to coat well. Spread to dry. Break apart; store in tightly covered container.

CHOCOLATE DIVINITY

YIELD: 36 Pieces

5 cups sugar
1 cup light corn syrup
1 cup water
½ teaspoon salt
4 egg whites

2 teaspoons vanilla
4 squares (4 ounces) unsweetened
   chocolate, melted
½ cup pistachio nuts,
   coarsely chopped

DIRECTIONS:

TEMPERATURE: 260°
Hard ball stage

In 3 quart saucepan, combine sugar, corn syrup, water, and salt. Cook stirring constantly until sugar dissolves. Cook over medium heat, without stirring, to hard ball stage (260 degrees). Meanwhile, in large mixer bowl, beat egg whites until stiff peaks form. Gradually pour syrup over egg whites, beating at high speed on electric mixer. Add vanilla and beat until candy begins to hold its shape, 5 to 6 minutes. Beat in chocolate, beat 2 to 3 minutes more if necessary. Pour into buttered 10 x 15 x 1½ inch jelly roll pan. Spread evenly in pan. Top with pistachio nuts. Cut in squares when firm.

ENGLISH TOFFEE

YIELD: 24 Pieces

1 quart pecans or walnuts
1 · 8-ounce Hershey bar
2½ cups sugar

½ cup water
¼ cup light corn syrup
1 pound butter (not margarine)

DIRECTIONS:

Prepare nuts, 3 cups chopped coarse and 1 cup chopped fine. Butter a 10 x 15 inch cookie sheet with sides, or large roaster. Spread the coarsely chopped nuts in pan, save the finely chopped nuts for the topping. Grate chocolate bar by hand or in a blender. Save for topping.

In a large pan combine sugar, water, syrup and butter and cook to 280 degrees. Pour over nuts, then sprinkle grated chocolate over candy and then finely chopped nuts. When cool, break into pieces.

HINT:

Nuts and chocolate may be prepared while candy is cooking.

LICORICE CARAMELS

YIELD: 50 to 60 Caramels

1 cup butter or margarine
1 · 14-ounce can sweetened condensed
   milk
1½ cups light corn syrup

¼ teaspoon salt
2 cups sugar
¾ teaspoon black food paste coloring
¾ teaspoon anise oil or anise flavoring

DIRECTIONS:

Slowly melt butter in heavy large pan. Use fork to swirl butter up sides of pan to prevent sugar crystals. When melted, add rest of ingredients, except food paste and flavoring.

Turn heat to medium—medium high, cook and stir constantly with flat bottom wooden spoon. (Do not cook on high, stir the whole time) Cook to 234 degrees. Remove from heat; add food paste and flavoring, mix in. Pour into 9 x 13 inch pan that has been buttered.

Let set ovennight in a cool place. Cut in squares and wrap in waxed paper.

HINT:

For great caramel apples, omit black food paste and anise oil, and add 2 teaspoons vanilla.

PEANUT BRITTLE

YIELD: 1½ to 2 pounds

3 cups sugar
1 cup glucose or 1¼ cups white
   karo syrup
1 cup water
¼ cup butter

½ teaspoon salt
1 teaspoon soda
1 teaspoon vanilla
1 pound raw spanish peanuts

DIRECTIONS:

Grease 2 cookie sheets or marble slab with margarine. Combine sugar, syrup and water in large heavy saucepan (3 quart size). Cook over high heat and stir until boiling. Turn down to low, cover and steam for 3 minutes. Remove lid, turn heat to medium high, cook until starts to thicken. Add peanuts, do not stir until it boils again, then stir gently from bottom of pan to keep from burning. Cook to 280 degrees and add butter. Cook to 295 degrees and remove from heat.

After removing from heat, add salt, soda and vanilla, which have been mixed together. Stir to mix in. Pour onto buttered marble slab or cookie sheets and stretch as thin as possible with tongs or forks. When cool break into pieces.

SOUR CREAM FUDGE

SERVES 12

32-ounces of white chocolate
1 · 7-ounce jar marshmallow cream
1 tablespoon vanilla
2 cups walnuts, chopped

4 cups sugar
¼ pound butter
1 pint sour cream

DIRECTIONS:

Combine white chocolate, marshmallow cream, vanilla, nuts. Set aside. Combine sugar, butter, sour cream in saucepan. Heat until mixture boils, stirring constantly. Cook 5 minutes while boiling. Fold into chocolate mixture until smooth.

Pour into buttered 8 x 8 inch dish. Cool in refrigerator. Cut into pieces.

ALMOND COOKIES

YIELD: 3 Dozen Cookies

"Easy and great tasting."

1 cup butter or margarine, softened
1 cup sugar
1 egg, beaten
¾ cup ground blanched almonds
   (3 ounces)

1 teaspoon almond extract
2½ cups flour
1½ teaspoons baking powder
dash of salt
36 to 40 blanched almonds

DIRECTIONS:
OVEN TEMPERATURE: 350°

Cream butter and sugar together in large bowl. Beat in egg, ground almonds, and extract.

Stir together flour, baking powder and salt. Gradually stir into butter mixture.

Knead into a ball. Then shape into 1½ inch balls. Flatten with a smooth bottom glass lightly dipped in flour to keep from sticking. Top with 1 whole blanched almond for each cookie. Cookies should be about an inch apart on baking sheet. Bake at 350 degrees for 10 to 12 minutes or until pale golden at edges.

CARROT COOKIES WITH ORANGE FROSTING

YIELD:

1 cup butter
¾ cup sugar
1 egg
1 cup cooked mashed carrots
2 cups flour
¼ teaspoon salt
2 teaspoons baking powder
1 teaspoon vanilla extract

Icing
¼ cup butter
2 cups powdered sugar
3 tablespoons orange
  juice
1 tablespoon orange
  rind

DIRECTIONS:
OVEN TEMPERATURE: 375°

Cream butter and sugar; add egg and carrots.

Sift flour, salt, baking powder together and add to butter mixture. Add vanilla.

Drop by teaspoon onto cookie sheet and bake at 375 degrees for about 10 minutes or until done. Test for doneness as you would a cake.

Icing: Cream butter and sugar, add orange juice and rind. Spread on cookies.

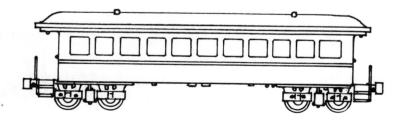

CHOCOLATE COVERED CHERRY COOKIES

YIELD: 56 Cookies —
One for each cherry

"This is a great recipe."

2¼ cups flour
¾ cup cocoa
¼ teaspoon salt
¼ teaspoon baking powder
¼ teaspoon baking soda
¾ cup margarine, or butter, softened

1½ cup sugar
2 medium eggs
2¼ teaspoon vanilla
2 · 6½-ounce jar maraschino cherries
1 · 6-ounce package semi-sweet chocolate chips
½ cup sweetened condensed milk

DIRECTIONS:

OVEN TEMPERATURE: 350°

In small bowl stir flour, cocoa, powder, salt, baking powder and soda; set aside.

In a large bowl, mix butter and sugar on low speed until fluffy. Add eggs and vanilla. Gradually add dry ingredients. Shape dough into 1 inch balls. Place on ungreased cookie sheet. Press down center of dough with thumb.

Drain marashino cherries, reserving juice. Place one cherry in center of each cookie.

In small saucepan combine chocolate chips and sweetened condensed milk. Heat until chocolate is melted. Stir in 3 teaspoons of reserved cherry juice. Spoon about 1 teaspoon frosting over each cherry. Bake in oven at 350 degrees for 10 minutes.

CHOCOLATE SNOW CRACKLES

YIELD: 3 Dozen Cookies

3 eggs
½ cup oil
2 cups sugar
2 teaspoons vanilla
7 tablespoons cocoa

½ teaspoon salt
2 teaspoons baking powder
2-2½ cups flour
powdered sugar

DIRECTIONS:

OVEN TEMPERATURE: 350°

Mix eggs, oil, sugar, and vanilla. Add cocoa, salt and baking powder. Blend in 2 cups flour. Add more if dough is sticky.

Chill 1 hour or longer. Roll into 1 inch balls; roll in powdered sugar and place on cookie sheet. Cookies will spread and "crackle" as they bake. Bake at 350 for 6 to 8 minutes.

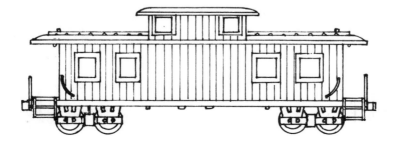

DOUBLE-CHOCOLATE CRINKLES

YIELD: 70 Cookies

4-ounces unsweetened chocolate
½ cup shortening
2 cups sugar
2 teaspoons vanilla
4 eggs

2 cups all-purpose flour
2 teaspoons baking powder
½ teaspoon salt
1 · 6-ounce package chocolate chips
1 cup powdered sugar, sifted

DIRECTIONS:

OVEN TEMPERATURE: 375°

Melt chocolate and shortening together in the top of a double boiler over hot, but not boiling, water. Stir in sugar. Place mixture in a medium bowl. Cool. Beat until blended. Add vanilla. Beat in eggs, 1 at a time, mixing well after each addition.

In another medium bowl, sift flour, baking powder and salt. Stir flour mixture into chocolate mixture. Stir in chocolate chips. Refrigerate dough several hours or overnight.

Lightly grease baking sheets, set aside. Break off small pieces of chilled dough and form into 1 inch balls. Place powdered sugar in a shallow bowl. Roll cookie in sugar, covering them completely. Place cookies 2 inches apart on prepared baking sheets. Bake 10 minutes at 375 degrees. Cookies will be very soft, but will firm as they cool.

DOUBLE PEANUT BUTTER COOKIES

YIELD: 2 Dozen

1½ cups sifted flour
½ cup sugar
½ teaspoon soda
½ teaspoon cinnamon
¼ teaspoon salt

½ cup shortening
½ cup crunchy peanut butter
¼ cup light corn syrup
1 tablespoon milk
extra peanut butter

DIRECTIONS:

OVEN TEMPERATURE: 350°

Sift dry ingredients. Cut in shortening and peanut butter until crumbly. Blend in syrup and milk.

Shape in 2 inch roll and chill 1 hour. Slice in ⅛ inch thick, slices.

Place slices on ungreased cookie sheet. Spread with ½ teaspoon peanut butter. Top with another slice and seal edges with fork.

Bake at 350 degrees for 12 minutes.

GINGER COOKIES

YIELD: 4 Dozen Cookies

"Chewy"

¾ cup shortening or margarine
1 cup sugar
¼ cup molasses
1 egg
2 cups flour

2 teaspoons baking soda
½ teaspoon salt
¾ teaspoon ginger
1 teaspoon cinnamon

DIRECTIONS:

OVEN TEMPERATURE: 350°

Cream shortening and sugar. Add molasses and egg mix. Add dry ingredients and mix all. Roll into balls and roll in sugar. Place on a lightly greased cookie sheet and bake at 350 degrees for 7 to 10 minutes. Don't overbake. They should be chewy.

MELT-A-WAYS

YIELD: 5 Dozen

"Everyone's favorite little bite."

1 cup butter
¾ cup sifted
  cornstarch
⅓ cup powdered
  sugar
1 cup flour

Melt-A-Way Frosting
3 ounces cream cheese
1 teaspoon vanilla
1 cup powdered sugar
couple drops of milk
couple drops of coloring

DIRECTIONS:

OVEN TEMPERATURE: 350°

Beat butter until very soft. Add cornstarch, sugar and flour. Mix very well. Drop ½ to 1-inch balls on ungreased cookie sheet. Bake at 350 degrees for 10 to 12 minutes or until set and very lightly browned. Cool.

Combine all ingredients for frosting and beat until smooth. Drop a dab on top of each cookie.

TIP:

Let cookies cool on a wire rack — in a single layer, never stacked or overlapped, and cool completely before stacking them on a plate or storing them. To keep cookies fresh, store them in an airtight container, but do not store moist cookies in the same container with crisp cookies.

RUGGELA

YIELD: 50 Cookies

1 cup butter or margarine
8-ounces cream cheese
2 cups flour
¾ cup sugar

1 tablespoon cinnamon
¾ cup finely chopped nuts
1 to 2 tablespoons milk

DIRECTIONS:

OVEN TEMPERATURE: 375°

Mix butter and cream cheese; mix in flour. Divide into four balls. Wrap each ball in waxed paper and refrigerate over night.

Roll each ball into large circle on floured board. Brush surface of dough with milk. Sprinkle with a mixture of sugar, cinnamon and nuts. Cut circles into 12 to 16 pie shaped wedges. Roll crescent from outside circle toward center. Place on baking sheet point down and bake at 375 degrees for 20 to 25 minutes, or until lightly browned.

May be reheated to freshen, but not usually necessary.

HINT:

These freeze well.

SESAME SEED COOKIES WITH BROWNED BUTTER SESAME ICING

YIELD: 3 Dozen

"Toasted nutty flavor."

Cookies
½ cup butter or margarine
⅓ cup sesame seeds
½ cup butter
1 cup sugar
1 egg and 2 tablespoons water
2 cups flour
1 teaspoon baking powder

¼ teaspoon salt
Icing
3 cups powdered sugar
3 tablespoons milk
1 teaspoon vanilla
Browned butter and sesame mixture
    (remaining from making cookies)

DIRECTIONS:

OVEN TEMPERATURE: 350°

Brown ½ cup butter and sesame seeds over low heat until golden. Set aside.

Mix butter, sugar, and egg mixed with water. Add 2 tablespoons seeds to sugar mixture (from browned butter mixture). Stir dry ingredients together; blend into sugar mixture.

Drop by spoonfuls on ungreased baking sheet. Flatten dough with bottom of greased glass dipped in sugar. Bake at 350 degrees for 8 minutes for a chewy cookie, or until lightly browned for a regular cookie.

Icing: Blend all ingredients together until smooth. Frost cookies.

SOFT SUGAR COOKIES

YIELD: 3 Dozen Large Cookies

4 cups flour
¾ teaspoon salt
4 teaspoon baking powder
1 cup sugar

½ cup margarine or butter
2 eggs
½ cup milk
1 teaspoon vanilla

DIRECTIONS:

OVEN TEMPERATURE: 350°

In small bowl, mix 2 cups of the flour with salt, baking powder and set aside.

In large bowl, cream margarine and sugar. Add eggs, milk and vanilla. Gradually mix dry ingredients into wet. The dough will be sticky and moist. Add remaining two cups flour to make dough easy to handle. Roll out and cut with cookie cutters.

Bake on ungreased sheet at 350 degrees for 8 minutes. Frost.

WINNIE'S COOKIES

YIELD: 3 to 4 Dozen Cookies

"Meringues"

4 egg whites (room temperature)
¼ teaspoon cream of tartar
½ teaspoon salt
1 teaspoon vanilla

¾ cup sugar
12-ounce package semi-sweet
    chocolate chips

DIRECTIONS:

OVEN TEMPERATURE: 225°

Beat egg whites until frothy, add cream of tartar, salt and vanilla. Beat well.

Add sugar gradually and beat until batter peaks. (Must beat until sugar is dissolved for successful cookies.) Stir in chocolate chips.

Drop by teaspoon on cookie sheet that has been covered with brown paper. (A cut up grocery bag is fine.)

Bake at 225 degrees for 1 hour, turn off oven and leave in oven for 1 more hour. Remove from oven, cool 5 minutes, put in airtight container.

TIP:

For delicately browned cookies, choose shiny baking sheets. Darker surfaces absorb heat more quickly, and cookies tend to over-brown on the bottom.

BEST BROWNIES

YIELD: 3 Dozen Brownies

"You'll always get compliments on these brownies."

1 cup margarine, softened
2 cups sugar
⅓ cup cocoa
¼ teaspoon salt
1 teaspoon vanilla
4 eggs
1½ cup flour
1 cup chopped walnuts

3 cups miniature
   marshmallows

Best Brownie Frosting
½ cup margarine
1⅔ cups powdered sugar
⅓ cup cocoa
⅓ cup evaporated milk

DIRECTIONS:

OVEN TEMPERATURE: 350°

Mix all ingredients except marshmallows. Bake in 9 x 13 inch greased pan at 350 degrees for 20 to 30 minutes or until done. Place miniature marshmallows over brownies and place in oven until melted. (3 minutes)

Frosting: Combine all ingredients; mix until smooth. Frost cooled brownies.

HINT:

For a thinner brownie, bake in a 11 x 15 x 1 inch or sheet cake pan.

CARAMEL BROWNIES

YIELD: 20 Brownies

"Wonderful . . ."

60 light caramels
½ cup evaporated milk
1 · 18½-ounce package German
   chocolate cake mix

¾ cup melted butter
1 cup chopped nuts
1 cup semi-sweet chocolate chips
⅓ cup evaporated milk

DIRECTIONS:

OVEN TEMPERATURE: 350°

In a heavy saucepan combine caramels and ½ cup evaporated milk. Stir until melted and set aside. Grease and flour 9 x 13 inch pan. In a large bowl combine cake mix, melted butter, ⅓ cup evaporated milk and nuts. Press ½ of dough into the pan – reserve the rest for topping. Bake at 350 degrees for 4 minutes. Sprinkle chips over baked crust, spread caramel mixture over chips. Crumble the remaining dough over caramel. Return to oven and bake for another 18 to 20 minutes. Cool slightly, then refrigerate 30 minutes or until caramel is firm.

CREME DE MENTHE SQUARES

YIELD: 2 Dozen Squares

"Too, too much!"

1¼ cups butter or margarine
½ cup unsweetened cocoa powder
3½ cups sifted powdered sugar
1 egg, beaten

1 teaspoon vanilla
2 cups graham cracker crumbs
⅓ cup green Creme de Menthe
1½ cups semi-sweet chocolate chips

DIRECTIONS:

Bottom layer: In sauce pan combine ½ cup of the butter and cocoa powder. Heat and stir until well blended. Remove from heat, add ½ cup of the powdered sugar, egg and vanilla. Stir in graham cracker crumbs, mix well. Press into bottom of ungreased 9 x 13 inch baking pan.

Middle layer: Melt ½ cup butter in small bowl. Combine with Creme de Menthe. At low speed, beat in remaining 3 cups powdered sugar; beat until smooth. Spread over chocolate layer. Chill 1 hour.

Top layer: In small saucepan combine ¼ cup butter and chocolate chips. Cook and stir over low until melted. Srpead over mint layer. Chill 1 to 2 hours. Cut into squares and store in refrigerator.

ERICA'S APPLE BARS

YIELD: 2 Dozen Cookies

"Easier than it looks."

Crust
¾ cup butter
½ cup sugar
1 egg
2¼ cups flour
½ teaspoon baking powder
½ teaspoon salt

Filling
4 cups apple slices

¾ cup sugar
¼ cup flour
1 teaspoon cinnamon

Frosting
1 cup powdered sugar
1 teaspoon vanilla
1 tablespoon water or
   milk

DIRECTIONS:

OVEN TEMPERATURE: 350°

Cream butter and sugar together, then add egg and mix well. Add flour, baking powder, and salt and mix all together. Remove approximately ⅓ of the dough and put aside. Press remaining ⅔ of dough in ungreased 9 x 13 pan. Bake crust at 350 degrees for 12 to 15 minutes, or until golden brown.

Meanwhile, combine sugar, flour and cinnamon, then add sliced apples. Coat apples thoroughly. Arrange apples on cooked crust. Crumble remaining ⅓ of dough over apples. Bake another 15 to 20 minutes or until golden brown.

When cooled, mix powdered sugar and vanilla with water to dribbling consistency. Drizzle icing over cookie.

HINTS:

Apples may be grated for a smoother texture.

LEMON FINGER CHEESE BARS

YIELD: 36 to 40 Bars

"Rich, different and delicious!"

⅔ cup butter
1 cup brown sugar, packed
2 cups flour
1 cup chopped nuts
2 · 8-ounces packages cream cheese, softened

1 cup sugar
¼ cup milk
½ teaspoon lemon peel
4 teaspoons lemon juice
2 eggs

DIRECTIONS:

OVEN TEMPERATURE: 325°

Beat together butter and brown sugar. Blend in flour and nuts. Reserve 2 cups of this, press the rest in 9 x 13 inch pan. Bake at 325 for 15 minutes.

Beat cream cheese and sugar. Add milk, lemon peel, juice and eggs. Beat until smooth. Pour over crust. Sprinkle remaining crumbs on top. Bake at 325 degrees for 35 minutes. Cool. Cut into small bars.

LEMON SQUARES

YIELD: 16 Squares

"Tried and true."

1 cup flour
¼ cup powdered sugar
½ cup butter
2 eggs

1 cup granulated sugar
½ teaspoon baking powder
2½ tablespoons fresh lemon juice
dash salt

DIRECTIONS:

OVEN TEMPERATURE: 350°

Sift flour and powdered sugar into medium bowl. Blend in butter with fingers until well mixed. Pat evenly into 8 x 8 inch pan. Bake at 350 for 20 minutes.

While baking, beat eggs, add remaining ingredients and pour over baked crust. Return to oven for 20 to 25 minutes.

Cool on rack. Cut into 16 squares. Sprinkle with sifted powdered sugar.

TIP:

Bar cookies are sometimes cakelike, sometimes chewy, usually moist. But watch out for overbaking, which turns them dry, crumbly, and difficult to cut neatly.

NANIMO BARS

YIELD: 2 Dozen Bars

"It's yummy!"

1 cup plus 1 tablespoon butter
¼ cup sugar
5 tablespoons cocoa
1 teaspoon vanilla
1 egg, beaten
2 cups graham cracker crumbs
½ cup chopped walnuts

1 cup flaked coconut
2 tablespoons vanilla instant pudding
  mix
3 tablespoons milk
2 cups powdered sugar
4 squares semi-sweet chocolate

DIRECTIONS:

In a double boiler combine ½ cup butter, sugar, cocoa and vanilla. Heat until melted. Stir in the egg and cook 5 minutes, stirring constantly. Fold in the nuts, crumbs and the coconut, remove from heat. Press into the bottom of a 9 x 13 inch buttered pan. Chill for 15 minutes.

Cream ½ cup butter; add pudding mix, milk and powdered sugar. Beat until smooth. Spread over crumb mixture. Chill 15 minutes.

Melt chocolate with 1 tablespoon butter over low heat. Spread over top. Chill. Cut into squares. Keep refrigerated.

OATMEAL FUDGE NUT BARS

SERVES 24

"A favorite of the sustainers."

1 cup butter or margarine
2 cups brown sugar
2 eggs
2 teaspoons vanilla
2½ cups flour
½ teaspoon salt
1 teaspoon soda
3 cups quick rolled oats

Fudge Nut Filling:
1 can sweetened condensed
  milk
1 · 12-ounce package chocolate
  chips
2 tablespoons butter
1 cup walnuts, chopped
1 teaspoon vanilla

DIRECTIONS:

OVEN TEMPERATURE: 350°

Cream butter and sugar. Mix in eggs and vanilla. Sift flour, salt and soda. Stir in oats. Add dry ingredients to creamed mixture and mix well. Set aside.

Filling: Mix condensed milk, chocolate chips and butter in bowl. Melt in microwave or in top of double boiler. Stir in nuts and vanilla. In bottom of greased 15 x 10 inch pan spread ⅔ of oatmeal mixture. Cover with chocolate filling and dot with remaining oatmeal mixture. Bake for 25 to 30 minutes. Do not overbake. Cool and cut into squares to serve.

ORANGE MINCEMEAT SQUARES

YIELD: 64 Squares

1½ cups flour, sifted
1 cup brown sugar, firmly packed
¾ teaspoon salt
⅔ cup shortening

2 cups rolled oats
⅓ cup orange juice
1 tablespoon grated orange rind
1½ cups mincemeat

DIRECTIONS:
OVEN TEMPERATURE: 350°

Mix flour, brown sugar and salt. Cut in shortening until mixture is consistency of corn meal. Stir in uncooked, rolled oats. Add orange juice. Blend thoroughly. Pack ½ of mixture into greased 8-inch square pan.

Stir grated rind into mincemeat. Spread over oat mixture in pan. Cover with remaining oat mixture, pressing lightly. Bake in 350 degree oven 35 minutes. Cool in pan. Cut into small squares.

PEANUT BUTTER FUDGE BARS

YIELD: 60 Bars

"Make ahead and freeze."

1 · 18½-ounce package yellow cake mix
1 cup peanut butter
½ cup butter or margarine, softened
2 eggs

Filling:
1 cup semi-sweet chocolate chips
1 · 14-ounce can sweetened condensed milk
2 tablespoons butter or margarine
1 package coconut pecan or coconut almond frosting mix

DIRECTIONS:
OVEN TEMPERATURE: 350°

Combine cake mix, peanut butter, butter and eggs and mix with pastry blender or fork until well mixed. Press ⅔ of mixture into 10 x 15 inch pan. Prepare filling.

Combine chips, milk, and butter; melt over low heat stirring until smooth. Remove from heat. Stir in frosting mix. Spread over dough. Crumble remaining dough over filling. Bake at 350 degrees for 18 to 20 minutes. Cool — cut into bars.

TIP:
To soften hard peanut butter, add 1 tablespoon hot water to the jar and mix.

SY'S TURTLES

YIELD: 30 Bars

"Freezes well."

1½ cups flour
1½ cups quick oats
⅓ teaspoon salt
⅔ teaspoon soda
1½ cups brown sugar

1 cup butter or margarine
48 light carmels (1 pound)
7½ tablespoons milk
1 · 6-ounce package semi-sweet
   chocolate chips

DIRECTIONS:

OVEN TEMPERATURE: 350°

Mix flour, oats, salt, soda, brown sugar and butter until crumbly. Pat one half of mixture into an ungreased 9x13 inch pan. Bake at 350 degrees for 10 minutes.

Melt carmels with milk in saucepan over low heat. Sprinkle chocolate chips on top of baked crust and drizzle with carmel sauce. Sprinkle remainder of crumbs over all.

Bake at 350 degrees for 15 minuters. Cool completely. Cut into 30 bars.

HINT:

Carmel may be melted in microwave.

VIENNESE BROWNIE

YIELD: 1 Dozen Brownies

"Delicious layered brownie."

1 · 8-ounce package cream cheese,
   softened
⅓ cup sugar
1 egg
2 · 1-ounce squares unsweetened
   chocolate

½ cup butter
2 eggs
1 cup sugar
¾ cup flour
½ teaspoon baking powder
½ teaspoon salt

DIRECTIONS:

OVEN TEMPERATURE: 350°

Grease an 8 x 8 x 2 inch pan. Combine cream cheese, sugar and 1 egg. Set aside. Melt chocolate and butter. Beat 2 eggs until fluffy, add 1 cup sugar and chocolate mixture. Add dry ingredients, stir to blend.

Pour half of chocolate mixture into greased pan. Spread with cream cheese mixture. Top with remaining batter.

Bake 40 minutes at 350 degrees.

Frost if desired, but very rich without.

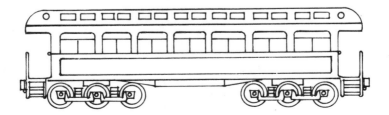

AUNT MINNIE'S COOKIES

YIELD: 6 Dozen

"A favorite of Anne B. Hoover 1982-84 president of Association of Junior Leagues."

4 cups flour
1 pound butter
1 cup sugar

6 egg yolks
(reserve egg whites)
2 teaspoon vanilla

DIRECTIONS:

OVEN TEMPERATURE: 375°

Using a food processor with metal blade blend the flour and butter. Add sugar, egg yolks and vanilla. Blend until dough forms a ball. Remove from bowl and refrigerate covered for 1 hour.

Roll out on lightly floured surface and cut into desired shapes with cookie cutters. Brush with beaten egg whites and sprinkle with colored sugar sprinkles. Bake on an ungreased cookie sheet for 8 to 10 minutes at 375 degrees.

BRANDY BARS

YIELD: 40 Bars

1½ cups currants
1½ cup raisins
1½ cup halved candied cherries
1½ cup candied pineapple
1½ cup sweet Sherry or Brandy
½ cup butter
1½ cup packed brown sugar
2 eggs

2 cups sifted flour
1 teaspoon cinnamon
1 teaspoon cloves
1 teaspoon allspice
1 teaspoon soda
1 teaspoon salt
dash of nutmeg

DIRECTIONS:

OVEN TEMPERATURE: 325°

Mix fruits in a bowl, add the wine or Brandy, cover and let stand 24 hours.

Cream butter and sugar, add the eggs. Sift the flour with the other dry ingredients and beat into the creamed mixture. Add the drained fruit. Spread the mixture into a buttered 9 x 13 inch pan and bake in a 325 oven for 45 minutes. When cool, cut into squares. Frost if you like, with powdered sugar creamed with butter and lemon juice and the liquor drained from the fruit.

CHEWY GINGERBREAD COOKIES

YIELD: 5 Dozen

⅓ cup shortening
1 cup brown sugar
1½ cups molasses
⅔ cup cold water
6 cups flour
2 teaspoons soda

1 teaspoon salt
1 teaspoon allspice
1 teaspoon ginger
1 teaspoon cloves
1 teaspoon cinnamon

DIRECTIONS:

OVEN TEMPERATURE: 350°

Cream shortening, sugar, and molasses. Add cold water and mix until blended. Stir in dry ingredients. Chill dough. On floured surface, roll out dough until approximately ¼-inch thick. Cut into desired shapes and bake on greased cookie sheet for 12 minutes at 350 degrees. When cool, decorate with icing.

DIAGONAL COOKIES

YIELD: 6 Dozen Cookies

"Delightful for holiday season."

1¼ cup butter, softened
½ cup sugar
2½ cups flour
⅛ teaspoon salt
¼ cup raspberry jam

Glaze
½ cup powdered sugar
1 tablespoon hot water
1 teaspoon vanilla

DIRECTIONS:

OVEN TEMPERATURE: 375°

Lightly grease cookie sheet. Using electric mixer, cream together butter and sugar. Gradually add flour and salt. The mixture will resemble fine crumbs. Work the crumbs between the palms of your hands until their warmth turns the mixture into a dough.

Roll dough into long logs about the diameter of a nickel. With blunt edge of knife press a slight dent down length of each log.

Bake in 375 degree oven for 10 minutes. Remove and fill dent with jam. Return to oven and bake about 10 minutes longer or until edges are light and golden color. Remove from oven and brush with glaze. Cut in 1 inch diagonal slices.

A very festive cookie.

FRUITCAKE BARS

YIELD: 3 Dozen Bars

"Perfect for Christmas."

1 cup golden raisins
1 cup chopped dates
1 cup mixed, chopped candied fruit
¼ cup brandy
4 eggs
1 cup sugar

1 teaspoon vanilla extract
1½ teaspoons grated orange peel
½ teaspoons salt
¾ cup all purpose flour
1½ cups chopped walnuts

DIRECTIONS:

OVEN TEMPERATURE: 350°

In a small bowl combine raisins, dates and candied fruit with brandy. Stir, cover and set aside for 24 hours.

Preheat oven to 350 degrees. Grease and flour a 10½ x 15½ inch jelly-roll pan. In large mixer bowl with mixer at medium speed, beat eggs until mixed. Add sugar, vanilla, orange peel and salt; continue beating until combined.

Stir in flour marinated fruit and walnuts. Spread evenly in prepared pan. Bake 30 to 35 minutes. Cool in pan and cut into bars.

PECAN PIE COOKIES

YIELD: 4 Dozen Cookies

"Festive cookie."

1 cup butter	**Pecan Filling**
½ cup sugar	½ cup powdered sugar
½ cup dark corn syrup .	¼ cup butter
2 egg yolks (save egg whites)	3 tablespoons dark corn syrup
2½ cups flour	½ cup pecans, chopped

DIRECTIONS:

OVEN TEMPERATURE: 375°

Mix butter, sugar, syrup, yolks and flour until well blended. Refrigerate for 2 hours.

Meanwhile, prepare and chill filling. Combine all but pecans in saucepan. Stir and cook over medium heat until it reaches a full boil. Remove and add pecans. Chill.

Beat egg whites with fork. Use 1 tablespoon of dough for each cookie, roll in balls, and dip in egg white. Place on cookie sheet and bake at 375 degrees for 5 minutes.

Remove from oven – place ½ teaspoon pecan filling (chilled and rolled in a ball) in center of each cookie. Return to oven. Bake 5 minutes longer. Cool 5 minutes on cookie sheet.

SPECULAAS

YIELD: 3 Dozen Cookies

½ cup unsalted butter, room temperature	1 egg white mixed with 1 tablespoon water
1¼ cups brown sugar	
1 egg, lightly beaten	**Icing:**
1 teaspoon Cognac	⅓ cup soft butter or margarine
2 cups flour	3 cups confectioner's sugar
2 teaspoons cinnamon	1½ teaspoons vanilla
½ teaspoon allspice	about 2 tablespoons milk
½ teaspoon baking powder	

DIRECTIONS:

OVEN TEMPERATURE: 350°

Cream butter until light and fluffy. Add the sugar beaten egg and Cognac. Mix in the remaining dry ingredients. Cover and refrigerate 1 hour.

Roll dough into ¼ inch thickness and cut with cutters to desired shapes. Place on cookie sheets and brush lightly with egg white mixture. Bake for 10 to 15 minutes at 350 degrees. Cool on racks. Frost with butter icing.

BUTTER ICING:

Blend butter and sugar. Stir in vanilla and milk; beat until icing is smooth and of spreading consistency.

ALMOND BLITZ TORTE

SERVES 10-12

Cake:
½ cup butter
¾ cup sugar
4 eggs, separated
1 cup almonds, ground
1 cup pastry flour
1 teaspoon baking powder
⅛ teaspoon salt
5 tablespoons milk
1 teaspoon vanilla
1 cup sugar

Chocolate Custard:
1½ ounces semi-sweet chocolate
1 cup milk
6 tablespoons granulated sugar
1½ tablespoons cake flour
¼ teaspoon salt
1 egg yolk
½ teaspoon vanilla
⅓ cup whipping cream, whipped
1 cup whipping cream, whipped

DIRECTIONS:

OVEN TEMPERATURE: 350°

Cream the butter with ¾ cup sugar. Add well-beaten egg yolks, ¾ cup almonds, and sifted flour, baking powder, and salt. Add this alternately with the milk and vanilla. Beat vigorously and pour into two buttered and floured 9 inch cake pans.

Beat 4 egg whites, gradually beat in the sugar until stiff meringue forms. Spread the meringue over the batter in the pans, sprinkle with the remaining almonds, and bake in a preheated 350 degree oven for 30 minutes or until a knife inserted in the cake comes out dry.

Melt the chocolate and milk in a double-boiler. Add the sugar, flour, and salt. Cook until thickened, stirring constantly. Stir in the slightly beaten egg yolk and cook 2 minutes. Remove from the heat and stir in the vanilla. Cool and fold in ⅓ cup whipping cream, whipped.

To assemble: Place one layer of cake, half the chocolate custard, half the additional whipped cream, another cake layer, more custard, and decorate with the remaining whipped cream.

BAKED APPLES WITH BRANDY CREAM TOPPING

SERVES 4-6

"A delicious baked apple."

4 large apples (1¾ pounds)
  peeled and sliced thin
1 teaspoon lemon juice
¼ to ½ cup sugar (depending on taste)
3 tablespoons butter
¼ cup heavy cream

Topping:
3 ounces cream cheese
  (room temperature)
½ cup heavy cream
¼ cup sugar
1 tablespoon brandy

DIRECTIONS:

OVEN TEMPERATURE: 400°

Butter 1½ quart glass baking dish. Place apples in dish, sprinkle with lemon juice and sugar. Mix to distribute sugar. Dot with butter.

Bake in pre-heated oven 400 degrees for ½ hour. Turn oven to 500 degrees, pour cream over apples and bake 5 minutes or until golden brown. Serve with brandy cream sauce topping.

Topping: Beat cream cheese and cream together. Add sugar and beat until smooth. Blend in brandy.

BEAUPA'S CHOCOLATE ROLL

"Worth the effort"

Chocolate Roll
6 eggs plus 1 extra egg white
1 cup powdered sugar
½ cup ground chocolate
½ teaspoon salt
1 rounded tablespoon flour
½ teasoon vanilla

Chocolate Sauce
12 ounce semi-sweet chocolate
2 ounces unsweetened chocolate
½ pint heavy cream
2 tablespoons cognac, Grand Marnier
or vanilla

Filling:
1½ pints whipping cream – whipped with 1 to 2 tablespoons sugar, and 1 teaspoon vanilla.

DIRECTIONS:

OVEN TEMPERATURE: 350°

Beat the egg whites with a pinch of salt until stiff – set aside. Beat the egg yolks until lemony, add vanilla, flour, sugar, and chocolate. Beat until thoroughly mixed. Fold ¼ of the egg whites into the chocolate mixture and mix well. Fold the rest of egg white into the mixture, carefully so it does not all deflate.

Pour into a jelly roll pan 12 x 15 which has been buttered and then lined with buttered parchment paper. Bake in a preheated 350 degree oven for 20 to 25 minutes. When done turn out onto a towel which has been sprinkled with powdered sugar. Roll up lengthwise and cool.

Make the chocolate sauce by melting the chocolate on top of a double boiler. Stir in the cream, stirring constantly. When smooth, remove from heat and add cognac.

Beat whipping cream for filling until stiff. Spread a thin layer of chocolate sauce on the chocolate roll. Put ⅔ of the filling on top of the chocolate roll, and roll up lengthwise. Decorate with remaining whipped cream, and drizzle with ¼ cup chocolate sauce. Serve with remaining sauce poured over each slice.

BETH'S RUM PUDDING

SERVES 6

1 envelope unflavored gelatin
  (1 tablespoon)
½ cup boiling water
¼ cups cold water
3 eggs (separated)

dash of salt
1 cup sugar
½ pint whipping cream
dash of salt
½ cup light rum

DIRECTIONS:

Dissolve gelatin in boiling water. Add cold water and set aside.

Separate eggs, add a dash of salt to each yolk. Beat yolks; add ½ cup sugar, and stir in gelatin mixture. Mix well. Set in freezer 15 minutes.

Beat egg whites until stiff, add ½ cup sugar.

Beat ½ pint whipping cream, add dash of salt, remove yolks from freezer and beat until fluffy again. Fold in egg whites and whipped cream. Add ½ cup light rum. Pour into serving dishes and garnish with nutmeg.

BLENDER POTS
DE CREME

SERVES 8

"Quick, easy and elegant."

¾ cup milk
1 cup chocolate chips
1 egg
2 tablespoons sugar

pinch of salt
1 teaspoon vanilla or Grand Marnier
whipped cream for topping (optional)

DIRECTIONS:

Heat milk just to boiling. Place all other ingredients in blender and add hot milk.

Blend at low speed for one minute.

Pour at once into 8 demitasse cups. Chill 2 hours. Add dollop of whipped cream when serving.

BLUEBERRY
CHEESE BLINTZES

Crepes
3 eggs
⅓ cup cooking oil
½ cup milk, room temperature
½ teaspoon salt
1 cup flour

Filling
1 pound carton cottage cheese

3 eggs
½ pound Swiss cheese grated
juice of two lemons

Sauce
2 teaspoons sugar
juice of 1 lemon
2 · 16-ounce cans blueberries
1 · 16-ounce can blueberry pie filling

DIRECTIONS:

OVEN TEMPERATURE: 350°

Crepe: Beat well. Refrigerate for 2 hours. Cook crepe in small skillet until golden on each side. Remove to paper towel.

Filling: Blend all ingredients in blender until smooth and fluffy. Fill crepes with mixture and roll. Bake in pyrex dish at 350 degrees for 15 to 20 minutes.

Sauce: Heat until bubbly. Spoon over blintze. Sprinkle with powdered sugar.

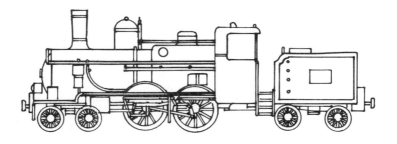

BRANDY ALEXANDER DESSERT

SERVES 8

"Unbelievably delicious!!!"

½ cup Brandy
1 quart vanilla ice cream
½ cup Créme de Cacao

garnish: chocolate shavings for
decoration

DIRECTIONS:

Combine all ingredients in a blender and blend until smooth. Pour into chilled or frosted wine glasses and sprinkle with chocolate shavings.

CARROT PUDDING WITH BUTTER RUM SAUCE

SERVES 6

"Hearty steamed pudding."

1 cup bread crumbs
1 cup grated potatoes
1 cup grated carrots
1 cup grated apples
1 cup raisins
1 cup chopped nuts
1 cup flour
1 cup sugar
1 teaspoon cinnamon
½ teaspoon nutmeg
½ teaspoon cloves
1 teaspoon salt

1 teaspoon soda combined with 2
tablespoons water
3 tablespons melted shortening

Butter Rum Sauce
4 tablespoons brown sugar
2 cups water
½ cup sugar
¼ cup butter
3 tablespoons cornstarch
¼ cup water
1 teaspoon vanilla
1 teaspoon rum flavoring

DIRECTIONS:

Combine bread crumbs, potatoes, carrots, apples, raisins, and nuts. Sift together flour, sugar, and spices. Add flour mixture to ingredients along with soda, water and shortening. Combine all ingredients and blend well. Fill greased, 48 ounce shortening can two thirds full. Cover with foil. Steam in 2 to 3 inches water in covered pan for 3 to 3½ hours. Serve with Butter Rum Sauce. Refrigerate.

Butter Rum Sauce: Combine brown sugar, water, sugar, and butter in saucepan. Bring to a boil. Add cornstarch, dissolved in the ¼ cup water. Cook one minute or until boiling and thickened. Add vanilla and rum flavoring. Serve over carrot pudding.

CHOCOLATE CHEESECAKE

SERVES 12

"Rich!"

Crust:
1 · 8½-ounce box Nabisco thin
   chocolate wafers
¼ teaspoon cinnamon
½ cup butter, melted

4 · 8-ounce packages cream
   cheese

4 eggs
2 cups sugar
1 tablespoon cocoa
1 tablespoon vanilla
1 · 12-ounce package semi-sweet
   chocolate morsels, melted
2 cups sour cream

DIRECTIONS:

OVEN TEMPERATURE: 350°

Crust: Place wafers in blender and grind. Combine butter and cinnamon with crumbs. Line bottom and sides of a 10-inch spring form pan. Chill.

Filling: With mixer, beat cream cheese until fluffy. Add eggs one at a time alternating with sugar. Add cocoa and vanilla. Mix well and fold in melted chocolate. Stir in sour cream and pour into chilled crust. Bake 1 hour 10 mintues at 350 degrees. Cool, then refrigerate.

HINT:

The longer this sets, the better it is; this may be prepared 5 or more days in advance.

CHOCOLATE FONDUE

9-ounces Hershey milk chocolate
1 square German chocolate

2 tablespoons cola or coffee
½ cup light cream

DIRECTIONS:

Combine all ingredients in double boiler and cook over low flame until melted and smooth.

To serve pour into fondue pot or chafing dish and keep warm over low flame. Serve a variety of bite sized fruit, frozen, ice cream balls or angel food cake cut into bite sized chunks.

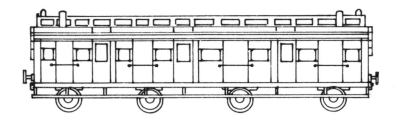

CREAMY RICE PUDDING

SERVES 8

4 cups milk
¼ cup rice, uncooked
¼ teaspoon salt
½ cup sugar
2 tablespoons butter

½ to 1 cup raisins
1 large egg
1 teaspoon vanilla
¼ teaspoon nutmeg

DIRECTIONS:

OVEN TEMPERATURE: 350°

Combine milk, rice, salt, sugar, butter and raisins and pour into greased 1½ quart casserole. Bake uncovered 2½ hours at 350 degrees. Stir frequently during baking time.

Beat egg well with fork, add vanilla and nutmeg. Add some of the hot pudding to egg mixture, whipping it constantly. Pour egg mixture into baking dish and bake for 10 minutes.

DELICIOUS CHEESECAKE

SERVES 15

"Lovely dessert for a large group"

Crust:
1½ cups graham cracker crumbs
⅓ cup melted margarine
¼ cup powdered sugar

Filling:
3 · 8-ounce packages cream cheese
3 cups powdered sugar
1 · 3-ounce package lemon gelatin
1 cup boiling water
1 teaspoon vanilla

1 · 8-ounce container frozen whipped
  topping
Topping:
  (optional)
8 ounces sour cream
⅓ cup powdered sugar
or
1 · 4¾ ounce package Danish Dessert
  (raspberry)
1 · 10-ounce package frozen
  raspberries

DIRECTIONS:

Mix crust ingredients together. Press in 9 x 13 inch pan and refrigerate. Dissolve gelatin in boiling water. Set aside to cool. Blend softened cream cheese with powdered sugar. Mix in slowly the cooled gelatin, vanilla and whipped topping. Pour over crust.

Refrigerate for at least 3 hours. Add either topping if desired.

Blend sour cream and powdered sugar until smooth. Spread on cheesecake or cook Danish Dessert with ½ cup less liquid than recipe calls for. Stir in raspberries. Spread on cheesecake and refrigerate.

HINT:

Can be made ahead and frozen without topping.

ENGLISH TRIFLE

SERVES 10

"... A La Microwave"

1 · 4¾ ounce package raspberry
Danish Dessert
2 cups hot water
1 · 10-ounce package frozen
raspberries
1 · 3¾ ounce package vanilla, banana

or coconut pudding (instant)
2 large bananas
1 · 10½ ounce prepared sponge cake
1 · 8-ounce container frozen whipped
topping

DIRECTIONS:

In 2 quart glass bowl mix Danish Dessert with 2 cups hot water. Bake on full power for 3 minutes.

Mix berries into dessert, set aside.

Make pudding according to directions on package. Slice bananas into puddings. Set aside.

Tear up pre-made sponge cake into thumb size pieces.

In a clear bowl (minimum 3 quart size) place half of the cake pieces on the bottom. Continue to layer with half of pudding, half of Danish Dessert, half of whipped topping. Repeat, layering in same order with remaining ingredients. Refrigerate until serving.

HINT:

Steps 1 through 3 may be done a day in advance. Assembly can be completed early in the day.

GRANDMA'S APPLE DUMPLINGS

SERVES 8

8 apples, peeled and cored
2 cups flour
1 teaspoon salt
2 teaspoons baking powder
¾ cups shortening
½ cup milk
sugar
cinnamon
butter

Syrup
2 cups sugar
2 cups water
½ teaspoon nutmeg
3 tablespoons red cinnamon
candy
¼ cup margarine

DIRECTIONS: OVEN TEMPERATURE: 350°

Sift flour, salt and baking powder together. Cut shortening into flour with pastry blender. Add milk, enough to make soft dough. Divide the dough into eight pieces and roll to 8 inch square or large enough square to wrap apple.

Place an apple on the pastry and sprinkle with sugar, cinnamon, and a small pat of butter. Bring each corner of square to top of apple; pinch edges of pastry together firmly, to cover apple completely.

In a small saucepan boil syrup ingredients together.

Place pastry covered apples into greased baking pan and pour syrup over the apples. Bake at 350 degrees until browned and apples are cooked through, about 35 minutes.

GALATOPETA

"Custard a la Grecque"

1 quart milk
1¾ cups sugar
¾ cup farina (cream of wheat may be
   substituted)
1 cup butter
10 eggs, separated
2 teaspoons grated orange rind
1 teaspoon vanilla
2 jiggers fruit liqueur (optional)
cinnamon
1 pound Filo pastry leaves (cover
   Filo with a slightly damp cloth so it

won't dry out)
1 cup melted butter

Spiced Syrup
1 cup water
1½ cups sugar
1 teaspoon vanilla
2 jiggers orange liqueur
   (optional)
3 whole cloves
1 cinnamon stick
2 teaspoons orange peel

DIRECTIONS:

OVEN TEMPERATURE: 350°

In large saucepan heat milk and half of the sugar over low heat until warm. Add farina slowly, stirring constantly with wooden spoon until thickened and smooth. Add butter and stir until completely blended. Remove from heat, add vanilla, orange rind and liqueur. Stir well and allow to cool.

Beat egg yolks and remaining sugar with mixer until frothy. Beat egg whites until stiff and fold into yolks. Add farina mixture and stir well.

Grease a 9 x 12 x 2 inch baking pan and place about 10 sheets of the filo leaves in the bottom of the pan, each individually brushed with melted butter. Pour the cooled custard mixture into the pan, and spread evenly. Cover the custard with remaining filo sheets, brushing each sheet with melted butter.

With a sharp knife, cut the top layer of pastry into 3 inch squares. Bake at 350 degrees for 1 hour, remove from oven and pour the cool syrup over the pan, so it saturates the filo and custard thoroughly. Cool before serving.

Spiced Syrup: Bring to boil all ingredients except vanilla and liqueur. Simmer over low heat about 15 minutes. Add vanilla and liqueur. Cool.

GRANDMA GREAT'S LEMON DESSERT

YIELD: 8 Servings

"Very lemonly."

4 eggs, separated
1 cups sugar
2½ lemons

1 pint whipping cream
2 cups graham cracker crumbs

DIRECTIONS:

Beat egg yolks. Add sugar and juice of lemons. Cook over medium heat until thickened, stirring constantly. Cool. Whip cream. (Do not sweeten.) Beat egg whites. Fold whipped cream into cooled lemon mixture. Fold in egg whites.

Line 9 x 9 inch pan with 1 cup graham cracker crumbs. Pour lemon mixture over crust. Top with 1 cup crumbs. Chill several hours.

ICE CREAM MOLD

"Lovely"

½ gallon ice cream (such as French Vanilla, Praline, Coffee)

Filling:

1½ pounds semi-sweet chocolate bits   ½ cup Grand Marnier
3 egg yolks   1 cup whipping cream
6 egg whites   ¼ cup sugar
½ cup strong coffee

Note: Only half of this amount is needed for the mold. The rest can be saved in the freezer.

DIRECTIONS:

Spray ½ gallon mold lightly with Pam. Let ice cream soften and spread around bottom and sides of the mold leaving a cavity in the center. Cover with saran wrap and freeze.

Filling: Melt chocolate with coffee and liqueur – beating with whisk until smooth. Add egg yolks one at a time and cool. Beat egg whites until stiff, adding sugar, a little at a time. Whip cream until stiff and fold into egg whites; fold in chocolate. Chill in freezer, fill cavity of ice cream mold. (You may wish to make 2 molds and save one for later.) Freeze and cover bottom with ice cream layer.

HINT:

To unmold – dip mold in pan of hot water briefly and decorate with chocolate sauce and nuts.

LEMON BAVARIAN CREAM

SERVES 10

"Attractive filled with fresh berries"

1 envelope gelatin   1 cup whipping cream
¼ cup lemon juice   1 tablespoon grated lemon peel
3 eggs   2 cups strawberries, sliced and
¾ cup sugar   sugared

DIRECTIONS:

Soften gelatin in lemon juice for 5 minutes. Place bowl in hot water and stir until dissolved. In large bowl, beat eggs until frothy. Beat in sugar slowly and continue to beat for 5 minutes, or until very thick.

In medium bowl, beat cream until stiff. Fold in lemon peel, gelatin mixture, and fold cream into eggs, until well combined. Chill in five cup ring mold 4 hours or overnight. Unmold and fill with strawberries.

LUSCIOUS LAYERED DELIGHT

SERVES 16

Crust:
1 cup flour
¼ pound margarine
½ cup chopped nuts

Filling:
8-ounce package cream cheese

1 cup powdered sugar
1 · 8-ounce container frozen whipped
topping
1 · 6-ounce and 1 · 3-ounce package
chocolate pudding (instant)
4 cups milk
1 cup cream

DIRECTIONS:

Mix crust ingredients together and press in a 9 x 13 inch pan. Bake at 350 for 15 minutes. Cool.

Mix cream cheese with powdered sugar. Blend in cool whip. Spread on crust.

Make pudding according to package directions, using only 3 cups milk. Spread over cheese layer.

Whip cream, sweeten as desired. Spread on pudding layer.

Refrigerate at least 3 hours before serving.

VARIATIONS:

1. Delicious topped with toasted almonds, chocolate curls, crushed lemon or peppermint candy. 2. Try Lemon or Pastachio Pudding.

MOOGOO MUD PIE

SERVES 20

"Very rich . . . men love this dessert"

1 · 15-ounce package chocolate
Oreo cookies
⅓ cup melted butter
½ gallon ice cream – can use butter
pecan, maple nut, vanilla, etc.
1 ounce semi sweet chocolate

¼ cup butter
⅔ cup sugar
1 teaspoon vanilla
⅛ teaspoon salt
5 ounces evaporated milk
¼ cup slivered almonds

DIRECTIONS:

Crush cookies in blender, 5 at a time. Mix crumbs with melted butter and press into the bottom of a 9 x 13 inch pan.

Soften ice cream and spread over cookie crust. Freeze.

Melt chocolate; add butter, sugar, vanilla, salt and milk. Boil slowly for 8 to 10 minutes. Remove from heat and cool. Spread over frozen pie. Sprinkle with almonds and return to freezer.

HINT:

The chocolate sauce may be doubled.

MOUSSE IN CHOCOLATE SHELL

SERVES 10

"Very fancy and delicate."

14 ounces semisweet chocolate
½ teaspoon ground cinnamon
40 cup cake liners
3 tablespoons water
2 tablespoons coffee-flavored liqueur
  or Grand Marnier

½ teaspoon grated orange peel
3 egg whites
¼ cup sugar
1 cup whipping cream
thin strands of orange peel

DIRECTIONS:

Place 8 ounces of the chocolate and cinnamon in top of double boiler. Melt over low heat. Cool. Using double muffin liners, paint melted chocolate with a paint brush around bottom of liner and half way up sides. Chocolate should be about ⅛ inch thick. Set cups in muffin tin and refrigerate at least 1 hour. (May be wrapped air tight and chilled up to 3 weeks.) Peel paper off.

Filling: Melt remaining chocolate and water in top of double boiler. Stir in liqueur and grated peel. Cool. Beat egg whites until soft peaks form. Gradually add sugar until stiff peaks form. Whip cream and fold into chocolate, fold in beaten egg whites. Fill cups, chill for several hours before serving. May be made several days in advance.

NEW YORK CHEESECAKE

SERVES 12

"This is a heavy cheesecake."

Basic Crumb Crust
1½ cups graham cracker crumbs
6 tablespoons butter, melted
¼ cup granulated sugar

Cheesecake
2 pounds cream cheese

¾ cup granulated sugar
2 large eggs, slightly
  beaten
1 teaspoon vanilla extract
2 tablespoons cornstarch
1 cup sour cream

DIRECTIONS:

OVEN TEMPERATURE: 450°

Crust: Preheat oven to 350 degrees. Place crumbs in mixing bowl and add butter and sugar; blend well. Press the crumb mixture in the bottom and partly up the sides of a greased 9 inch springform pan. Bake for 10 minutes and cool before filling.

Cake: Preheat oven to 450 degrees. In a large mixing bowl, beat together the cream cheese and sugar until smooth and light. Beat in the eggs, vanilla, and cornstarch only until thoroughly mixed. Stir in the sour cream until the mixture is well blended. Pour the mixture into the prepared crust and bake for 45 minutes. Watch the cake carefully after 30 minutes and if it is browning too quickly on top place an aluminum foil tent over the top, being careful not to touch the top of the cake. Let cake cool completely and refrigerate several hours before serving.

NUTTY CHOCOLATE LOG

SERVES 8

"Tastes like German chocolate."

¼ cup butter
1 cup flaked coconut
1 cup chopped nuts (walnuts,
  almonds, or pecans)
1 cup chocolate chips (milk
  or semi-sweet)
1 · 14-ounce can condensed milk
3 eggs

1 cup sugar
¾ cup flour
⅓ cup cocoa
¼ teaspoon salt
¼ teaspoon soda
⅓ cup water
1 teaspoon vanilla
⅓ cup powdered sugar

DIRECTIONS:

OVEN TEMPERATURE: 375°

Line 10 x 15 inch jelly roll pan with foil. Melt butter in pan. Sprinkle with coconut, nuts and chocolate chips. Pour condensed milk evenly over coconut mixture.

In medium mixing bowl, beat eggs until fluffy. Add remaining ingredients, except powdered sugar. Beat 1 minute. Pour evenly over condensed milk.

Bake at 375 degrees for 18 minutes. Remove from oven. Sprinkle with powdered sugar. Cover with smooth dish towel; invert on cookie sheet. Roll up jelly roll fashion from narrow end. Leave wrapped, until cool. Don't wrap towel with cake.

OBSCENELY RICH (AND EASY) CHOCOLATE TRIFLE

SERVES: 40-50

"Absolutely gorgeous."

3 · 18-ounce chocolate cake mixes
2 · 8-ounce containers frozen
  whipped topping

2 · 16-ounce cans chocolate syrup
nuts (optional)
Creme de Menthe (optional)

DIRECTIONS:

Prepare cakes according to package directions. Line the bottom of a large trifle bowl with a layer of cake slices. Pour some of the chocolate syrup mixed with the Creme de Menthe over the cake. Spread a layer of the whipped topping. Repeat layers several times ending with the whipped topping.

HINT:

This can be made a day ahead. Try using fruit, cherries or raspberries between the syrup and whipped topping.

The recipe may be reduced to desired number of servings.

BURDETT'S BURNT ALMOND FUDGE ICE CREAM

YIELD: 5 Quarts

"Scrumptious texture and flavor"

3 cups sugar
1 cup cocoa
1 teaspoon salt
4 eggs, beaten
8 cups milk
6 cups cream

¼ cup chopped maraschino cherries
¾ teaspoon almond extract
1½ cups almonds, roasted in oven at
    300 degrees for 15 minutes or
    until browned

DIRECTIONS:

Combine sugar, cocoa, salt, eggs and 4 cups of the milk. Boil until mixture coats spoon. Cool.

Add remaining ingredients and mix in a 5 to 6 quart ice cream freezer following freezer instructions.

HINT:

For a richer ice cream, use more cream, less milk.

ORANGE BANANA ICE CREAM

YIELD: 6 Quarts

"Refreshing, fruity, and delicious!"

2 quarts whole milk
4 · 13-ounce cans evaporated milk
4 cups sugar
1 tablespoon vanilla

1 cup orange juice
1 cup lemon juice
4 bananas, mashed

DIRECTIONS:

Combine all ingredients and mix well. Pour into ice cream freezer. Freeze ice cream according to ice cream freezer instructions.

ORANGE CRUSH ICE CREAM

YIELD: 5 Quarts

3 cups sugar
1 · 6-ounce can frozen orange juice
juice of 1 lemon
1 cup whipping cream

1 · 14-ounce can sweetened
    condensed milk
1 · 12-ounce can Orange Crush soda
2 quarts milk

DIRECTIONS:

Mix all the ingredients in a 5 to 6 quart ice cream freezer. Freeze according to freezer instructions.

PUMPKIN ROLL

SERVES 15

3 eggs
1 cup sugar
⅔ cup pumpkin
1 tablespoon lemon juice
¾ cup flour, sifted
1 teaspoon baking powder
2 teaspoons cinnamon
1 teaspoon ginger
½ teaspoon nutmeg

½ teaspoon salt
1 cup chopped nuts

Spread
1 cup powdered sugar
1 · 8-ounce package cream cheese
4 tablespoons soft butter
1 teaspoon vanilla

DIRECTIONS:

OVEN TEMPERATURE: 375°

Beat eggs for 5 minutes, then gradually add sugar. Stir in pumpkin and lemon juice.

Fold flour, baking powder, cinnamon, ginger, nutmeg, salt, into pumpkin mixture.

Spread mixture on greased 10 x 15 inch jelly roll pan. Top with 1 cup nuts.

Bake at 375 degrees for 12 to 15 minutes.

Immediately remove and invert on dish towel. Sprinkle with powdered sugar and roll up. Cool.

Unroll and spread with powdered sugar, cream cheese, butter and vanilla, which has been mixed together.

Roll up again. Chill or freeze.

HINT:

Best if set for 2 or 3 days.

RASPBERRY ICEBOX DESSERT

SERVES 9-10

2 cups Vanilla wafer crumbs
½ cup butter
1 cup sugar
2 eggs

1½ cups fresh raspberries (approx.)
  DO NOT WASH
1 cup whipping cream, whipped,
  and sweetened
1 teaspoon vanilla

DIRECTIONS:

In an 8 x 8 inch pan, layer 1 cup wafer crumbs.

Cream together butter, sugar, and eggs until light and fluffy. Spread carefully over vanilla wafer crumbs. Place raspberries in rows completely covering creamed mixture. Cover raspberries with sweetened whipped cream, to which vanilla has been added. Sprinkle 1 cup vanilla wafer crumbs over whipped cream. Refrigerate several hours.

RASPBERRY WALNUT DESSERT

YIELD: 15 Squares

1¼ cups flour
⅓ cup powdered sugar
½ cup butter
¾ cup ground walnuts
1 · 10-ounce package frozen
    raspberries
2 eggs (at room temperature)
1 cup sugar
¼ cup flour
½ teaspoon salt

½ teaspoon baking powder
1 teaspoon vanilla
whipped cream to top
2 tablespoons cornstarch
½ cup sugar
raspberry juice
½ cup water
½ tablespoon lemon juice
1 drop red food coloring
    (optional)

DIRECTIONS:

OVEN TEMPERATURE: 350°

Combine flour, sugar and butter; press into 9 x 13 inch baking pan. Bake at 350 degrees for 15 minutes.

Grind walnuts in blender or processor, drain thawed raspberries reserving juice. Blend walnuts and berries together with back of spoon until mixed. Spread on crust.

Beat eggs with sugar until light and fluffy. Add flour, salt, baking powder and vanilla. Blend. Pour over nut mixture evenly. Bake for 30 minutes. Cool. Cut into 15 squares. Top with whipped cream, drizzle raspberry sauce over cream.

Sauce: Mix cornstarch and sugar, blend in raspberry juice and water. Cook until thick and clear. Remove from heat and add lemon juice and coloring. Do not refrigerate.

STRAWBERRY ALMOND CREPES

YIELD: 20 Crepes

1 · 8-ounce package cream cheese,
    softened
1 cup sour cream
½ cup powdered sugar

⅛ teaspoon almond flavoring
3 cups sliced fresh strawberries
¼ cup sliced almonds
20 prepared crepes

DIRECTIONS:

Place cream cheese in small mixing bowl; beat until smooth. Add sour cream and powdered sugar; beat until fluffy, scraping bowl often. Fold in almond flavoring. Refrigerate until thickened. Layer filling, strawberries and almonds in each crepe; fold over. Top with remaining filling and strawberries. Garnish with almonds and powdered sugar.

VARIATIONS:

Substitute canned sliced peaches, or fruit cocktail, frozen blueberries or raspberries for strawberries.

HINT:

Prepare filling and refrigerate. Fill crepes when ready to serve.

FROSTED GRAPES

SERVES 4-6

1 pound seedless grapes
1 egg white

1 cup sugar
1 small paper sack

DIRECTIONS:

Wash grapes, pat dry.

Beat egg white with fork. Break grapes in small clusters (4 to 6). Dip in egg white. Shake in sack with sugar a few clusters at a time.

Place on cake rack, let dry at least an hour.

HINT:

Great dessert with cheese or beautiful garnish on dinner plate.

NUTTY PINEAPPLE

SERVES 6

"Perfect accompaniment for outdoor cooking."

1 medium-size ripe pineapple
¼ cup butter or margarine
¼ cup shredded coconut

2 tablespoons finely chopped almonds
1 tablespoon light brown sugar

DIRECTIONS:

Cut off leafy top of pineapple. Cut pineapple lengthwise into 6 wedges; cut off the core of each wedge. Slash the flesh vertically down to, but not through, the skin at ¾ inch intervals.

In small sauce pan heat butter until melted. Brush half over wedges. To butter remaining in saucepan, add coconut, almonds, and brown sugar; stir until well mixed. Spoon some mixture into slashes.

Place pineapple on grill over medium coals, cut-side down. Grill 5 minutes, turn and grill 5 more minutes until lightly browned and heated thoroughly.

Serving Suggestion: Good with barbequed ham slice. Serve with ice cream or dessert after cook-out.

TIP:

When a recipe calls for shortening, margarine or butter, do not substitute oil, even when the shortening, margarine or butter is melted.

SHERRIED GRAPES

SERVES 4

"A light finish to a heavy meal."

2 pounds grapes (green, seedless)
1½ cups pale sherry

1 cup sour cream
½ cup brown sugar

DIRECTIONS:

Remove grapes from stems. Wash and puncture each one with a toothpick. Place grapes and sherry in covered bowl and chill at least 2 hours.

To serve, garnish with sour cream and generously sprinkle with brown sugar.

WINE SPICED PEACHES

SERVES 8

1 · 1 pound 13 ounce can peach halves
2 tablespoons sugar
2 · 3-inch cinnamon sticks, broken
  in half

2 tablespoons orange juice
½ cup Sauterne wine

DIRECTIONS:

Drain peaches, reserving ⅔ cups syrup.

In saucepan, combine syrup with sugar, add cinnamon pieces. Place peaches in medium size bowl. Bring to boil and boil 5 minutes. Remove from heat. Blend in orange juice and wine.

Pour over peaches. Cover and chill overnight.

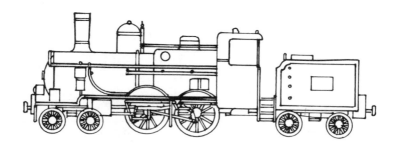

EXTRA SPECIAL PIE CRUST

YIELD: 1 · 9-Inch Double Crust Pie

"Great for quiche and quick cooking pies."

2½ cups flour
1 teaspoon salt
1 cup shortening

1 egg yolk
milk (evaporated is best)
1 teaspoon baking powder

DIRECTIONS:

Mix flour, salt and shortening with a pastry blender, to fine crumbs, set aside. Place egg yolk in a measuring cup and beat with a fork; fill to ½ cup with milk. Add baking powder and stir well. Pour liquid over dry ingredients and mix with two knives in a cutting motion. (Pastry may be chilled at this point).

Roll out onto lightly floured surface. Enough for a double crust pie. This crust browns easily.

"FLAKY" PIE CRUST

YIELDS: 9 to 12 Inch Pie

2½ cups flour
½ teaspoon salt
1 cup shortening

1 egg
1 tablespoon vinegar
⅓ cup cold water

DIRECTIONS:

Mix flour, salt and shortening. Add egg, vinegar, and cold water and mix until all ingredients are wet. Roll out with flour and bake according to your pie recipe. Makes one double pie plus one single crust.

NO-ROLL PIE CRUST

YIELD: 1 · 8 to 9-Inch Crust

"E-Z"

1½ cups flour
½ teaspoon salt
2 tablespoons sugar

½ cup salad oil
2 tablespoons milk

DIRECTIONS:

OVEN TEMPERATURE: 375°

Combine all ingredients. Spread in pie plate. For baked crust: Prick with fork, bake 375 degrees for 25 minutes. For unbaked crust: Pour in pie filling and then bake as directed.

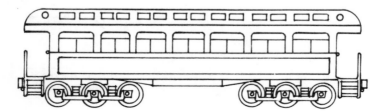

APPLE-WALNUT CREAM PIE

YIELD: 1 · 9-Inch Pie

"Delicious with ice cream, whipping cream or cheese."

One unbaked 9-inch pie shell
6 to 9 apples – MacIntosh or Jonathan
  are best
1 cup sugar
3 tablespoons flour
¼ teaspoon salt

½ teaspoon cinnamon
¼ teaspoon nutmeg
2 eggs
1 cup cream
1½ teaspoon vanilla
½ cup coarsely chopped walnuts

DIRECTIONS:

OVEN TEMPERATURE: 450°

Slice apples (pared and cored) very thin into pie shell, filling nice and full. Mix together sugar, flour, salt, cinnamon, and nutmeg. Beat together eggs, cream, and vanilla. Add sugar mixture and mix well. Pour over shell filled with apples; dot with butter and sprinkle with nuts.

Bake at 450 degrees for 10 minutes, reduce heat to 350 degrees and continue baking for 45 minutes or until apples are tender and top is browned.

CHANTILLY BROWNIE PIE

YIELD: 1 Pie

½ cup butter
2 · 1 ounce squares unsweetened
  chocolate
1 cup sugar
2 eggs, beaten
1 teaspoon vanilla
¾ cup flour
½ cup chopped nuts

Chantilly Cream
1 cup whipping cream
½ cup confectioners sugar
½ teaspoon vanilla
1 cup sour cream
chocolate curls or crumbs
  (optional)

DIRECTIONS:

OVEN TEMPERATURE: 350°

Melt butter and chocolate over low heat. Stir in sugar and cool. Beat in eggs and vanilla. Stir in flour and nuts. Pour into buttered, 10 inch pie plate. Bake at 350 degrees for 20 minutes or until pick comes out clean. One or two hours before serving, add Chantilly Cream.

Chantilly Cream: Whip cream until soft peaks form. Add sugar and vanilla, beat until stiff. Gently fold in sour cream. Spread over brownie pie. Decorate with chocolate curls or crumbs. Refrigerate.

TIP:

When cooking with fresh fruits, a dash of salt and 2-3 teaspoons fresh lemon juice will enhance the flavor and preserve the fruit.

CHOCOLATE CREAM PIE

YIELD: 1 Pie

Crust
1½ cups graham cracker
  crumbs (about 20 crackers)
3 tablespoons sugar
⅓ cup melted butter or margarine

Filling
1 cup butter
1½ cups sugar

3 squares unsweetened chocolate,
  melted and cooled
2 teaspoons vanilla
4 eggs

Toppings
½ pint whipping cream
almond shavings (optional)
strawberries (optional)

DIRECTIONS:

OVEN TEMPERATURE: 350°

For crust — Heat oven to 350°. Mix crumbs, sugar and butter. Press mixture firmly and evenly against bottom and side of 9-inch pie pan. Bake in 350° oven for 10 minutes. Cool.

For filling — Cream butter and sugar. Blend in chocolate. Add vanilla. Add eggs, one at a time, beating 4 to 5 minutes after each addition.

Pour into baked and cooled pie crust and chill several hours.

Top with whipping cream, almonds and/or strawberries before serving.

DELECTABLE PINEAPPLE PIE

YIELD: 1 · 10-Inch Pie

¾ box (7 ounces) vanilla wafers
½ cup butter
2 cups powdered sugar
2 eggs

1 · 20 ounce can sweetened
  crushed pineapple
½ pint whipping cream

DIRECTIONS:

Crush wafers. Place half in 10-inch pie pan. Reserve remainder. Cream butter, sugar and eggs. Place on crumbs. Drain pineapple and spread on top. Whip cream and cover pineapple mixture. Sprinkle with remaining crumbs and refrigerate until serving time.

HINT:

Very rich. Does not keep well. Should be eaten the day prepared.

TIP:

When making pie crusts, keep ingredients as cold as possible. Use chilled shortening and ice water and handle pastry as little as possible. Chill pastry before rolling.

CHOCOLATE MOUSSE PIE

SERVES 12

"Magnificient Mousse"

Crust
3 cups chocolate wafer crumbs
½ cup unsalted butter, melted

Filling
1 pound semi-sweet chocolate
2 eggs
4 egg yolks
2 cups whipping cream
6 tablespoons powdered sugar
4 egg whites, room temperature

Chocolate Leaves
8 ounces semi-sweet
   chocolate
1 tablespoon (scant)
   vegetable shortening
Camellia or other waxy
   leaves

Topping
2 cups whipping cream
sugar to taste

DIRECTIONS:

For crust – Combine crumbs and butter. Press on bottom and completely up sides of 10-inch springform pan. Refrigerate 30 minutes or chill in freezer.

Filling – Soften chocolate in top of double boiler over simmering water. Let cool to lukewarm 95 degrees. Add whole eggs and mix until thoroughly blended.

Whip cream with powdered sugar until soft peaks form. Beat egg whites until stiff but not dry. Stir a little of the cream and egg whites into chocolate mixture to lighten. Fold in remaining cream and egg whites until completely incorporated. Turn into crust and chill at least 6 hours or preferably overnight.

Chocolate leaves – Melt chocolate and shortening in top of double boiler. Using spoon, generously coat underside of leaves. Chill or freeze until firm.

Cream top – Whip remaining 2 cups of cream with sugar to taste until stiff.

Loosen crust on all sides using sharp knife; remove springform. Spread all but about ½ cup cream over top of the mousse. Pour remaining cream into rosettes in center of pie. Separate chocolate from leaves starting at stem end. Arrange on top of mousse.

CINNAMON PEAR PIE

YIELD: 1 · 9-Inch Pie

"Let your friends try to guess the ingredients."

Pastry for double 9 inch pie
5 cups pears – Anjou or Bosc
¾ cup sugar
3 tablespoons flour
⅛ teaspoon salt

1 tablespoon lemon juice
4 tablespoons cinnamon red hot
   candies
2 tablespoons butter

DIRECTIONS:

OVEN TEMPERATURE: 425°

Peel, core and slice pears.

Mix with sugar, flour, salt, lemon juice and candies. Spoon into pastry lined pie plate. Dot with butter. Cover with top pastry. Flute or crimp edges. Bake at 425 degrees for 45 to 50 minutes.

DIXON'S FAMOUS LEMON CREAM CHEESE PIE

YIELD: 2 · 8-Inch Pies; 12 Servings

2 · 8-inch baked pie crusts

Filling
1¼ cups sugar
¼ cup corn starch
3 eggs beaten and strained
juice from 2 lemons
1¼ cups water

1 teaspoon vanilla
yellow food coloring (optional)

Cream cheese mixture:
6 ounces cream cheese
¾ cup powdered sugar
¾ teaspoon vanilla
¾ cup whipping cream, whipped

DIRECTIONS:

In a double boiler mix sugar and cornstarch. Add eggs, lemon juice, and water Cook until thickened. Remove from heat and add vanilla and a couple drops of yellow food coloring if desired. Cool.

Beat cream cheese until fluffy. Add sugar and vanilla. Beat well. Fold in whipped cream.

Fold cooled lemon filling into cream cheese mixture. Chill.

EMERALD CREME PIE

YIELD: One Nine Inch Pie

"Perfect for Bridge Luncheon."

1½ cups fine chocolate wafer crumbs
6 tablespoons butter or margarine,
  melted
1 envelope (1 tablespoon) unflavored
  gelatin
2 tablespoons sugar
¾ cup water

1 cup light cream
¼ cup green Creme de Menthe
¼ cup white Creme de Cacao
1 · 3½ ounce package vanilla flavored
  whipped topping mix
strawberries and whipped cream
  for topping (optional)

DIRECTIONS:

Combine crumbs with butter. Press firmly into a nine inch pie plate. Chill until set.

Mix gelatin with sugar in medium saucepan, add water. Heat and stir until gelatin is completely dissolved. Add cream and liqueurs. Blend well. Chill until thick and syrupy. (About 1 hour)

Prepare topping mix according to package directions. Combine with gelatin in large mixer bowl. Beat at medium speed for 1 minute. Chill until mixture mounds when spooned, about 10 minutes. Spoon into crust. Chill for about 4 hours or until firm. Can be garnished with whipped cream and strawberries if desired.

FRESH STRAWBERRY PIE

YIELD: 1 Pie

"Light and airy. A chiffon type pie."

Crust
¾ cup graham cracker crumbs
⅓ cup butter, melted
¼ cup finely chopped nuts
¼ cup flaked coconut
2 tablespoons sugar

Filling
1 · 3-ounce package vanilla pudding

1 · 3-ounce package strawberry
   gelatin
1¼ cup milk
½ cup frozen lemonade
   concentrate
1 cup whipping cream
1 teaspoon vanilla
1 cup sliced strawberries

DIRECTIONS:

OVEN TEMPERATURE: Crust – 350°

Crust: Combine all ingredients together. Press onto bottom and sides and 9 inch pie plate. Bake 8 to 10 minutes at 350 degrees or unti golden brown. Cool completely. Refrigerate while preparing filling.

Filling: Combine pudding mix and jello in saucepan. Stir in milk. Cook over medium heat, stirring constantly, until mixture reaches full boiling. (Mixture will appear curdled while cooking, but this does not affect end product). Remove from heat. Stir in lemonade concentrate. Chill mixture until slightly thickened, stirring often.

Meanwhile — Whip cream until soft peaks form; add vanilla. Continue to beat until stiff. Whip cooled pudding mixture until fluffy, fold in whipped cream. Fold in strawberries. Turn into chilled crust. Refrigerate several hours before serving.

FROZEN PUMPKIN PIE

YIELD: 1 · 9-Inch Pie

"A break from the traditional."

Crust
1 cup ginger snap crumbs
½ cup ground pecans
¼ cup sugar
¼ cup softened butter

Filling
1 cup canned pumpkin

½ cup brown sugar
½ teaspoon salt
½ teaspoon ginger
½ teaspoon cinnamon
¼ teaspoon nutmeg
1 quart French vanilla ice
   cream

DIRECTIONS:

OVEN TEMPERATURE: 425°

Crust: Combine cookie crumbs, pecans, sugar, and butter. Press into bottom and sides of a 9 inch pie. Bake at 425 degrees for 5 to 7 minutes.

Filling: In a large bowl combine the pumpkin, sugar and spices. Stir in softened ice cream. Pour into cooled crust, and freeze overnight. Remove from freezer 15 minutes before serving.

GOLDEN APPLE PIE WITH RUM SAUCE

YIELD: 1 · 9-Inch Pie

Pastry for 9-inch double crust pie
7 cups Golden Delicious Apples
¼ cup packed brown sugar
2 tablespoons flour
½ teaspoon cinnamon
¼ teaspoon salt
⅛ teaspoon nutmeg
2 eggs, beaten
¼ cup ground walnuts
1 tablespoon rum

2 tablespoons butter

Rum Sauce
1 cup sugar
¾ cup water
½ teaspoon cinnamon
¼ cup water
2 tablespoons cornstarch
¼ cup rum

DIRECTIONS:

OVEN TEMPERATURE: 425°

Pare apples, slice thin, combine with sugar, flour, cinnamon, salt, nutmeg and eggs. Spoon into pie plate lined with pastry. Sprinkle with nuts and rum – dot with butter. Roll remaining pastry – prepare lattice crust.

Bake 425 degrees for 55 minutes. (If crust browns too much, cover edges with foil or pie tape half way through.) Serve with rum sauce.

Rum Sauce: Boil sugar, water and cinnamon in saucepan. Blend water and cornstarch together and stir into hot sugar mixture. Cook until thickened. Stir in rum. Cool slightly. Serve warm with pie.

GOURMET PEACH PIE

YIELD: 2 · 9 inch Pie

Crust
½ cup butter
¼ cup powdered sugar
¼ teaspoon salt
1 egg yolk
1 cup flour

Hard Sauce
½ cup butter

¼ teaspoon salt
2 cups powdered sugar
4 teaspoons whipping cream
1 teaspoon vanilla

Peach Filling
3 or 4 fresh peaches
1 cup whipping cream

DIRECTIONS:

OVEN TEMPERATURE: 350°

Crust: Mix and cut in flour with pastry blender. Spread with hands on bottom and sides of 2 9-inch plates (very thin crust). Bake at 350 degrees for 12 minutes or until light golden brown. Place in refrigerator to chill.

Hard Sauce: Cream butter; add salt and sugar. Cream until well blended. Add cream a drop at a time. Add vanilla. Spread on bottom and sides of chilled pie shell. Chill again.

Peach Filling: Slice and drain peaches. Place in chilled shells. Top with sweetened whipped cream.

LATTICE STRAWBERRY- RHUBARB PIE

YIELD: 1 · 9-Inch Pie

"Serve warm with vanilla ice cream."

1½ cups sugar
¼ cup flour
¼ teaspoon salt
½ teaspoon nutmeg
2 eggs, beaten
3 cups fresh or frozen rhubarb
 (½ inch pieces)

1½ cups fresh or frozen strawberries,
 sliced
1 tablespoon butter
pastry for 1 double crust pie,
 1 pie shell and strips for
 lattice crust

DIRECTIONS:

OVEN TEMPERATURE: 400°

In mixing bowl stir together sugar, flour, salt, nutmeg. Add beaten eggs, stir in fruits, let stand for 20 minutes. Spoon into pie crust. Dot with butter.

Arrange lattice strips on top. Flute edges.

Bake 400 degrees for 45 minutes. Reduce heat to 350 and bake 15 minutes more until browned.

HINT:

In early days rhubarb was called "Spring Tonic." Grandma said it purified your system. Utah rhubarb is ready the end of April or first part of May.

LEMON CHESS PIE

YIELD: 1 · 9-Inch Pie

Crust
1 cup flour
¼ cup sugar
1 teaspoon grated lemon peel
½ cup butter, softened
1 egg yolk, slightly beaten
¼ teaspoon vanilla

Filling
2 cups sugar

2 tablespoons flour
¼ cup lemon juice
4 eggs, beaten
½ cup melted butter
2 teaspoons vanilla
1 to 4 tablespoons lemon peel
 (as desired)
¼ cup evaporated milk
½ teaspoon salt
whipped cream for topping (optional)

DIRECTIONS:

OVEN TEMPERATURE: Crust – 400°
Pie – 375°

Crust: Combine flour, sugar and lemon peel. Cut in butter until mixture is crumbly. Add egg yolk and vanilla, blend. Pat into 9 inch pie pan and bake for 8 minutes in a 400 degree oven.

Filling: Combine all ingredients in mixing bowl and mix together for 2 minutes. Pour filling in pie crust and bake 15 minutes at 375 degrees. Then lower heat to 300 degrees and bake 35 to 45 minutes to a golden brown. Serve hot or cold, with whipped cream if desired.

MANDARIN ORANGE PIE

YIELD: 1 · 9-Inch Pie

Shell
3 egg whites
¼ teaspoon cream of tartar
1 cup sugar

Filling
1 · 3⅛-ounce package lemon pudding
  mix

½ cup sugar
¼ cup water
3 egg yolks
1 · 11-ounce can mandarin oranges
  (reserve juice)

2 teaspoons lemon juice
1 cup cream, whipped

DIRECTIONS:

OVEN TEMPERATURE: 275°

Beat egg whites and cream of tartar to soft peaks. Gradually add 1 cup sugar. Beat to stiff peaks. Spread on bottom and sides of well greased 9-inch pie pan. Bake 1 hour at 275 degrees. Turn off heat. Leave in oven 2 hours or overnight.

Combine pudding, sugar, water and egg yolks. Drain oranges and add enough water to drained liquid to make 1½ cups juice. Add to pudding mix. Cook as directed on pudding package. Cool. Add lemon juice. Fold in half of the whipped cream and ¾ cups broken orange sections. Reserve 8 to 10 slices for top. Spoon into shell and garnish with ½ remaining cup whipped cream and orange sections. Refrigerate until served.

MRS. FIELDS MOCHA PIE

YIELD: 1 · 10 inch pie

One pound Mrs. Field's chocolate
  chip cookies
¼ cup butter
1 cup semi sweet chocolate
  chips
3 egg yolks
1 cup whipping cream
1½ tablespoons expresso instant coffee
  (or favorite instant coffee)
3 egg whites
¼ cup sugar

Topping
2 cups heavy whipping cream
1 tablespoon sugar
1 teaspoon vanilla
½ cup semi-sweet chocolate chips,
  grated in food processor
or:
2 cups heavy whipping cream
1 tablespoon sugar
½ cup fresh-squeezed orange juice,
  grated orange peel

DIRECTIONS:

Grind cookies in food processor. Lay in 10-inch pie pan, bake in 275 degree oven for 10 minutes. Remove from oven; place parchment paper over 10-inch pie pan. Place a 9-inch pie pan on top and press until crust binds together. Set aside to cool Melt butter and chocolate chips together over very low heat. Mix in egg yolks, stirring until well blended.

Beat cream until stiff, blend in instant coffee. In separate bowl, beat egg whites until stiff, gradually add sugar, beating until sugar is dissolved.

Combine cream and egg white mixture, blend well. Fold in chocolate and blend. Spoon into pie crust. Refrigerate until serving. (At least three hours.)

Topping: Whip cream; add sugar and vanilla. Spread on pie, sprinkle with chocolate. Or: whip cream with sugar and orange juice. Garnish with grated orange peel.

Courtesy of Debra Fields, Park City, Utah.

RED RASPBERRY CREAM CHEESE PIE

YIELD: 1 · 9-Inch Pie

1 · 9-inch pie crust baked and
   cooled
6-ounces cream cheese, softened
⅔ cup whipping cream
1 quart fresh red raspberries

1 cup sugar
½ cup unsweetened pineapple juice
¼ cup cornstarch
unsweetened whipped cream for
   garnish

DIRECTIONS:

In medium bowl beat together cream cheese and whipping cream. Spread over bottom of pie shell; chill.

Reserve half the raspberries. In large bowl mash remaining raspberries. Stir in sugar; let stand 1 hour.

Sieve berry mixture. In a sauce pan combine cornstarch and pineapple juice; stir in berry mixture. Cook and stir over medium heat until thickened and bubbly. Reduce heat; cook and stir 2 more minutes. Remove from heat; let cool.

Spread ¾ of thickened berry mixture over cream cheese layer in pie shell. Arrange 1½ cups of reserved berries over top of pie. Spoon the remaining cooked berry mixture over the whole berries. Chill about 2 hours or until set. Garnish with whipped cream and whole berries.

STRAWBERRY GLAZE PIE

YIELD: 1 · 9-Inch Pie

1 · 9-inch baked pastry shell,
   brushed with butter
1½ quarts strawberries, washed and
   hulled
1 cup sugar

3 tablespoons cornstarch
½ cup water
1 tablespoon lemon juice
whipped cream

DIRECTIONS:

Crush enough strawberries to make 1 cup. Combine sugar and cornstarch in saucepan. Add crushed strawberries and water. Cook, stirring constantly, until thick. Blend in lemon juice. Cover. Cool to lukewarm.

Brush inside of baked pie shell with melted butter and chill. This coating keeps filling from soaking into crust. Place 3 cups whole or sliced strawberries in pastry shell. Pour glaze over berries. Chill. Serve topped with whipped cream.

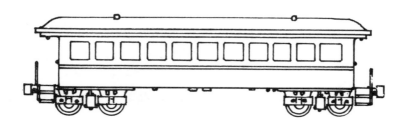

STRAWBERRY DELIGHT

SERVES 6

"A layered parfait"

1 quart strawberries
powdered sugar
Amaretto to taste
1 · 8-ounce package cream cheese

4 egg yolks
½ cup sugar
2 tablespoons cream
whipped cream for garnish

DIRECTIONS:

Clean strawberries and cut each berry in half. Cut into fourths if you have very large berries. Sprinkle with powdered sugar and Amaretto. Refrigerate at least one hour.

Combine cream cheese, Amaretto, egg yolks, sugar and cream in food processor.

Layer cream cheese mixture, strawberries, ending with berries. Top with a dollop of whipped cream and garnish with a berry.

STRAWBERRY TART

Crust
1 cup flour
1 egg yolk
⅛ teaspoon salt
2 tablespoons sugar
1 tablespoon cold water
6 tablespoons frozen butter

Filling
8-ounce cream cheese
¼ cup cream
1½ quarts fresh strawberries
1 cup sugar
4 tablespoons cornstarch
½ cup whipping cream

DIRECTIONS:

OVEN TEMPERATURE: 400°

Crust: Process ingredients for crust in a food processor. Place in a buttered tart pan. Prick, chill, and bake in a 400 degree oven for about 10 minutes.

Filling: Whip cream cheese and cream together; spread onto cooled crust. Wash and hull strawberries. Cut them in half and place half or more on top of cream mixture. Purée the remainder, then place in a pan. Bring to a boil, then add 1 cup sugar and cornstarch. Cook until thick. Cool. Pour over the rest. Chill. Decorate with sweet whipped cream.

TIP:

Sweeten whipped cream with powdered sugar to retain volume, and use super-fine sugar for meringues.

BOLOGNA RIBBONS

SERVES 1

"A fun snack for picky eaters."

1 slice bologna
1 slice processed cheese

5 toothpicks

DIRECTIONS:

Roll cheese and bologna together into the tightest roll possible. Secure roll with 5 toothpicks evenly spaced. Slice between the toothpicks across the roll.

Turn each roll on its side so design of bologna and cheese can be seen.

CANDYCANE POPCORN

SERVES 20

"Excellent for holiday party!"

4 quarts popped popcorn
2 cups whole nuts
  (pecans, cashews, peanuts)
3 cups miniature marshmallows
1½ cups spiced gumdrops

1 cup margarine
1½ cups sugar
½ cup light corn syrup
1 teaspoon vanilla

DIRECTIONS:

Mix popcorn, nuts, marshmallows and gumdrops in large mixing bowl. Melt margarine in heavy saucepan and add sugar and corn syrup. Bring to a boil, stirring, and simmer 3 minutes. Add vanilla, blend well. Pour over the popcorn mixture, and mix well. Let stand 2 minutes to cool. With hands dampened in cool water, shape into a candy cane. Arrange on a baking sheet to set. Wrap in plastic to store. Store in cool place.

CARAMEL CORN

YIELD: 2-3 Gallons Popcorn

"Makes enough for an army of children."

½ cup butter
1 cup light syrup
1 pound brown sugar (2¼ cups)

1 · 14-ounce can sweetened
  condensed milk
2-3 gallons popped corn

DIRECTIONS:

Place butter, syrup, and brown sugar in medium size saucepan. Boil 6 minutes. Remove from heat. Add milk stirring vigorously until mixed. Pour over popped corn and stir to coat.

CARAMEL HEAVENLIES

YIELD: 3½ Dozen Triangles

"Great for kids to make at Christmas."

12 double graham crackers
2 cups (4 ounces) miniature
   marshmallows
¾ cup butter
¾ cup firmly packed brown sugar

1 teaspoon cinnamon
1 teaspoon vanilla extract
1 cup sliced almonds
1 cup flaked coconut

DIRECTIONS:

OVEN TEMPERATURE: 350°

Preheat oven to 350 degrees. Arrange graham crackers in single layer in a 10½ x 15½ inch jelly-roll pan. Sprinkle with marshmallows.

In medium saucepan combine butter, brown sugar and cinnamon. Cook over medium heat stirring constantly, until sugar is dissolved. Remove from heat and stir in vanilla.

Spoon evenly over marshmallows; sprinkle with almonds, then coconut. Bake 12 to 14 minutes or until lightly browned. Cool in pan or wire rack. Cut into 3 inch squares, then cut each square in half to form triangles.

CHOCOLATE MOUNTAINS

YIELD: 4 Dozen Cookies

"There's a surprise inside!"

½ cup shortening
½ cup evaported milk
2 tablespoons water
1 egg
1 teaspoon vanilla
2 cups flour
½ teaspoon soda
½ teaspoon salt
1 cup sugar

½ cup cocoa
½ cup chopped walnuts (optional)
24 large marshmallows (cut in half)

Frosting:
¼ cup butter
3 tablespoons evaporated milk
3 tablespoons cocoa
2 cups powdered sugar

DIRECTIONS:

OVEN TEMPERATURE: 350°

Beat shortening, milk, water, egg and vanilla. Add remaining ingredients except marshmallows, blend well.

Drop by teaspoon on greased cookie sheet.

Bake 8 to 10 minutes at 350 degrees. Take from oven. Quickly place marshmallow half (sticky side down) on each cookie. Let cool.

For frosting bring to a boil butter, milk and cocoa. Add sugar and blend.

Frost over marshmallow like mountain.

CHOCOLATE WAFFLE COOKIES

YIELD: 28-30 Waffles

3 · 1-ounce squares unsweetened chocolate
1 cup margarine
4 eggs
1½ cups granulated sugar
2 cups flour
1 teaspoon vanilla
¾ teaspoon salt

Frosting
1 · 14-ounce can sweetened condensed milk
2 · 1-ounce squares unsweetened chocolate
1 tablespoon water
½ teaspoon vanilla
⅛ teaspoon salt

DIRECTIONS:

Melt chocolate and margarine together. In separate bowl beat eggs. Add sugar. Pour chocolate mixture into sugar and egg mixture, add flour, vanilla and salt. Cook in waffle iron at medium-high heat for 2 minutes. Lightly frost.

Frosting: In a double boiler over rapidly boiling water, combine milk, chocolate, water, vanilla and salt. Cook, stirring constantly until thick enough to spread (about 15 minutes). Cool at room temperature.

CHRISTMAS HOLLY WREATHS

YIELD: 18 Wreaths

30 large marshmallows
½ cup margarine
1 teaspoon vanilla

2 teaspoons green food coloring
4½ cups corn flakes
candy red hots

DIRECTIONS:

Melt marshmallows and margarine together over low heat. Add vanilla and food coloring. Pour over corn flakes. Gently blend together. Drop by tablespoon full onto waxed paper and shape into wreaths. Add red hots for holly berries.

DELUXE CHOCOLATE PUDDING

SERVES 6-8

1 · 4½-ounce package instant chocolate pudding
1 cup milk
2 cups chilled whipping cream
whipped cream or chocolate curls for garnish

DIRECTIONS:

In large mixing bowl, combine pudding and milk and mix at low speed. Add 2 cups whippping cream and beat about 2 minutes on medium speed or until soft peaks form. Pour into dessert dishes and chill at least 15 to 20 minutes. Garnish with whipped cream or chocolate curls.

EDIBLE WITCHCRAFT

SERVES 1

1 fat carrot	1 prune
3 toothpicks	2 sheets black construction paper
12 raisins	1 twig
3 cloves	black yarn

DIRECTIONS:

Cut the bottom off carrot at the widest part. Trim off the top to a blunt point, so you have a piece about 6-inches long. Use a toothpick stuffed with raisins for each arm. Make the eyes and mouth with whole cloves. Break a toothpick in half and put a prune on one end to use for a nose.

For the hat, cut a shape out of black paper, using ¼ of an 8-inch circle. Curve around to make a cone that fits your carrot. Tape to secure. Remove and trace around the base on black paper. Draw a circle ½-inch larger around this. Cut out the center and around the brim making a lifesaver shape. Slip the brim onto the carrot, stopping above the eyes. Add cone of hat and tape together.

A broom can be made with a twig from a bush or tree, about 3½-inches long. Cut several lengths of black yarn and tie onto twig. Put the twig between the last two raisins on the arm.

Optional Edibles to go with witch:

A black cat can be made from a prune with a raisin head and a pipe cleaner for a tail and ears.

A spider can be made by opening an oreo cookie and laying 3 pieces of black string licorice (about 4-inches long) across the cookie, then putting the cookie back together. Use chocolate icing as glue to add M&M eyes to the spider.

GUESS WHAT BARS

SERVES 16

2½ cups flour	2 teaspoons baking powder
1 cup sugar	¼ teaspoon salt
4 tablespoons butter, softened	3 eggs
1 tablespoon anise seed	

DIRECTIONS:

OVEN TEMPERATURE: 375°

Mix 1½ cups of the flour with remaining ingredients on low speed until completely mixed. Beat on medium speed for 3 minutes. Stir in remaining 1 cup of flour and mix well. Wrap dough in waxed paper and refrigerate at least 1 hour.

Preheat oven to 375 degrees. Divide dough in half. On floured surface, shape each half into 12 x 2 inch logs.

Bake logs for 20 minutes or until lightly browned. Slice hot into 1 inch logs.

HOME-MADE BUTTER

YIELD: ½ Cup Butter

"Fun activity while bread is baking."

1 cup whipping cream   ⅛ teaspoon salt

DIRECTIONS:

Place the cream into a clean pint jar with a tight fitting lid. Add the salt. Twist the lid on tightly. Shake the container until the cream thickens to butter. Pour out the liquid and the butter is ready. Serve on bread or crackers.

KRAZY KRACKERS

YIELD: 4-5 Dozen

2¾ cups flour   ½ teaspoon baking soda
2-4 tablespoons sugar   ½ cup mayonnaise
½ teaspoon salt   1 cup plain yogurt

DIRECTIONS: OVEN TEMPERATURE: 400°

Sift together flour, sugar, salt, soda. With pastry blender, cut in mayonnaise until well mixed and coarse crumbs form. Stir in yogurt with hands. Firmly press dough into ball. Cut into 16 pieces, cut each into little pieces. Roll in flour. Roll out to ¹⁄₁₆ inch thickness. Bake on ungreased cookie sheet at 400 degrees for 6 to 7 minutes or until golden. Sprinkle with salt.

KID'S DO IT ICE CREAM

YIELD: 3 Cups

"A great activity for a summer afternoon."

1 cup milk   nuts or fruit as desired
½ cup sugar   1 egg (optional)
1 cup whipping cream   ice and rock salt for
½ teaspoon vanilla extract   freezing ice cream

DIRECTIONS:

Put all ingredients except ice and rock salt in 1 pound coffee can with a tight fitting plastic lid. Place lid on can. Place can with ingredients inside 3 pound coffee can with a tight fitting plastic lid.

Pack larger can with crushed ice around smaller can. Pour at least ¾ cup of rock salt evenly over ice. Place lid on 3 pound can. Roll back and forth on a table or cement slab for 10 minutes. Open outer can. Remove inner can with ingredients. Remove lid and use a rubber spatula to stir the mixture, scrape sides of can.

Replace lid. Drain ice water from larger can. Insert smaller can, pack with more ice and salt. Roll back and forth for 5 more minutes.

LAYERED FINGER JELLO
SERVES 10

"Very festive for children's party – they are beautiful and the kids love it!"

3 · 6-ounce packages gelatin (2 lime, 1 cherry are nice)
1 · 14-ounce can sweetened condensed milk
8 envelopes unflavored gelatin

DIRECTIONS:

First Layer – Mix 1 · 6-ounce package lime gelatin and 2 envelopes unflavored gelatin. Add 2⅛ cups hot water. Stir until gelatin is completely dissolved. Pour into lightly greased 13x9 inch pan. Allow to set until firm (1 to 1½ hours).

Second Layer – Mix 1 envelope unflavored gelatin and ½ cup hot water. Dissolve completely. Allow to cool but keep stirring. Add ½ can sweetened condensed milk. Pour over first layer. Set. (Sets very quickly – about 10 minutes)

Third Layer – Mix 1 · 6-ounce package cherry gelatin with 2 envelopes unflavored gelatin. Add 2 cups hot water. Stir until completely dissolved. Allow to cool. Pour onto milk layer.

Fourth Layer – Repeat instructions for Second Layer.

Fifth Layer – Repeat instructions for First Layer.

MAMA T'S DOUBLE DUTCH PIZZA
YIELD: 30-40 Servings

"A children's pizza delight!"

¾ cup margarine
1 cup sugar
1 egg
1 teaspoon vanilla
1½ cups flour
¼ cup cocoa

½ teaspoon baking soda
¼ teaspoon salt
¾ cup M&M candy
½ cup walnuts, chopped (optional)
¼ cup miniature marshmallows
¼ cup flaked coconut (optional)

DIRECTIONS:
OVEN TEMPERATURE: 350°

Blend together margarine and sugar until light and fluffy. Blend in egg and vanilla. Combine flour, cocoa, soda, and salt and add to the egg-sugar mixture. Mix well. Stir in ½ cup candy, ¼ cup chopped nuts.

Place dough on foil lined 12 or 13¼ inch pizza pan, spreading to 1½ inch from edges of pan.

Sprinkle with remaining nuts, candy, marshmallows and coconut. Bake at 350 degrees for 20 minutes or until edges are set. Do not over bake.

Cool 10 minutes in pan. Gently remove pizza with foil liner to wire rack. Cool thoroughly. Cut and serve.

NATURE CENTER INDIAN FRY BREAD

YIELD: 20 · 2-Inch Patties or 8 Servings

"This is always a favorite when children visit the Ogden Nature Center. The bread is cooked on the open camp fire so it would be great to take along on a camping trip."

2 cups flour
½ cup dry milk
1½ tablespoon baking powder
¾ teaspoon salt

2 tablespoons shortening
¾ cup luke warm water
1 cup vegetable oil

DIRECTIONS:

In mixing bowl mix together flour, milk, baking powder, and salt. Cut shortening into dry ingredients. Add warm water. Knead until smooth. If dough is too tough add more warm water. Dough should be elastic but not sticky. Allow to stand 30 minutes or overnight. Pat into 2 inch patties. (Children love doing this.)

Heat oil in skillet; drop patties into oil and cook until golden, about 1 minute per side. Drain on paper towel and serve with honey butter.

NO BAKE COOKIES

YIELD: 64 Medium Sized Cookies

2 cups sugar
½ cup butter
½ cup milk
1 teaspoon vanilla
1½ cups oatmeal

1½ cups wheaties
1 · 12-ounce package chocolate
  chips
½ cup chopped nuts

DIRECTIONS:

Combine oatmeal, wheaties, chocolate chips, and nuts. Heat sugar, butter, milk and vanilla. Cook for 1 minute and pour over oatmeal mixture. Drop quickly by spoonfuls onto wax paper. Chill.

ORANGE COCONUT BALLS

YIELD: 3 Dozen 2-Inch Balls

1 · 6-ounce can frozen orange juice
½ cup butter or margarine
1 · 12-ounce box Vanilla Wafer cookies

1 pound powdered sugar
1 cup shredded or flaked coconut

DIRECTIONS:

Thaw orange juice. Crush cookies finely. Blend orange juice, butter, crushed cookies, powdered sugar together thoroughly with spoon. Roll into 1½-inch balls with hands. Roll balls in coconut to coat. Chill until firm.

PEANUT BUTTER BONBONS

YIELD: 3 Dozen Bonbons

1½ cups powdered sugar
1 cup graham cracker crumbs
  (about 12 squares)
½ cup margarine or butter

½ cup peanut butter
1 · 6-ounce package semisweet
  chocolate chips
1 tablespoon shortening

DIRECTIONS:

Mix powdered sugar and cracker crumbs. Heat butter and peanut butter over low heat until melted, stir into crumb mixture. Shape mixture into 1-inch balls. Heat chips with shortening. Dip balls into chocolate with tongs until coated.. Place on waxed paper. Refrigerate until firm.

PLAY CLAY

"Great for group projects. The entire batch can be colored turquiose and molded into Indian beads, using toothpicks to make holes. Combined with colored macaronis it makes a perfect squash blossom necklace."

2 cups baking soda
1 cup cornstarch

1¼ cups water

DIRECTIONS:

Combine soda, starch, and water. Mix until smooth. Boil one minute to the consistency of mashed potatoes. Stir constantly. Spoon out onto plate. Cover with damp cloth and cool. Knead lightly and roll out on wax paper to cut with cookie cutters or mold by hand. Patterns can be drawn or pressed into the clay using toothpicks or buttons with fun patterns. Dry 24 to 48 hours.

Dried pieces can be painted with tempera or water colors, then coated with spray varnish or clear nail enamel. The clay can also be colored by adding powdered tempera or food coloring while cooking.

DO NOT EAT.

PORCUPINE CARAMELS

YIELD: 130 Treats

"Great treat for a school class!"

1 · 14-ounce can sweetened condensed
  milk
½ cup butter

1 package Kraft caramels
1 · 16-ounce package marshmallows
1 · 13-ounce package Rice Krispies

DIRECTIONS:

Melt condensed milk, butter and caramels in a heavy saucepan or double boiler. Cut marshmallows in half. Spread Rice Krispies on waxed paper. Dip pieces of marshmallows in caramel mixture and toss in Rice Krispies until well coated. Store in a box, not in plastic or airtight container.

SAUSAGE BALLS

SERVES 8

1 cup biscuit mix
1 · 12-ounce tube Jimmie
  Dean Sausage

14-ounces grated cheddar
  cheese

DIRECTIONS:
OVEN TEMPERATURE: 350°

Combine ingredients, form into balls. Bake in 350 degree oven for 15 minutes.

SPUD CHICKEN

SERVES 4

"Children will enjoy coating the chicken in preparation for baking."

12 Drumsticks or 1 to 2½ pound
  chicken cut into pieces

½ cup mayonnaise
1½ cups potato flakes

DIRECTIONS:
OVEN TEMPERATURE: 400°

Coat chicken pieces with mayonnaise and roll pieces in potato flakes to coat well.

Arrange chicken on a baking sheet in a single layer. Bake in 400 degree oven for 40 minutes or until golden brown.

THANKSGIVING CORNUCOPIA

YIELD: 1 Serving, 1 Cornucopia

"Another great idea for holiday parties."

1 sugar ice cream cone with pointed end
Assorted candies, nuts, miniature marshmallows, etc.
Frosting

DIRECTIONS:

Steam and turn the end of the cone up. Place frosting inside cone.
Add candies, nuts, marshmallows.

Spread frosting on a square piece of paper, 6 x 6 inches. Stick cornucopia on paper base for a festive table decoration.

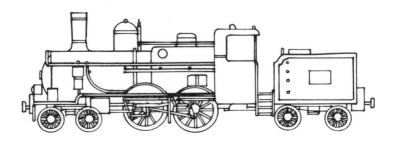

TURTLES

YIELD: 2 Dozen

2 · 1-ounce squares chocolate
⅓ cup margarine
2 eggs, beaten
¾ cup sugar

1 teaspoon vanilla
¼ teaspoon salt
1 cup flour

DIRECTIONS:

Melt together the chocolate and margarine. In medium size bowl combine sugar, vanilla, salt and flour. Mix well. Add chocolate and butter to mixture. Drop by teaspoon full onto waffle griddle heated to medium temperature. Cook 1 to 2 minutes.

Frost with chocolate frosting.

YUMMIE DECORATOR CLAY

YIELD: Plenty for 6 children to mold

"Colorful and fun to work with and tastes yummie!"

⅓ cup margarine, melted
⅓ cup light corn syrup
1 teaspoon vanilla
(*for brighter more vibrant colors, use food paste)

½ teaspoon salt
1 pound powdered sugar
food coloring or food paste

DIRECTIONS:

Using spoon, blend margarine, corn syrup, vanilla and salt. Mix in sugar. Knead until smooth. Add more powdered sugar if needed to make a non-sticky, pliable clay. Divide clay into number of colors desired. Add food coloring or paste. Knead until color is blended. The clay can then be molded to decorate cakes, cookies, cupcakes, crackers, etc. Use round toothpicks as forming tools.

Clay may be refrigerated in plastic bags for up to 2 weeks. Soften to room temperature before using.

TIP:

Chill eggs before separating whites and yolks.

HINTS ON DUTCH OVEN COOKING

The Dutch oven is probably the most useful utensil for campfire cooking. Nearly everything that can be cooked or baked in a home oven can be prepared over a fire in the Dutch oven. I have found the most convenient size of oven to be the 12 inch model with a flanged or flat rimmed lid which will hold the coals on top while baking. With this oven, I can prepare enough food for eight hungry adults.

The type and numbers of coals used are very important in achieving and maintaining the correct baking temperature. The best coals are those that have burned down to glowing, not flaming, embers. They should be placed both beneath and on top of the oven. The bottom layer should be approximately as wide as the diameter of the oven. The top layer should have considerably more coals on it, causing most of the baking heat to come from there.

Two variables which will most affect the success of your baking are the altitude at which you bake and the heat of the coals you use. The higher your campfire, the longer your baking time and the hotter your coals should be. I recommend brushing off the top coals, lifting the lid and checking the progress of your baking about every 15 to 20 minutes so that you can adjust the heat if necessary.

Only practice can help you become proficient with Dutch oven baking. But the results — succulent stews, mouth-watering desserts or whatever you desire — are always pleasant and delightful surprises to any camping experience.

Sally Neill
Calvin Alpine Outfitters

APPLE CRISP

SERVES 6-8

"Another campfire Dutch oven treat."

6 large Granny Smith apples
1 cup raisins
¾ cup flour

1 cup brown sugar
1 tablespoon cinnamon
butter or margarine

DIRECTIONS:

Generously butter a 12 inch Dutch oven and slice apples into it. Sprinkle raisins among apples.

Combine flour, sugar and cinnamon and pour over apples. Dot with butter.

Place covered Dutch oven in fire pit on top of hot, but not flaming, coals. With shovel, generously cover top of oven with additional coals. Let bake for 30 minutes or until apples are soft and juicy.

BLUEBERRY MUFFINS

SERVES 8

"For the campfire"

2 cups flour
¼ cup sugar
4 teaspoons baking powder
¾ teaspoon salt
1 egg

⅓ cup cooking oil
2½ tablespoons dry milk, mixed with
    water to yield ½ cup milk
1 · 15-ounce can blueberries, drained

DIRECTIONS:

Mix flour, sugar, baking powder and salt. Beat together, egg, milk and oil and add to flour mixture. Gently add blueberries. Pour batter into greased 8 x 8 inch aluminum pan. Place entire pan into Dutch oven, cover and bake 25 minutes or until inserted wooden pick comes out clean.

CAMPER SPUDS

1 potato per person
Cheddar cheese, grated
green onion, chopped

salt and pepper
butter or margarine

DIRECTIONS:

Slice each potato into strips as you would for preparing French fries and place on a piece of aluminum foil. Top each potato with 2 tablespoons each of grated cheese and chopped onion. Season to taste and dot with butter. Wrap each potato tightly in foil and place in hot coals on edge of fire for 20 to 30 minutes. Turn after 15 minutes. Test with a fork for doneness.

CAMPFIRE SQUASH

SERVES 8

6 yellow crooked neck squash,
  sliced
1 large onion, chopped

soy sauce
seasoning salt
butter

DIRECTIONS:

Place squash and onion on large piece of heavy-duty foil; Season with soy sauce, seasoning salt and dot with butter. Wrap tightly and place in campfire where it can simmer for 20 to 30 minutes.

VARIATIONS:

Add other vegetables, cauliflower, zucchini, carrots. Melt cheese on top.

CHERRY UPSIDE DOWN CAKE

SERVES 8

"A cake to cook in a Dutch oven over a campfire"

1 package lemon cake mix
3 eggs
$\frac{1}{3}$ cup salad oil

$1\frac{1}{4}$ cups water
$\frac{1}{4}$ cup butter or margarine
2 · 16-ounce cans pie cherries, drained

DIRECTIONS:

Blend cake mix, eggs, oil and water. Beat 3 minutes by hand. Melt butter in preheated Dutch oven; when bubbling, pour cherries evenly over bottom of pot. Remove from heat and pour in cake batter. Cover and bake for 25 minutes or until wooden pick inserted in center comes out clean. Let cool 5 minutes; invert onto platter to serve.

CUCUMBER AVOCADO SALAD

SERVES 8

2 large cucumbers
2 large avocados

Creamy Italian salad dressing

DIRECTIONS:

Peel cucumbers and avocados and dice into large pieces. Marinate for 15 minutes in creamy Italian dressing. Serve.

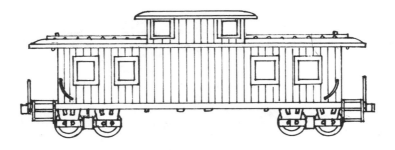

DUTCH OVEN BARBECUED CHICKEN

SERVES 6-8

"Excellent with quick-cooking long grain/wild rice!"

1 · 18-ounce jar hickory smoke
  barbecue sauce
1 envelope dry enchilada sauce mix
2 cups water

7 chicken breasts
7 chicken legs
4 chicken wings

DIRECTIONS:

Combine sauce, enchilada mix and water. Add chicken pieces and bake in Dutch oven approximately 2 hours, stirring occasionally.

ENCHILADA PIE

SERVES 6-8

2 pounds ground beef
1 medium onion, chopped
2 · 10-ounce cans mild enchilada
  sauce
9 · 8 inch flour tortillas

1 teaspoon salt
1 · 10¾-ounces can tomato soup
1 cup water
2 cups Cheddar or mozarella cheese
  shredded

DIRECTIONS:

Working over an open fire, brown ground beef with salt and onion in a Dutch oven. Drain off drippings. Add tomato soup, enchilada sauce and water. Simmer 5 minutes.

Spoon ¾ of the mixture into a medium size bowl. Arrange 2 to 3 tortillas over mixture remaining in Dutch oven. Alternate meat, cheese and tortillas in three layers.

Replace lid on Dutch oven. Simmer 7 to 10 minutes or until cheese melts and tortillas soften. Serve pie with remaining tortillas as side bread.

SHRIMP-FILLED AVOCADOS

SERVES 8

"Impressive gourmet lunch, especially when served on mountain peaks!"

6 to 8 avocados
1 · 8-ounce jar mayonnaise
juice of ½ lemon

¾ teaspoon curry powder
1 tablespoon soy sauce
3 · 4½-ounce cans tiny shrimp

DIRECTIONS:

Cut avocados in half and remove pits. Combine mayonnaise, lemon juice, curry and soy sauce. Add shrimp. Spoon mixture into avocados and serve with a spoon.

HAM AND VEGETABLE STEW

SERVES 6-8

"Good served with warm tortillas or sheepherders' bread on a cool mountain evening."

3½ pounds ham, cut into bite-sized pieces
2 · 16-ounce cans green beans or 1½ pounds fresh green beans
2 large onions, chopped
1 large head cauliflower, cut into pieces
2 medium yellow or zucchini squash, sliced
1 · 2-ounce package country vegetable dry soup mix

DIRECTIONS:

Put cubed ham into Dutch oven and add approximately 2 inches of water. Bring to a boil and let simmer for ½ to 1 hour with lid on. Add beans, onions, cauliflower, squash and dry soup mix. Cook until vegetables are done. Add more water during cooking if necessary.

MEATLOAF IN AN ONION

SERVES 6

1 pound lean ground beef
1 egg
¼ cup cracker crumbs
¼ cup tomato sauce

⅛ teaspoon pepper
½ teaspoon salt
½ teaspoon dry mustard
6 large onions, peeled

DIRECTIONS:

Cut six 12 inch squares of heavy foil and set aside. In a bowl, mix ground beef, egg, cracker crumbs, tomato sauce, pepper, salt and dry mustard. Set aside.

Cut onions in half horizontally and remove centers, leaving a ¼ inch shell. Chop onion centers and stir 2 tablespoons into meat mixture. Spoon meat mixture into the onion halves and place two halves together.

Wrap onions securely in foil squares. Cook on coals for 14 to 20 minutes on each side.

TIP:

Dutch ovens clean easily with hot water and a scouring pad. Soap should not be used as it permeates the cast iron.

OMELET SANDWICH

SERVES 4

"Wrap this sandwich in newspapers and it will stay warm for hours. A great treat to take along on a winter picnic or on a cross-country skiing trip."

1 loaf circular bread
  (either home-made or from store)
1 green pepper, sliced
½ cup mushrooms, sliced

1 onion, sliced
3 eggs
½ cup milk or water
  (optional)

DIRECTIONS:

Halve the bread horizontally, scoop out inside, leaving ½ inch shell. Stir fry pepper, mushrooms, and onions until soft. Set aside.

Beat eggs, add milk or water if desired, and beat together. Fry eggs, adding vegetables when eggs are nearly set.

Stuff the bread shell with warm omelet.

QUICK CINNAMON ROLLS

YIELD: 8 Servings

For the campfire

3 tablespoons dry milk mixed with
  water to yield ⅔ cup milk
2 cups biscuit mix flour

4 ounces raisins
1 cup brown sugar
2 tablespoons cinnamon

DIRECTIONS:

Blend milk and biscuit mix; pat out in a rectangular shape on a floured, flat surface. Spread raisins and brown sugar over the dough. Sprinkle with cinnamon.

With floured hands, roll the dough into a cylinder beginning with the long side. Cut cylinder into 8 rolls and place in bottom of a greased 8 x 8 inch aluminum pan. Place entire pan into Dutch oven. Cover and bake about 20 minutes or until done.

TIP:

Eggs pack easily when broken into a large plastic bottle. They will last 5-7 days if kept as cool as possible.

SHEEPHERDERS' BREAD

YIELD: 1 Very Large Loaf

"This bread is best made at home and then packed in a Dutch oven when camping. Leftover bread makes EXCELLENT French toast."

3 cups very hot tap water
½ cup butter or margarine
⅓ cup sugar
2½ teaspoons salt

2 packages active dry yeast
9 to 9½ cups flour
salad oil

DIRECTIONS:

In large bowl, combine water, butter, sugar, and salt. Stir until butter melts; let cool to about 110 degrees. Stir in yeast, cover, and let it stand until bubbly (5 to 15 minutes.)

Beat in about 5 cups of flour to make a thick batter. Stir in enough of the remaining flour (about 3½ cups) to make a stiff dough. Turn dough out onto a floured board; knead until smooth and satiny (10 to 20 minutes), adding flour as needed to prevent sticking.

Turn dough over in a greased bowl; cover and let rise in a warm place until doubled, (about 1½ hours.) Punch dough down and knead on a floured board to form a smooth ball.

With a circle of foil, cover inside bottom of a 12-inch diameter Dutch oven; grease foil, inside of oven, and under side of lid with oil. Place dough in oven and cover with lid. Let rise in a warm place until dough begins to push up lid (about 1 hour.)

Bake, covered with lid, in a 375 degree oven for 12 minutes. Remove lid and bake for 30 minutes or until loaf is golden brown.

TURKEY AU GRATIN SOUP

SERVES 4-6

4 to 5 cups diced, cooked turkey
4 cups water
4 chicken bouillon cubes
½ teaspoon ground marjoram
½ teaspoon ground oregano

1 · 5½-ounce package au gratin
    potatoes and sauce mix
1 large carrot, sliced
½ cup dry white wine

DIRECTIONS:

Combine all ingredients and stir. Bring to a boil over a fire. Cover and let simmer 20 minutes or until potatoes are done.

COOKBOOK COMMITTEE

ENGINEER
Mary King

CONDUCTOR
Kathy Morris

REPAIRMAN
Lucia Child

CREW
Yacko Bryner
Mimi Bulkley
Linda Campbell
Susan Findlay
Ann Parker-Judd
Linda Lambert
Lorraine Merrill

Sally Neill
Margaret Pappas
Myrth Priest
Laurie Ruskin
Rindy Smith
Lizbeth Sneddon
Marcia Hawks Summers

CONTRIBUTORS

PHOTOGRAPHS COURTESY OF:

Golden Spike Empire   Snow Basin Ski Resort   Utah Travel Council

Virginia Abajian	Cathay Christiansen	Ruth Ford
Kathy Adams	Nancy Christiansen	Gloria Froerer
Marilyn Agricola	Margaret Cole	Joyce Galetka
Di Allison	Linda Collins	Connie George
Dareth Anderson	Joan C. Colvin	Rebecca Gillespie
Nanette Anderson	Cheryl Connors	Kathy Goddard
Beverly Aoki	Mary Coscia	Kay Goldie
Kathy Austin	Connie Cox	Greenery Restaurant
Greta Ball	Pam Crandall	Patti Grinnell
Priscilla Barenholtz	Chantal Cunningham	JoAnne Gross
Lois Anderson Barker	Helen Curtis	Addie Lou Hancey
Sue Barker	Sue Curtis	Lyn Handley
Holly Bauman	Trish B. Dahl	Beverly Hansen
Helen Baur	Joan Dallof	Jeanie Hansen
Mary Benowitz	Judy Davenport	Joyce Pugmire Hansen
Anne Bergera	Barbara Dehaan	Edna Hardy
Kathy Black	Litz Dee	Jane Hartman
Pat Black	Chris Deeter	Leigh Ann Havas
Barbara Bowman	Susan E. Denkers	Susan Heald
Jean Bradshaw	Dolly DeVine	Joan Hellstrom
Carol Brewer	Barbara Dobb	Shirley Hemmingway
Jane Brewer	Joan Dolph	Linda Henderson
Linda Bright	Janet Dopp	Carol Herold
Pam Brimhall	Ruth Eccles	Jodee Hoellein
Ruth Brockman	Carol Eckhardt	Carol Hoffman
Colleen Brown	Chris Eggert	Lucille Holley
Claudia Brewster-King	Ana Maria Eldredge	Anne Hoover
Erica Bryner	Harry Eldredge, Jr.	Rita James
Todd Bulkley	Helen Eldredge	Brenda Jensen
Helen Burdett	Karen Fairbanks	Kathy Jensen
Anne Burk	Gloria Farkas	Sandy John
Pam Carlson	Janis Farrell	Pat Jones
Mary Carney	Lenore Ferro	Jun Kawaguchi
Susan L. Cathcart	Debra Fields	Kazuko Kawaguchi
Judi Baur Chartrand	Carolyn Firmage	Phyllis Keiter
Lucia Child	Catherine Ford	Peggy Kelly

Karen B. Kimose
Golda King
Jane T. King
Lynzee Krakover
Lavon Lake
Ila Lambert
Andrea Lane
Sami Lapine
Frankie Larsen
Marya Lee
Lori Leetham
Dori LeVanti
Suzanne Lindquist
Geri Lingren
Nikki Lovell
Calene Lucero
Glenda Lynn
Elmeda MacNamara
Sharon McFarland
Fran Madlang
Kathy Majerek
Kathy Mangione
Market Street Grill
Sharon Olsen Markos
Cora Marks
Betty Marsh
Nancy Martin
Lynn Massie
Pat Mencimer
Lorraine Merrill
Kathy Miller
Linda Miner
Judy Mitchell
Jill Moore
Kiele L. Moore
Stephanie Moore
Bea Morris
David Morris
Diane Naisbitt
Elizabeth Neill
Kwee Thai Neill

Bonnie E. Nelson
Donna Nelson
Melba Nelson
Kathie Nelson
Maurine Newton
Bev Nye
Linda K. Oda
Dixie Owens
Carol Pack
Janet M. Palmer
Deed Parrett
Annette Parker
Sandi Paulsen
Janet Petersen
Nancy Petersen
Kathy Peterson
Joan Petty
Connie Poce
Katherine Poce
Patrick Poce
Selinda Powell
Mabel Powelson
Marsha Prantil
Joyce Price
Loma Prince
Lani Prout
Marian Pugmire
Faye Purdy
Connie Ray
Maurine J. Redd
Pat Rees
Pat Richter
Debbie Rocco
Pam Rogers
Amparo Rosen
Shelia Runyon
Marilyn Sandberg
Denise Schmutz
Kathy Schreck
Leslie Leishman Scilley

Kathlyn Scott
Pete Seibert
Susan Shaw
Carrie Sheldon
Judy Sherman
Cheryl Shimer
Lawanna Shurtliff
Nancy Sivulich
Mimu A. Sloan
Carol Lynn Smith
Susan V. Smith
Susan Spence
Beverly S. Spencer
Marjorie Spencer
Susan Stacey
Lynne Starley
Bonnie Swanson
Barbara Taylor
Phyllis Taylor
Roni Taylor
Barbara Tenniss
Delphia Thomas
Ruth Toller
Elizabeth Tullis
Nadine Udy
Tina Verhaal
Fern Waddoups
Kirt Walling
Julie Watkins
Sandy Watson
Lisa Waters
Sharon Webb
Susan Westenskow
Jane Wheeler
Sue Williams
Herb Wong, Ph.D.
Celia Woodcock
Dixie Wright
Lyn Wright
Mary Yoachum